BEING MARRIED

YOUR GUIDE TO A HAPPY MODERN MARRIAGE

SHARON ARIS

First published in Australia in 2005

Copyright © Sharon Aris 2005

All rights reserved. No part of this book may be reproduced or transmitted in any form or by any means, electronic or mechanical, including photocopying, recording or by any information storage and retrieval system, without prior permission in writing from the publisher. The *Australian Copyright Act 1968* (the Act) allows a maximum of one chapter or 10 per cent of this book, whichever is the greater, to be photocopied by any educational institution for its educational purposes provided that the educational institution (or body that administers it) has given a remuneration notice to Copyright Agency Limited (CAL) under the Act.

Allen & Unwin
83 Alexander Street
Crows Nest NSW 2065
Australia
Phone: (61 2) 8425 0100
Fax: (61 2) 9906 2218
Email: info@allenandunwin
Web: www.allenandunwin.c

National Library of Australia
Cataloguing-in-Publication ent

N E EDUCATION & LIBRARY BOARD	
9081657	
Bertrams	27.11.06
306.81	£8.99
WHD	

Aris, Sharon
 Being married: your guide to a happy modern marriage.

ISBN 1 74114 321 7.

 1. Marriage. 2. Marriage – Case studies. 3. Communication in marriage. 4. Man–woman relationships. I. Title.

301.81

Typeset in 11/15 Memento by Midland Typesetters, Maryborough, Vic
Printed by Griffin Press, Netley, SA

10 9 8 7 6 5 4 3 2 1

Contents

Acknowledgements		iv
Introduction		1
1	Why Marry?	8
2	Nice Day for a White Wedding	35
3	The Honeymoon is Over	52
4	The Art of Marital Warfare	72
5	Men v. Women: Can we be on the same side?	93
6	SEX: Are we having fun yet?	123
7	Show Me the Money	150
8	All Work, No Play?	172
9	The 'C' Word: Children	195
10	The Sticking Point	226
Conclusion: Having it all		256
Notes		268

Acknowledgements

This book started as a conversation between Danni Townsend and myself about why we had each married and why we were glad we had. It was a dialogue that continued for many months and is indeed still going. As it turned out, although the idea for the book was jointly conceived, Danni had to leave the project when she and husband David had a special project of their own in the form of young Ellery, but the many ideas we discussed form the basis of this book.

I owe an enormous debt of gratitude to all the couples who were willing to talk to me about the intimate, sometimes funny, sometimes painful yet always enlightening details of their marriages. Your honesty and trust leaves me humble and inspired and I thank you all.

I also owe a lot to the many experts who were willing to share their insights and research. I learned from all, but in particular I would like to thank John Gottman and William Doherty who were encouraging and unselfish with their time and reflections. Robyn Parker and Dr Michelle Simons from the Institute of Family Studies also gave Danni a wonderful interview at the start of this project that helped frame its direction and Ann Hollands from Relationship Australia was most helpful.

This book went through several drafts as we worked to find

the best tone. Through it all the smart and sassy Jo Paul, my publisher at Allen & Unwin, was patient, helpful and perceptive. Karen Gee, my copy editor, did a wonderful job smoothing the rough edges and asking all the right questions, and also thanks to Colette Vella and Gina Iverarity, who worked on an earlier draft. And to Senior Editor Joanne Holliman who shepherded the production process with panache.

This rewriting process also got me thinking about the editors I have worked with over the years and who have made me a better writer. I would like to particularly acknowledge Shelley Gare, Ashley Hay, Michael Duffy, Max Suich and Rob Johnson, who have always made any work I submitted better for their touch.

It is this final editor, Rob Johnson, I owe the greatest debt, and not just because he married me. Through the whole long process he encouraged me forward when I couldn't see the way, read and re-read each draft and kept believing in it, even when I didn't. He makes me a better writer and a better person.

Sharon Aris
July 2004

For my husband Rob Johnson, who
makes my being married a joy.

Sharon Aris is a freelance writer and television producer. She is the author of *It's My Party and I'll Knit If I Want To* and *Top Jobs*, and holds a Masters degree in Policy and Applied Social Research.

Sharon is (very happily) married and lives with her husband Rob, cat Crouching Tiger and the lovely baby Olivia.

Introduction

> Okay, life's a fact, people do fall in love, people do belong to each other, because that's the only chance anybody's got for real happiness.
> **—Holly Golightly, *Breakfast at Tiffany's*, 1961**

They say every girl grows up knowing exactly what she wants her wedding to be like, from dress to decorations. Not me. It wasn't so much that I was anti-wedding or anti-marriage but during my twenties I honestly didn't give it much thought. I had other things to do—travel, get a career, then get another one, party. A wedding in white and settling down simply weren't on the radar. Then something changed. To be honest, I still don't entirely understand what, but it did.

After being with Rob for seven years, for some reason, just living together stopped being good enough. It wasn't as if we weren't committed to each other: we'd travelled together; we were buying a house; we'd supported each other through two degrees, the writing of two books and a career change. But somehow, in some way, I started wanting more. I'd feel inexplicable jealously waft over me as we went to the weddings of friends who did the whole engagement party, hens' night, kitchen tea and big-fat-wedding routine. I started to feel like I'd been gypped, that I'd been done out of something. I became fixated. 'Where's my fucking diamond?' I began to mutter, though I pretended it was a joke. For two years I was 'only kidding' about the ring. And about getting married. Then we went on holidays and I issued an ultimatum: 'Either you decide this is permanent or I'll leave.' Rob had until the end of the year to decide. The deadline passed and I pondered my next move. Then on Valentine's Day he proposed. I got my diamond.

Rob, of course, remembers none of this. He just remembers that somewhere along the line he decided to marry me.

Marriage has a big image problem. See the newspaper headlines and you could be forgiven for thinking marriage is in trouble, is bad for you and is on the way out. 'Young men in fear of a life stifled by marriage', 'Marriage is the weakest contract of all', 'Women reject the chore of marriage', 'Call for inquiry into the decline of marriage'[1] and that's just from one group of newspapers over six months.

I had my own anti-marriage list: I was a feminist (and women lose from marriage, right?); I didn't think you had to be married to prove commitment; I didn't think premarital sex was wrong and I didn't think children born to de facto couples were bastards; I didn't like it that gay friends couldn't also be married; most marriage promoters left me cold—they were either politicians I disliked or moralists I didn't trust (do it, they pronounced through thin, dour, lips, it's *good for you*, sounding the death knell to an interesting life); I didn't need to be a fairy-dressed princess-for-a-day; I'd never pictured myself behind the picket fence; my friends weren't only smug-marrieds—they were also de facto, still single and single again and I liked them all just fine; and when people talked about family values they didn't seem to be talking about anything that looked like my life (I didn't go to church, want a 4WD, do school fetes, Tupperware or *The Wiggles*). Oh, and I never wanted to be 'a wife'. And yet, and yet and yet, somehow I still wanted it. Wanted to be married. Whatever that was. But I don't think I was the only one who was confused.

Reading the statistics you may well conclude that marriage is on the endangered list: currently, marriage rates are at 100-year lows while the divorce rate is hitting 100-year highs.[2] Marriage is on shaky ground right? Well, it certainly has an image problem. But of course the picture isn't that simple. In fact, contradicting the doomsayers most of us want to get married and most of us will. In Australia, around eight in ten people will marry by the age of fifty and, of those who haven't, most will be in some kind of committed relationship, either as a prelude or an alternative to marriage.[3] So despite the bad publicity, marriage is still something we want.

Four and a half years ago on a small island in Sydney Harbour, Rob and I married. We hired a ferry to get there, Rob wore a blue suit and gold tie, and I was dressed goddess-like in topaz taffeta. We giggled through the richer or poorer bit in the vows (richer? We are *writers* for goodness sake). We fought with our families over the guest list. We made our friends dress up. We had a cake and speeches. Everyone laughed at our jokes. It was a great party. And we're glad we did it. We still take walks around the bay to look at our island and reminisce. We've become marriage promoters. 'Get married,' we tell our friends, 'You'll have the best time.' And it has, somehow, made a difference to our relationship.

How and why fascinates me. Is there something transforming in saying vows? Or is it standing in front of a crowd of people who know you best and promising that this relationship is for keeps? What is the magic dust that made our relationship better after marriage—and, even more significantly, how do we hold onto that?

I started asking those questions and soon found I had a hundred more. Like, 'if vows are so important, why is it that so many marriages fail?' Because the hard truth is a lot of marriages do founder: around 42 per cent of Australian, 55 per cent of American, 42 per cent of English and 37 per cent of German marriages now end in divorce.[4] Even if every couple walks down the isle thinking it won't happen to them, those aren't good odds in anyone's language.

My biggest question of all was, 'how do you stay married?'

So I started reading the books. From the earnest title on the front, to the thoughtful author's frown on the back, the news sounded grim: you've got to 'work on it'; 'marriage isn't easy'; what to do when 'passion dies'. Could it be that bad? The books made it sound like it's just possible to stay married, if you had enough gritty determination, and that being married is as much work as the salt mines and about as much fun too. I wasn't interested in that. I didn't just want to be married, I wanted to be *happily* married. Surely there is something you can do to make it succeed?

So I started this quest, to find out how to be happily married. But where to look? I thought the obvious place to start would be with the experts on what went wrong—divorcees. Researchers have been swarming over divorce for decades, so thanks to them we know an awful lot about what makes marriage risky. Here's a short list of the hazard lights for divorce:

- marriage at a young age
- early pregnancy
- low income or poor economic circumstances
- a low level of education
- living together before marriage
- premarital birth
- parents who've divorced
- non-traditional family values
- previous marriage
- the wife's employment.[5]

Already I had hit a roadblock. Many of these potholes are difficult to miss. Did you have the misfortune to be born into a dysfunctional family?[6] Maybe you came from a poor background, married early, have been married before, or had a child previously? What are you going to do then—just give up? Add a desire for a career and having 'non-traditional values' and just excuse me a moment while I speed-dial my divorce lawyer. Maybe, this line of inquiry wasn't as helpful as I'd have liked.

Well then, how about looking at what divorcees say went wrong with their marriages? Maybe they can offer some clues. Here the list runs to poor communication, basic unhappiness, loss of love, incompatibility, infidelity, mental illness, emotional problems, conflict over men and women's roles or spouse's poor personality traits.[7] Kind of hard to pin down really isn't it? How do you prevent basic unhappiness? Or emotional problems? Again, not as helpful as you might hope.

There's another problem, too. If you take a quick look at a list of marriage deal-breakers it starts to feel naggingly familiar. Uneven distribution of housework? Join the club. Fight nasty? Who doesn't? Don't share common interests? I'm never going to find dude-style gross-out comedies entertaining. Which is to say, what divorcing couples say were the straws that broke the camel's back are the same things that many of us learn to live with in our relationships.

In short, while divorce studies, the volume of which could usefully brick up the family court, tell us lots of about what can go wrong and are no doubt terribly useful for social policy and general education, when it comes down to brass tacks they don't really tell us how to make our marriages succeed.

Time, I decided, for a change of tack. Instead of looking at all the 'why I got divorced' surveys, I started to look for 'what I did right' marriage studies. Interestingly, there's a lot less research here. Here's a short list of attributes researchers say you'll find in happy couples:
- feeling respected and appreciated
- having trust and being faithful
- having a good sex life
- having good communication
- cooperation and mutual support
- enjoying time together

- having a sense of spirituality
- sharing values
- the ability to be flexible when confronted with change.[8]

Now we're actually getting somewhere, even if this list boils down to the old-fashioned Dear Prudence advice of 'choose well', 'don't cheat', 'compromise' and 'have fun together'. Indeed, in exactly that vein, researchers have also quizzed old-timers with long marriages about what made their marriages last, and here is what they said helped them go the distance:

- having the ability to change and adapt to change, and having the ability to live with the unchangeable
- assuming the marriage would last
- trust
- a balance of power
- enjoying each other
- valuing shared history
- luck
- seeing their spouse as their best friend, and liking their spouse
- seeing marriage as a long-term commitment
- seeing marriage as a sacred institution
- agreeing on aims and goals
- spouses becoming more interesting to each other
- wanting the relationship to succeed.[9]

It's hard to disagree with anything on this list. But here's the tricky bit: how do you actually live that today? It looks easy written down, but somehow I suspected that memorising that list really wasn't going to be a huge amount of help because it still doesn't tell you how you actually live it. To that end I decided there was nothing for it but some good old-fashioned David Attenborough-style observation. I would visit the happily married species in its natural habitat. I would observe, make notes, draw pictures and diagrams. I would talk to the experts who have spent years putting the happily marrieds into captivity then prodding and poking them to see how they reacted. And I would go straight to the source—people who say they have happy marriages.

I started collecting stories from couples. Many were friends, others heard about the project as word rippled out, some came from support agencies or through professional recommendation. A few were simply in the right place at the right time when I bowled up with my tape recorder, and all were generous to a fault. They let me into their beds and their bank accounts. I got the low-down on their fights and their make-ups. I watched them create a marriage and a family and a community without losing their sense of themselves in the process.

I began to put together a map of what this marriage ecosystem looks like: from the first days when a couple decides to get married to the first big test—the wedding; how the limits are thrashed out once the honeymoon is over; what they said a marriage really needs to stay healthy. I looked at whether there were two species in the marriage pond or just one, and asked the hard question about how a marriage ecology survives foreign invaders like work or money or, most challenging of all, children. I started to learn what the rules were. What the conditions that make it flourish are. What really threatens it.

It's been fascinating journey and one I hope you'll enjoy as much as I have.

To sum it up

- Marrying is the start, not the end.
- Marriage, as it turns out, is fun.
- Knowing what causes divorce doesn't help you much with how to be married.
- Listing what makes a good marriage and living it are two different things.
- Happily ever after is where this story begins.

1

Why Marry?

We told our friends we were getting married while on a wine-tasting weekend in the country. There were four couples and we'd spent the time eating, drinking and playing cards. We were a tight group—three de factos, one married. When we made our announcement they all looked shocked. Then they divided into two camps. The married couple popped some champagne, said it was terrific and then told us marriage had made their relationship better. The de facto couples looked at us dumbfounded, as if we were betraying them. They soon came around, but it was clear that in deciding to make the public choice we'd stepped across a line. And indeed we had.

So why do we still marry? Today you don't need that piece of paper to buy a house or to have a child, and living together is so common that it attracts little more than a yawn outside the most conservative of families. Is it that we simply want to cater to the inner prince or princess and flounce about for a day? Are we just a generation of Muriel Heslops looking to marry because it would make us someone important? I don't think we're so hopeful. A post-divorce generation, we know if we marry to become someone the statistics don't offer good odds—at least a third of all marriages end in divorce.

Still, we're not cynical of relationships either (even if we have good reason to be) but we are wary. We've seen the marriage casualties, often lived with them. So we go for a handy halfway: we move in together. After all, can't two people who love and support each other, plan with each other without all the expense and family dramas that actually getting married entails? Well, yes. There are plenty long-term de facto couples out there proving it's possible. But for a lot of other couples—and I was a part of one—a relationship that begins as a de facto of convenience (and let's face it, it's convenience—financial, sexual, housing—as much as love that propels you into moving in together[1]) stops being quite enough. The short answer to 'Why marry?' is that marriage starts to look like it will add, well, something to your life.

Take Natalie, 31, an events manager, and Michael, 40, an IT professional. They met six years ago on a diving holiday in Vanuatu. Their holiday romance was meant to end when Michael returned home to the United Kingdom three months later, but two months after that Natalie followed him to London and they've been together ever since. Shortly after Natalie arrived in England they endured the death of Michael's father and then spent the next few years travelling the world as Michael chased IT job contracts. Landing back in Australia just before the Sydney Olympics, Natalie scored a job as an organiser for the SOCOG ceremonies and the couple finally settled down and bought a house. A relationship that had weathered so much surely didn't need a simple piece of paper to prove anything, right? Not quite. Natalie, as it turned out, really, *really* wanted that ring on her finger.

'I decided well before Mike to get married,' she says with a grin. 'But I really don't know why it was important to me. I'm a product of my upbringing, maybe it was a security thing—every time Michael couldn't get a job we'd be forced to move to another country. As contractors we were running out of options. We could live in Australia as de factos, but we couldn't move anywhere else.' So their decision was partly for pragmatic reasons. Though Natalie does own up to also wanting a princess moment.

Then she hit a road block. Michael said that he was already committed to the relationship—they had joint bank accounts, a joint car lease, a mortgage and he supported Natalie when she was unemployed. Why go to all the bother? 'He kept saying, "Don't ask me, don't ask me",' Natalie remembers. But Natalie was determined and one day—'Finally!'—she put down the hard word.

'It's been five years, we lived in two countries, we've travelled together and we've been through some pretty tough times,' she told him. 'We've survived all of that and I don't see a reason why you wouldn't marry me.' For good measure she added that if Mike didn't know by now whether he wanted to marry her he probably never would and, depending on his response, it would be her choice whether she stayed or moved on.

It didn't go well. 'He was really cross,' says Natalie, who then gave him a week to think about it and made him sleep in the spare room so he could get used to being alone. Tough, some would say, but fair.

At the end of the week Michael took Natalie out to dinner but he didn't say anything about marriage. Natalie gave him one last extension, to the end of the weekend. The next night he took her out again, to their favourite restaurant, and proposed. 'We don't talk about that week,' she says, grinning. 'We just say we got married and it was all very lovely.' And, she adds, they haven't fought like that since.

A life of choices

> Choose life. Choose a job. Choose a career. Choose a family. Choose a fucking big television. Choose washing machines, cars, compact disc players and electrical tin openers. Choose good health, low cholesterol and dental insurance. Choose fixed-interest mortgage repayments. Choose leisurewear and matching fabrics. Choose DIY

and wondering who you are on a Sunday morning. Choose sitting on that couch watching mind-numbing spirit-crushing game shows . . . Choose a future. Choose life . . .
—**Mark 'Rent-boy' Renton,** *Trainspotting,* **1996**

Natalie's story got me thinking. In our world of no guarantees the flip side to all the hard-won freedoms of our generation is choice. But all that choice has made us a bit weary. We've all got a bit of Mark 'Rent-boy' Renton in us because we are, more than anything, a generation of choosers. Every turn we have made has been about making a good choice. Do you work long hours to buy a house in your choice of suburb or save for a trip to Europe, or Asia, or America? Do you stay in a safe job or move to a riskier, more lucrative one? Shares or a mortgage? Public or private health? All this decision-making has taught us to keep our options open, because we never know when the next opportunity—or threat—will come our way.

Living lives of constant choice has infected our relationships. We get involved but not too involved—we could still move for work, or travel overseas. Mr Okay is okay, but don't shut the door in case Mr Incredibly Right comes along. We make have-it-both-ways relationships. We jump straight into living together, but keep risk at bay by splitting bills and housework down the middle and keeping two names on the rental agreement. Being de facto is one great hedge. You're there, but you've never, definitely, publicly made a final choice. We live this way often all the way through our twenties while there is a steady slippage of friendships, relationships and partnerships as we try to get ahead, to express ourselves, try to make it, or at least make money, all the while hedging our bets. We're happy and it seems to work, for a while.

Then something shifts. We start thinking about really settling down. Maybe we fall spectacularly in love, or maybe it's just a vague feeling of needing more commitment. That checklist starts humming in our heads: have a career, *get married,* surround yourself with babies. Perhaps it's turning thirty, or a friend having a baby, or a peer getting *your* dream job, but there's a 'wake up' moment. You realise you want something more than what you have now. And the deadline is looming. Because it's never been the case that we don't want long-term, committed relationships. We do. Despite the myths, generation X-ers and Y-ers emphatically do want commitment: surveys show we're the group *most* likely to regard marriage as a life-long commitment.[2] Indeed, if anything, we take it more seriously.

Choosing to marry becomes one of the big events in a lifetime of choices. It's certainly one of the biggest choices we've made thus far. So it's not surprising we feel a little daunted, especially because it's so optional, which somehow makes the idea even more powerful and more scary. Because there's also a flip side—if it doesn't work out, it's no one's fault but your own, because *you made that choice*. What do the old-timers tell us first about marriage? Choose well. They knew it and we know it. You made your bed, now lie in it. Choosing love, choosing marriage becomes both cynical and curiously romantic at the same time. We believe in love—and we believe in hope—but please God, we plead, let this be right, otherwise I'll have no one else to blame but myself. We take it desperately seriously. Despite the divorce rate, no one goes down the aisle thinking 'I'll try again if this doesn't work out'. We still see tying the knot as permanent, it still means finally closing the door to other possibilities, and it still means choosing one other person and saying this is it.

What's love got to do with it?

When I began talking with couples about why they married, what struck me was how rarely anyone mentioned love. It's not that it wasn't there—marriage wouldn't even be a choice unless there was love—but it didn't seem to be the tipping point. Rather, it seemed like the journey to marriage was more about negotiating a series of

> **Why don't we marry?**
> *Top reasons Australians give for not marrying*
> Fear of divorce (26 per cent)
> Avoidance of commitment (26 per cent)
> Fear of making a mistake (24 per cent)
> Bad previous experience (24 per cent)
> Strong commitment does not mean marriage (23 per cent)[3]
>
> *Top reasons American men give for why they haven't married*
> Sex is available without marriage
> A man can acquire a wife without marriage through cohabitation
> Wishing to avoid the risk of divorce and its cost
> Wanting to wait before having children
> Marriage requires change and compromise
> A soulmate hasn't appeared
> There are few pressures to marry
> Not wanting a relationship with a woman who has children
> Wanting to own a house before finding a wife
> Enjoying being single[4]

stumbling blocks that had more to do with what you didn't want, than about articulating what you did.

For our generation, many of our models of marriage are anti-models—when we think of marriage we think of the marriages of our grandparents or our parents and we don't relate. We don't want to look back. We don't buy the rosy domestic picture of the 1950s or the groover swinging marriages of the 1970s. We've done a lot of hard work forging a new design—none of that 'two into one' sentimentality for us. Instead, we see ourselves and our spouse as two individuals, but still side by side, trying to head in the same direction. Then we ask ourselves, is it really possible to be married and be like that?

Take Mandy, a bride-to-be with feet so cold she could have had frostbite. Despite being in a committed relationship, for this journalist, then aged 33, getting married was a terrifying proposition. 'I was never going to get married,' says Mandy. 'I thought it would make me conservative.' And that was just the start. In fact, Mandy had a whole list of reasons to not marry that ranged from 'you don't need a piece of paper to legitimise the relationship' to being superstitious that if she did love someone enough to get married, something really bad would happen to him. Sound familiar?

But as she and Andrew, an IT professional, started talking about having children two events conspired to change Mandy's mind. First she went to a friend's commitment ceremony ('their politics couldn't come at marriage') where the husband made a speech that really moved her. She fell under the marriage spell as he talked about how much he loved his partner and child 'and that when his dad died he realised that his relationship was so important that he did want to have that other element of commitment.' Then Mandy's mother, who was studying to become a marriage celebrant, wrote an essay on the history of marriage. Reading it, says Mandy, 'made me realise that even though we say cynically that it's just about property and a woman passing from father to husband, marriage is actually a ceremony that's been around for thousands of years. It is a celebration of love and of building a life together.' For the first time, Mandy considered there might be more to being married than just living together.

Although Mandy and Andrew set a date, it would be wrong to say it all fell smoothly into place. As the wedding approached Mandy's feet got colder and new issues kept arising. 'I didn't want to be the centre of attention,' she says. 'And I didn't want to deal with all the politics of getting married—the whole family business.' She tried to call the off wedding. More than once. 'Mum got a few calls in the middle of the night,' she admits. The last time she attempted a cancellation was only a couple of weeks before the ceremony, her resolve to call it off weakening only when Andrew told her that if she cancelled now his mother would lose the catering deposit. Persistence won out. Two weeks later Mandy and Andrew finally walked down a red carpet together, with Mandy dressed in pink and gold, and, in front of a fountain, in a ceremony conducted by her mother, they married.

Now, three years and two children later, all her doubts have evaporated. The wedding, says Mandy, was a catalyst for change. Getting married made her confront her fears about the future and made her think about what she thought of herself. 'The funny thing about being married is that it has made me feel more secure,' she says. 'All those things I thought I didn't want—children, my own home, mortgage, marriage—have turned out to be wonderful. I'm happier now than I've ever been.'

Deciding to get married makes us confront what we really want from life, and face what we really fear. The glib say marriage is just a piece of paper, though no one says that about divorce. Deciding to get married forces us to look ahead, to say what we believe in and hope for. We put our heart on the line to get a stake in something real. For a generation that grew up in the dying days of the Cold War and became adults in the age of AIDS and terrorism, choosing to believe in a future together is a big deal.

But is it just an uncertain future we are so afraid of? Psychoanalyst Stephen Mitchell suggests in his book, *Can Love Last?* that committing to love itself is what scares us most because it's love that finds us at our most vulnerable with someone else. We pull both ways between security and adventure, he writes, and learning to love together is about living with that constantly shifting equilibrium. Living de facto can be a way to protect ourselves from that vulnerability, as can dull domesticity where daily routines strip love of desire and break its will. Either way, choosing to really love is scary. And marrying more than anything says, 'I choose to love you'.

The rituals of courtship

> 'I've got a new theory about marriage. Two people are in love, they live together, and then suddenly, one day, they run out of conversation. Totally. They can't think of a single thing to say to each other. That's it. Panic. Then suddenly it occurs to the chap that there is a way out of this deadlock ... ask her to marry him. Suddenly they've got something to talk about for the rest of their lives.'
>
> 'Basically you are saying marriage is just a way of getting out of an embarrassing pause in the conversation.'
>
> 'Yup. The definitive icebreaker.'

—Gareth and Charles, *Four Weddings and a Funeral,* **1994**

How did it come to this? How did deciding to get married become so, well, difficult? If people have been marrying for thousands of years, how is it we've made making that decision so hard? A big part of it is that we just don't have courtship like we used to. It used to be straightforward: boy meets girl; boy and girl date; they marry; and sex, kids and mortgage all come later. Today, there are many more steps and the order is different. After boy meets girl, courtship today looks a lot more like:

- begin sexual relationship (hopefully exclusive) with emotional intimacy
- relationship recognised socially by friends and family
- live together
- share finances
- buy a house
- marry (around eight in ten)
- have children (around eight in ten).[5]

That's a lot of steps with a surprising lack of ritual celebrations for any of them. No one recognises you with a 'congratulations you're having sex' card; your parents don't have you round for drinks to celebrate your joint bank account; and who can afford to throw a 'we're buying a house' party when they're hocked to the eyeballs?

So at what point do you actually know you're serious? It's tricky. All those extra, drawn out steps mean it's harder to get around to getting married because the goalposts keep shifting and it's hard to know when you're really a committed couple. Is it when you move in together, or when you buy your first whitegoods? Does merging two CD collections count? Or is it when the government recognises that you're a permanent couple (and thus entitled to half of the joint property) after you've been living together for two years? It's all a bit of an anticlimax really—somehow having equal dibs on the book collection doesn't quite seem special. Though there is something about putting together your joint finances that has a sobering effect.

Chris, 37, a marketing director, and Ann, a 34-year-old creative director, were together for six years before they decided to tie the knot at a ceremony in 1998. During that time they had already lived together, travelled together and bought property and shares together. So why get married? 'Tax advantages,' says Chris with a cheeky grin. He's the first of several guys to make this joke. (When I called the Australian Tax Office to find out if this was actually true, they helpfully told me that the tax laws around relationships are quite complex, that they couldn't really tell me if there are any tax advantages to being married and if I was genuinely interested I should contact a tax lawyer. My accountant, when quizzed, said there *may* be some advantages when setting up a family trust.)

'One of the reasons I thought it was important to get married is we had a lot of financial commitments together,' says Ann. 'But

I also couldn't imagine living without Chris and wanted an emotional commitment as well. That's very different to financial commitments.'

This became a familiar theme for a lot of couples: a 'debt until death' mortgage isn't quite the same as 'until death do us part' marriage. For most couples, commitment needs to include more than just joint finances.

Do de factos divorce more?

> It is easier to be a lover than a husband for the simple reason that it is more difficult to be witty every day than say pretty things from time to time.
> **—Honoré de Balzac, *The Physiology of Marriage*, 1829**

We don't necessarily yearn for a simpler time. Chris pointed out he had no nostalgia for a time when courtship was quicker and straightforward. 'Looking at my parents' generation, lots of couples divorced,' he says. 'Most got married before they were fully developed people. I'm hoping that because we took the time to become people first, we'll be more successful at being married.'

It's a good point. Taking time to get to know yourself and each other should mean that you're more prepared for marriage. This should also mean de facto couples have a better chance when it comes to staying together after getting married. But curiously, some research (mostly from the United States) suggests the exact opposite, that de facto couples who marry have a greater chance of divorcing.[6] Social researchers offer three possible explanations for this statistic:

- people who cohabit may be more skittish about commitment in the first place, or more likely to call it quits when problems arise
- cohabiters don't develop good conflict–resolution and support skills; instead they tussle for control and then carry these bad habits over to married life

- some de facto relationships are in their last stages of the relationship when the couple decided to marry and marriage failed to 'save' them.

It all sounds rather grim, especially if you're contemplating making the leap from defacto-dom. But it's not the whole story.

In all probability we're in the middle of a generational shift that is part of the 'new-deal' relationships we're forging. New Australian research indicates that living together in the 1990s didn't show up the same marriage failure risks as it had in the 1970s and 1980s. So while the earlier mob may well have been skittish committers, nowadays, as de facto is the pre-marriage step for more than 70 per cent of first-married couples in Australia and the United Kingdom,[7] it's just another step in the whole courtship ritual. Indeed, giving credence to the third theory (that de factos marry to save their relationship) when researchers added the total number of years couples lived together—in cohabitation or marriage—they couldn't distinguish relationship breakdown rates between the only marrieds and the de facto-to-marrieds.[8] And the really good news is that couples who have been living together before marriage have higher levels of relationship happiness and lower levels of relationship instability, disagreements and violent conflict than those who stay cohabiting.[9] Nor are all de facto relationships equal anyway. The ones far and away most at risk are the serial cohabiters—those who have lived with more than one partner,[10] which could suggest a lack of interest in building relationship skills.

Top three reasons people marry
To signify a life-long commitment
Security for children
To make a public commitment to each other[11]

Still not everyone takes the de facto path. Monica and Daniel are both professionals in the telecommunications industry. They met at work when they were put together on the same team and started dating a few months later. Then Monica proposed moving in together. It wasn't her first time—she had previously lived with a boyfriend for five years—so she didn't think it was a strange idea at all. Daniel, however, would have none of it.

'His response was "not until you have a ring on your finger",' says Monica. 'I was like "What?!"' Daniel, a devout Catholic, knew about Monica's previous boyfriend and he wasn't taking that same chance. It was marriage or nothing, which was rather confronting for Monica, who'd always maintained she didn't want to marry and didn't want kids. In fact, her previous boyfriend had asked her to marry him and she'd refused. Still, that first proposal had prompted a revelation—she hadn't wanted to marry *him* and that might have been the real reason she thought she didn't want children. So Daniel played a waiting game.

'It took him twelve weeks to ask me to marry him because it was a decision that I had to work through,' says Monica. 'He was quite smart. If he had asked me when I first talked about moving in together I'd probably have said no. But twelve weeks later I sort of thought "Why not? I've never felt like this about someone in my life".' Over those three months they also talked about having children, their careers, and future directions. Still, to be certain, when Daniel finally asked Monica she insisted on a twelve-month engagement.

Now married for five years and with two young sons, Monica sees a stark contrast between being married and just living together. 'Before I had been living on a day-to-day basis,' Monica observes. 'I didn't really appreciate the difference marriage can make until I went through the hard times—particularly when raising young children and having a career.'

Marriage, Monica believes, means she can put up with the bad times knowing it won't always be that way. 'I know it will be better than this for the rest of our lives. I can plan on that.' And there is the key. Beyond the dream wedding, the emotional bond and the public commitment, marriage offers something de facto relationships often don't. A future.

Indeed, it's often a crisis in the present that propels people into considering marriage and a future. For Georgina, 28, a television producer, and Martin, 35, a graphic designer, it was adversity that got them thinking. Together for seven years after meeting at university, they'd lived together in share houses, travelled and moved to the United Kingdom. Then, two years ago, they had a very bad year. Martin's father and sister both died within months of each other and then his work in design and animation dried up. He was out of the industry, unemployed, miserable and a long way from his friends. The only work he could find was in a pub so he and Georgina had to put their plans for owning a house on the backburner, along with their passion for travel.

But Georgina, during this time, was hitting her stride. She was working at the BBC in the documentary field, a position she'd long aspired to. One was on the up, the other very down and they weren't feeling like a successful dual-career, dual-income couple anymore.

'It was very depressing at times,' Georgina says. 'We did have a few big, teary fights.'

Their troubles could easily have torn them apart but instead they went back and took a long hard look at what really mattered. It was the relationship, a shared love of travel and a desire to have kids. So, right in the midst of the gloom, they decided to get married. They travelled back to Australia for the wedding and married at sunset in a waterside ceremony surrounded by their friends and family.

'For one glorious day,' says Martin, 'we were happy without limit. It was a surreal high point. If we had done it a year earlier it wouldn't have meant nearly as much. It was the fact that there were two of us in it that kept everything else at bay.' Martin continues, 'A friend asked me on the day "why get married?" I did the usual "I love her, she loves me" naff but then I thought "what this really is about is family". We plan to make a large family. In your twenties it's about your friends, but in my thirties family has become more important again and with Georgina I'm creating a family.'

> **Do de factos marry?**
> One in four cohabiting women say they don't expect to marry the man they're living with, so cohabiting isn't necessarily another step towards marriage. Around one quarter of couples will give different answers about their plans to marry in the future. Women are more likely than men to say that they expect to marry the person they're living with.[12]

The second time around

> The most superficial observer must have noticed that there is being gradually built up in the community a growing dread of the conjugal bond, especially among men, and a condition of discontent and unrest among married people, particularly women.
> —Maud Churton Braby, *Modern Marriage and How to Bear It*, 1908

While planning a future is great if you're a first timer, what if you've been married before? Wouldn't you be once bitten, twice shy? On paper, Tiffany, 36, a book editor and businesswoman, looks like she should be very marriage averse—not only did her parents divorce, but by the age of 30 she had two marriages behind her. But now married for five years to Andrew, a media consultant, she and Andrew—with children Holden, six, and Phoebe, three—are the very picture of domestic delight.

'I don't know whether it means I'm a hopeless romantic or quite pragmatic,' says Tiffany. 'People who have been divorced and say "that's put me off getting married" are basing their life on the principle that there's only one person out there for you. I think that's romantic claptrap,' she continues. 'I think it's a bit more like there's any number of people out there for you, and there's any number of people you can make it work with, but it comes to a point where you meet someone, and you think, "I can do this with this person, and I will". And it is a matter of will—it doesn't just happen. Marriage isn't the end or "happy ever after". Being married before didn't stop me being married again. Didn't even make me think twice about it to be honest.'

'Didn't cross my mind either,' says Andrew. 'Tiff's previous marriages make great stories for her, but I can honestly say I've never felt threatened. Maybe I have a healthy enough ego to think I'm different.'

'My parents divorced when I was twelve and they'd been together fourteen or fifteen years,' says Tiffany. 'I remember someone saying to me "do you think it affects you, being the product of a failed marriage?" and I don't actually regard my parents' marriage as being a failed marriage. They stayed together for fourteen years, had two fairly well-adjusted children and at a certain point it was no longer viable and they went their separate ways with very little animosity.' She pauses then asks, 'How do you define successful? Other people can be married for forty or fifty years and be pretty miserable and hate each other and people from the outside might say it's successful because of the time but it's not what I would consider successful.'

It's an approach reflected in Andrew and Tiffany's wedding vows, spoken at a cliff-top wedding overlooking the water.

'We said stuff about being individuals and that marriage makes us two individuals working together,' says Tiffany, 'not some icky thing about being two halves of something because we're not two halves, we're a team, not a unit. Our marriage is just one further step commitment-wise, and it's the public thing as well. We made the commitment and we're going to celebrate it.'

The starter marriage

Indeed, first-marriage breakdown makes people less skittish than you'd think: one in three marriages taking place in Australia in any year are remarriages for at least one of the partners.[13] But for those taking the plunge again, a lot seems to come down to how they see their first marriages and understanding what went wrong, even seeing the extra experience as a good thing.

David, 34, a writer, married to Jennie, 36, an advertising account manager, looks on his previous marriage positively. 'I by no means look on it as being a negative experience,' he says. 'In fact the positives totally outweigh the negatives. I look at it as "what could I have done better?" and "what am I going to do better this time around?" and try to be really honest about it. It would be so easy to say "oh it was the other person's fault and I was the perfect husband," but it's given me an insight into my own character, as well as shown me what's required of me to make a marriage work.'

Nor was David's previous marriage a deterrent to Jennie. 'It made me more positive,' she says. 'Everything he had gone through in his previous marriage had really helped him grow as a person.'

There's a name for this phenomenon: the starter marriage. It's a term coined to describe first-time marriages that last five years or less and do not produce any children. Author Pamela Paul has written a whole book on the subject. She thinks starter marriages have a lot to do with people focusing too much on a wedding and not enough on the marriage after, and having unrealistic expectations of what marriage can and cannot offer. A veteran of a starter marriage herself, Paul writes the good news is that these older and wiser divorcees can end up with the tools and experience needed to make the second trip down the aisle lasting and rewarding. This seems important because statistics also show second marriages have higher divorce rates than first.

Joanne, 36, a marketing manager, and Luke, 29, in information technology support, see it Paul's way. Both previously married, they got hitched two years ago when son Lachlan—now a tumbling tot in their cosy mountain cottage—was on the way. Both are thoughtful as to what went wrong the first time round. For Luke, his first marriage was about trying to fix a relationship already going off the rails: 'Gotta try something,' he says with a helpless shrug. Joanne, on the other hand, had married because she felt the pressure of a ticking clock.

'I was getting close to thirty and as a female I felt a lot of pressure to be married and to be in a certain place by that age.'

Meeting at work in the aftermath of the breakdown of their marriages, both say this time round everything is very different.

'You think about it more logically—can I spend the rest of my life with this person?' says Joanne. 'I know what it's like to walk away from a marriage and I never want to go through that again in my life.'

'Unlike the first time', Luke says simply, 'there was nothing to fix.'

> **Good news about marriage #1: marriage civilises men**
> Once married, men earn more, work more and attend church more often. They also frequent bars less often.[14] In fact, in a study of paroled men, University of Florida researchers found that the most hardened ex-cons were far less likely to return to their crooked ways if they settled down into the routines of a solid marriage. De facto relationships did not have the same crime-reducing effect.[15]

Creating a step-family

Getting over a starter marriage is easier when there are no two-legged reminders of the past. But what if there are? What is it like deciding to get married if you're going to be making a step-family? This is exactly what Sarah, 31, faced. Meeting Andrew, 47, at work ('He charmed me over the phone'), their decision to marry was complicated by the fact he had two almost-teenage children from his previous marriage. What's more, the acrimonious break-up of that marriage had left Andrew gun-shy of marrying again, to say the least.

'I was reluctant,' he admits. 'I just thought that Sarah and I had a pretty good relationship and, well, why change it?'

At first they didn't, simply living together as a part-time extended family. Then Sarah fell pregnant. Both agreed they didn't want to marry just because they were having a child. But that changed when they began talking about having another.

'I told Andrew that before I had my next baby I wanted to get married,' says Sarah. By then, Andrew was persuaded this relationship would stick.

'I think the time told,' he says. 'Everything had worked out. I had a reasonable balance with my own children and I thought that it was a good time to go again.' But there was one thing that Andrew insisted on before they took the plunge—counselling.

Andrew had spent six months in counselling after the breakdown of his first marriage. 'It was a huge help to sort through the things that I'd done wrong in life. I had to sort out what had gone wrong in my relationship and this counsellor really helped me to do that. To me it's like looking after the car,' he says. 'We'd been looking after the car fairly well, but I thought we might just get it checked over before we go on holidays—that's how I saw getting married again.' It was the counselling that finally sorted out their ongoing negotiations about the children from his first marriage.

'I really remembered the counsellor saying, "You know, Andrew's been married once and you've just got to let him deal with that",' Sarah says. 'She said, "That's his thing and that's over here in this square and you don't get involved" and from that day on I just stepped out and went "that's for you to deal with, it's nothing to do with me". Up until then I had let it affect me and it would always upset me. Getting married,' she adds, 'was more of a confirmation about how we felt about each other. It sort of put all the pieces of the puzzle together and while it didn't change our relationship, it probably made me feel more secure.'

Andrew agrees. 'I've had a fantastic opportunity for a great marriage and relationship,' he says. 'I think it's the best thing I've ever done.'

> **Good news about marriage #2: married people are healthier**
> Just 13 per cent of married men and women suffered stress compared to the 25 per cent of single men and women who are miserable when single. Women with children and a job have the fewest mental health problems of any other group of women.[16] This works second time around too! Relative to never-married or divorced people, people in second marriages are happier, live longer and have lower rates of many diseases and illnesses. And when they do develop health problems, they tend to recover faster and better from many illnesses than other adults.[17]

Improving the odds

It's not just those going round for a second time who see the benefits of pre-marriage counselling. Going hand in hand with our deliberate choosing to marry is wanting to do so with a plan, and around one in three couples marrying in Australia attend some form of relationship education.[18] This can range from filling in compatibility-type questionnaires to intensive weekends away with other couples. It's very popular with church groups and is becoming more widely common beyond them. It makes sense: with such a high divorce rate, why wouldn't you want to improve your odds?

Caroline Haski, a practicing therapist, conducts premarital education programs. Many of the participants are referred to her by Temple Emanuel in Woollahra, Sydney, which requires couples to undertake a premarital program before they can get married there. Like many premarital counsellors, Haski runs the Prepare program, a licensed format. In this program couples sign up for two to three sessions. At the first session each person completes an inventory that canvasses their attitudes, values and history on a range of issues. In the second, their inventories are mapped along the lines of emotional closeness in the couple and the closeness of the families they come from. The inventories look at their flexibility in decision-making, particularly in times of stress, and the values and attitudes that they've brought from their own families.

'It's really giving people information and enabling them to use the knowledge and skills they already have to address issues that can be universally present in long-term committed relationships,' says Haski. 'It's very useful for helping couples feel able to disclose what's really a sticking point or something that's been put on the back-burner—the experience where one partner says, "Oh, that used to be a problem, but we're past that now," and the look on their partner's face says, "Oh, no we're not".'

This was very much the experience of Andrew, a financier, and Eleanor, now a full-time mother with an active involvement in several charities. On the surface, from their waterfront flat overlooking the boats bobbing in a bay, they are the very picture of a stimulating modern marriage: their exchanges are lively and they swap fond looks as they constantly check what the other is thinking. With two young children and another on the way, they share parenting and both work on maintaining outside interests. But both fall over themselves to add it wasn't always this blissful.

It was, for a start, a turbulent courtship with several break-ups. And coming from two very different families—Eleanor is from a very religious Catholic family of six children, while Andrew's from 'a family shrub', his father having three children by three different marriages making ten siblings in total—they didn't have the same starting point on relationships.

'I never understood why people got married,' says Andrew. 'My father was a womaniser and a terrible role model in a lot of ways, and I never felt particularly inclined to get married.' Four years into his relationship with Eleanor a series of family crises, culminating in the death of Andrew's father, tipped the balance. Even though he and Eleanor were apart at the time, 'there was a strong sense that "this is the one",' says Andrew, 'even though we had travelled a rocky road together.'

Andrew proposed, Eleanor accepted, and a wedding date was set for six months' time. Then, 'I sort of freaked out,' says Eleanor. 'I grew up in a family with happily married parents. I saw how a good relationship can work, but how you have to work at it. If anything,' she continues, 'my fears were that I wanted so much to have that good marriage that I was petrified of not achieving it. We were coming from such different worlds, beliefs, family backgrounds. I was like, "Oh my God, is that going to work?"' She was, she confesses, driving Andrew mad being Miss Hypothetical—'just say this happens, what would you do?'

Then one day, Andrew turned to Eleanor and said, 'The ironic thing here is I have more faith in this relationship than you do and I believe we can work through these things together.' That stopped Eleanor in her tracks. The crisis propelled them into premarriage counselling, although Andrew was skeptical about it. 'I went in thinking "bet this is really rinky dink",' he says, screwing up his face. Still, he went. They filled out an 'agree', 'disagree' or 'uncertain' 140-point questionnaire that covered areas such as finance, family background and sexuality, had their answers collated and then sat down with the counsellor. 'We were about an hour into it,' recounts Eleanor, 'and the counsellor said "look, I just want to point out to you that most couples just come to one counselling session but you guys haven't even resolved the first issue. Are you happy to come back for a second session?"'

In those two sessions they covered things they'd been talking about for years, finally saying what they really thought. Like the issue of children. 'I didn't know whether I wanted to work after having children,' says Eleanor. 'Andrew's mother is very career driven, so I always worried that he wouldn't respect me if I wanted to stay at home. Even if I wasn't going to do that, I wanted to know it was an available choice,' she says. 'I brought that up as an issue and Andrew said, "I've told Eleanor not to worry about it, we'll deal with it." The facilitator said, "Look, Andrew, Eleanor is asking you for an answer now." We had discussed it for years, and Andrew thought he was answering it by saying, "don't worry about it", but I really needed reassurance.'

'Some things had become taboo topics,' agrees Andrew. 'As soon as Eleanor would raise one I'd half roll my eyes in a sort of "oh God, this is a topic I can't be bothered investing in" way. The best thing about that whole process was bringing [to the surface] any taboos we'd had in our interactions and finally settling a few matters, once and for all, which I hadn't realised were there in the first place.' A complete convert, Andrew says that these days, whenever he hears people talking about getting married, he implores them to try counselling. 'I was skeptical and I came out completely sold. It was fantastic, it really was.'

Haski has an expression she likes to pass on. 'No relationship really gets going until each person realises the person they married isn't going to be the parent they wished they'd had. Sometimes we gravitate towards people we think will make up, or compensate in some way, for what we think we missed out on. Or if we had great experiences we want to repeat them,' she explains. 'So there are also questions like "what do you want to bring from your family of origin to your marriage?" Those are very important. Not everyone comes from happy families, but perhaps there is something you can value even if you grew up in a problematic, stressful environment.'

Haski is at pains to point out that premarriage classes aren't counselling or advising. 'I'm not in the business of telling people what to do or to predict,' she laughs. 'A Rabbi friend told me he once said to a couple "don't get married, you're not meant for each other". They went off and were married by someone else. Then he said they stayed married for thirty years just to spite him.'

As for the million-dollar question, do premarital classes really make a difference? Well, everyone I spoke to who had done it was a fan, but in terms of research the jury is still out. Studies show couples who attend pre-marital workshops are mostly positive about the experience and rate their levels of communication and overall satisfaction 30 per cent higher than couples who don't.[19] They also show these courses are good at increasing awareness, improving communication and conflict resolution and at generally building relationship skills,[20] but there are no long-term studies to show whether or not they actually make marriages any more likely to last.[21]

Marriage in the noughties

> See, I've always been afraid of marriage because of, you know, ball and chain. I want freedom, all that . . . I suddenly saw it was the opposite: that is you got married to someone you know you love, you sort yourself out, it frees you up for other things.
> —**Nick Hornby,** *High Fidelity*, **1995**

Something else struck me when I was talking to all these couples about getting married: none of them mentioned that they were afraid of losing their freedom. They don't really see marriage as the end of something. It's not the ball and chain it used to be.

Something about marriage has shifted. At the very point in time when divorce rates are peaking and the marriage rate is dropping to record lows, we've finally got those old pictures out of our heads; we've stopped idealising marriage as a simple time of mowing the lawn on Sundays while a roast's in the oven, and we've stopped pretending that the 1970s playboy ended up doing anything but forlornly buying new playmates. In short, we've stopped looking back at what we imagined marriage and bachelorhood was and we've started looking forward, creating new versions of marriage. We know it was more complicated than then and we know we lead complicated lives now. Perhaps because the blinkers are off, though, we've given ourselves permission to simply be honest. We know as individuals we've negotiated a life without guarantees, so we need marriages that can navigate that fluid world outside, too.

You can see this in something seemingly simple like whether women change their names when they marry. It didn't even cross my mind that I would. I wasn't trying to change who I was, exactly the opposite: I was marrying someone who loved me for who I am. My name was part of who I was so why on earth would I want to change that? It also hadn't occurred to me that anyone would expect it. You can imagine what happened. Straight after we had exchanged our wedding vows my mother-in-law raced up to congratulate the new Mrs Johnson. 'But I'm not . . .' I choked.

It was the same for Mandy. 'I didn't even consider it,' she agrees. 'I'm 36, I'm going to change my name? No way.'

Perhaps it was because we were marrying later in life and already had a history. We weren't looking to jettison that and start afresh with a different identity. But in fact, Mandy and I are in the minority. For a generation raised by feminists, a surprising 86 per cent of brides still take their partner's surname.[22] It's when you talk to both groups about why that you start getting the idea of how we're re-inventing our relationships.

For some it is simple. 'I wanted to have the same surname as my children,' said Catherine. 'It's nice being a Reeves family,' said Joanne. For some it's more about creating a unit. They don't see it so much as joining their husband's family as making their own.

For others it's a welcome chance to start anew. Alicia had a turbulent childhood, raised by a single mum with money always tight and a very distant father. 'I didn't feel anything special about my surname,' she says. 'Why not give it up and start fresh? Create something new for the two of us.'

Others look to a middle ground, like Ann and Chris. 'For me it was very important Ann took my name. It meant a lot,' admits Chris. 'My attitude is that marriage is symbolic. So if you do the symbolic thing, you do it all.' They compromised.

'At work I'm Ann Gordon,' says Ann. 'But for everything we do together I'm Ann Armstrong.'

'Mrs A,' says Chris with a grin.

'Mrs A I don't mind,' says Ann.

Whether we change our names or not, we're saying exactly the same thing: our marriage is going to be what we make it. It's setting a standard for ourselves. We don't kid ourselves about this, we know we demand a lot from our marriages. We expect we'll have to work on them—but then, we've already worked to get this far. We've already set up a lot of the ground rules by the time we get hitched—mutual support, planning, investment—and only when they're working will we sign on the dotted line. We've decided we won't settle for freewheeling de facto-dom without end and we're looking for more than just a dependable spouse with a steady job. We want a soul-mate, a partner in crime, a supporter of our careers and an equal carer of the children, the pets and the house; someone who'll stimulates us, understand us and who dreams the same dreams. We want someone who won't tie us down but will be our refuge from the world. We are taking the individual freedoms we've found outside our relationship and turning those into freedom within. We're shaping marriage into a model that works for us.

We've changed the rules. The ecosystems of our marriages are more dynamic. We're coping with a world where jobs, investments, family and friends can be shifting, not the solid bedrock we may once have imagined it to be.

And whatever we're doing, however we're doing it, we're doing it right. In surveys of married people, at any one time 80 per cent or more say they are happily married. That's right. As it turns out, for most people, marriage really works.

To sum it up

- Being married is different to living together.
- Marriage is a choice, and choice can be scary.
- Marriage doesn't change who you are.
- Love is where you are most vulnerable.
- Joint finances aren't much of a commitment.
- Our marriages are different from those of our parents.
- Marriage gives you a future.
- Write your own rules.
- If you need help, bring in the experts.
- First marriages—the benefits of such an experience linger long after the scars have healed.
- Just because you've lived together doesn't mean you know how to be married.
- Only the two of you know if it's really right.
- Marriage isn't an end, it's a beginning.

2

Nice Day for a White Wedding

Wilt thou have this Woman to thy wedded Wife, to live together after God's ordinance in the holy estate of Matrimony? Wilt thou love her, comfort her, honour her, and keep her in sickness and in health; and, forsaking all other, keep thee only unto her, so long as ye both shall live?

The Man shall answer, I will.

Then shall the Priest say unto the Woman,

Wilt thou have this Man to thy wedded Husband, to live together after God's ordinance in the holy estate of Matrimony? Wilt thou obey him, and serve him, love, honour, and keep him in sickness and in health; and, forsaking all other, keep thee only unto him, so long as ye both shall live?

The Woman shall answer, I will.

—*The Book of Common Prayer,* **1622**

It's the opening day of the Sydney Bridal Show, held, more appropriately than perhaps intended, next door to the Fox movie studios.

Bursting through the doors are thousands of keen-eyed brides, trailed in order by their almost-as-enthused bridesmaids and slightly less eager grooms, and bringing up the rear are mothers with checklists and resigned, wallet-tapping fathers. All are set on the same mission: to create the perfect wedding.

Not that I've been here before. When it came to our wedding I wasn't nearly so organised—or so stereotypical. Sure, one friend tried to terrify me with copies of *Martha Stewart Weddings* (the dessert has to coordinate with the bridesmaids' outfits?) but I preferred the advice of another friend who said, 'Just look at the magazines—then do the opposite'. I was an individual, damn it! No cookie-cutter wedding for me. So apart from the ceremony, the wedding cake, the speeches and the invitations I was radically different. I didn't wear white and I wasn't given away. Okay, so it's hard to really buck the system but I tried.

Which is to say, I'm here today feeling a bit like a fish out of water. What I'm hoping to see is whether behind the rampant wedding industry—and make no mistake, weddings are very big business—there might be a hint of what the actual marriage might be like after the big day.

As I watch these eager groups plunge into bridal paradise, all I can see is that virginal white weddings are still in vogue—even if the flower girls are the couple's own kids. And it is still all about the bride, for, with the exception of some flash suits, flasher cars and a popular-with-the-boys chocolate fountain, the pink, white and crimson wares on display whisper repeatedly, 'it's *her* day'.

Solemnly consulting lists, bridal parties to-be promenade up and down the dress-strewn aisles, tasting cake samples here, pausing to read a poem sampler there. Choice reigns supreme. Is it to be roses or tulips? A formal table or simply cocktail? Harpist or a motorcycle escort? In one corner a bridal waltz is drowned out by the bridal rap being spun by a wedding DJ just across the way while Depilation Alley demonstrates that the amount of unsightly, unbridal hair to be removed is in direct proportion to the layers of wedding make-up to be piled on, ready for the photographers to create their studio-production magic. It's as if the movie *Murial's Wedding* never happened—there isn't a hint of irony in the whole place. The closest anyone comes to acknowledging that all might not be bliss after the big day is the purveyor of the Compatibility Blanket, which is split vertically down the middle so that one half is warm and the other cool.

It would be so easy to be cynical, watching these determined brides and attendants sally forth in tight wedge formation, if it weren't for something else. Rising above all the fat is a pure tears-in-your-eyes, choke-in-your-voice hope they all carry that takes my breath away.

Around six in ten couples in this auditorium will make it to their tenth anniversary. So already I know this room is filled with optimists. I get the feeling that everyone here believes that somehow the event they will conjure from the brochures, samples and giveaway bags will weave a special magic. That a perfect wedding day will help invoke a perfect marriage.

As the human tide turns towards the bridal fashion parade in the next pavilion, I see John and Sue Carroll handing out brochures from their Life Explored stall in the last aisle. Marriage counsellors, they're here touting premarriage counselling sessions.

'We're probably the only stall here offering something for life, not just [for] the day,' observes John. They've had a mixed reception.

'Some say "we don't need it because we've been living together for five years",' says Sue. 'Or parents say "I wish we had something like that".'

'Today's generation knows the divorce rate,' says John, 'they're looking for something more.'

This is why there is such an air of frantic, fingers-crossed hope pervading the place. With one in four of these marriages destined for divorce, who wouldn't want a little magic to see them on their way?

While I can pretend Rob and I weren't like this we really weren't so different. We might not have gone to the bridal expos, but just like most of our friends, when it came to our wedding we knew what we wanted—a party with our friends, nothing too fancy, and to dress up in a nice frock. Our wedding would be the perfect statement about who we were. And that would make it stick.

What a difference a day makes

> Another bride, another June
> another sunny honeymoon
> another season, another reason
> for makin' whoopee.
>
> A lot of shoes, a lot of rice
> the groom is nervous, he answers twice
> it's really killin', that he's so willin'
> to make whoopee!
> **—Gus Kahn, *Makin' Whoopee*, 1928**

Who were we kidding? Within a week or so of announcing the wedding date, we were presented with a handwritten list of 'must invites' by one set of parents and a typed list of reasons why our chosen venue was a bad idea by the other. While you might think your wedding is your day—and your first chance as a couple to make a public statement—it's really an event everyone wants a piece of. So at the very moment you're doing the most adult thing possible, your family is trying to impose their will on you more than ever. Forget that you moved out of home years before, that you've been living together forever or that you already own a house or have a child. The lead-up can easily feel like being trapped in a bad reality TV show.

In short, a wedding is one big load of expectations covered in meringue and white frosting. The stage is set for a classic showdown, featuring the dream themes of every soap-opera: family politics, fantasies, passions, values and huge expenses. If you're looking for a perfect wedding to be the good omen for a perfect marriage, you're on a road to nowhere.

Julia and Vikram's marriage almost didn't survive their wedding. Three years ago, Julia, a 29-year-old university administrator, met Vikram, 30, a barrister, while on holiday in India. After a whirlwind romance ignited during a Bollywood film, Julia convinced Vikram to come to Australia to study for his MBA. Here they lived together with her mother, but largely because Vikram's family was uncomfortable with this they decided to get married. Then they decided they'd do it in Bangalore, India, Vikram's home town.

It was to be an extravagant affair, with three full days of ceremonies. Julia was determined to get everything right, so she studied Hindu custom and prepared a rituals booklet for the thirty friends and family who travelled to India from Australia for the wedding. She and Vikram even attended cross-cultural counselling before they left Australia to iron out some misunderstandings. Of course she couldn't have been less prepared. Despite the giant arch picking out their names in marigolds, Julia had very little to do with her own wedding.

Julia spent the day before her wedding in typical Indian bridal fashion with her girlfriends, getting their hands and feet decorated in henna. Fun for the first hour, less so after the fifth, but being hand fed sweets was some compensation. On her wedding day Julia rose at 3.30 a.m. to begin preparations. Despite her protests she found herself wearing a heavy and uncomfortable headdress which soon added to the strain of wearing an unfamiliar-feeling red sari. Things were already out of her control.

'There were lots of people dressing me and putting on make-up, who didn't speak English,' Julia remembers. She was confused and didn't know what was going to happen next. 'I was kind of shoved out into the ceremony before I knew what was going on, and then basically had to just sit there for hours.'

With the ceremony almost entirely in Sanskrit, no one—not even her Indian family—really understood each part. Adding insult to injury, even though everyone had to participate, the guests could come and go while Julia had to sit still under the full glare of lights and video cameras on an already warm February day. All the while desperately needing to go to the toilet.

'I experienced extreme culture shock,' she says. 'Western brides are used to being in control on their wedding days. It's the exact opposite in India.'

Vikram, for his part, had been kept busy with family and preparations of his own.

'He didn't mediate on my behalf,' Julia says of the wedding planning and adds, still incredulously, 'On the evening of our wedding day he left to pick up his boss from the airport!'

'It was simply expected,' shrugs Vikram.

'The whole thing nearly ended there,' says Julia. 'It wasn't the happiest day of my life. I'm still angry about it,' she admits. 'Indian weddings aren't about the couple. It's really for the two families. I expected it to be my day, but there was no idea of that at all. It just felt like hundreds of people poking at me.'

While a wedding is a true rite of passage, it is not necessarily so in the way you are expecting. It can be a hothouse that germinates all the tensions lying dormant in your relationship, so at the very time when you think you'll be coming together, your differences are being floodlit. While Julia and Vikram are an extreme example, what they experienced is what most couples go through. Your wedding is only the start of a delicate negotiation cycle with family expectations that can last your entire marriage. In many ways the wedding is when you first start laying down the boundaries between your marriage and your family, which is the real rite of passage.

While losing control of your wedding doesn't have to spell doom for your marriage, it certainly gives you pause for thought about what the family boundaries are to be in your relationship. Julia and Vikram both know they haven't chosen an easy road trying to blend two cultures. And the jury is still out on where they will raise their children—Australia or India. Julia still fears that despite Vikram's family being liberal, she won't really have her freedom if they move to India. Vikram still misses the warm family clan he grew up with. Both acknowledge that finding a common communication style can be difficult; the happy medium sitting somewhere between Julia's western-style forthright immediacy and Vikram's philosophical eastern-style far-sightedness. They also know they'll have to keep negotiating that space in between. Their wedding brought up tensions that were going to surface anyway.

While she hasn't quite put it behind her, Julia was able to get some perspective after speaking to other Indian women. 'The older ones said, "we didn't even know our husbands",' she recounts. And back in Melbourne the pair had another ceremony, western and casual, for their friends. This time it was Vikram's turn to feel like a fish out of water.

'I'd never attended a western wedding,' says Vikram. 'Julia kept saying "what have you done for the wedding?" and I'd be "I don't know. What am I meant to do?"'

Now, they're looking past the wedding experiences and learning to turn their cultural differences into a strength, going back to the first principle of their relationship.

'The glue to our relationship is the Indian tradition that love is forever,' says Julia. 'It's very sincere and very refreshing. Vikram is a pillar. His mother said to me, "Don't even think it won't work out. Don't even entertain the idea." His conviction about us being meant to be is really incredible.'

Clashing wedding expectations don't necessarily come from outsiders such as your family. There are also your own expectations to deal with. Natalie and Mike (of the reluctant proposal in chapter 1)

> **The cost of love**
> The average cost of an Australian wedding is now $36 234, compared with $27 642 in 2000 and $22 751 in 1998.
> The average cost of an engagement ring is $2500.
> 54 per cent of brides will spend from $1000 to $3000 on their wedding dress.
> 57 per cent of brides expect to receive gifts in the $50 to $100 price range.[1]

thought that with his family in England and hers in Australia their best bet to avoid family politics was simply to elope. But checking through the tropical Asia–Pacific region Natalie soon found that if it wasn't monsoon season, the country was burdened with an impossible bureaucracy, a different religion or they had already been there before. Fate finally intervened. With Mike's IT contract about to run out, meaning they'd have to go back overseas for work, the couple finally settled on the perfect Pacific Ocean destination where there were no hassles—Sydney.

Now, however, they were back to square one on the family invite politics and had just seven weeks to organise the whole event. It was only then that Natalie realised that a big element in Mike's reluctance to get married wasn't his family's assumptions about the wedding, but his own.

'He was saying things like, "I'll have to get up and do a bridal waltz", "I'll have to wear a tux", and "I'll have to give this long speech",' she recounts. He also expected that the ceremony had to be in a church, they'd have a day-do and night-do, 200 guests and a buffet, just like at home in the United Kingdom.

'No, no, no,' said Natalie, who had something rather more casual in mind. 'Once we got going and he understood where we were heading, it was fine,' she says. 'It wasn't difficult for him, it was just different.'

Natalie and Mike threw away the rule book and the result was a barefoot wedding on the beach with twenty-five guests—four came out from England—and dinner at a long *Godfather*-style table in their favourite restaurant afterwards. Natalie wore a purple dress and carried long-stemmed oriental stargazer lilies. Mike wore a white shirt with a purple tie. They wrote their own vows—another thing Mike couldn't imagine—and the cake was a non-traditional chocolate mud.

'Halfway through the day Mike turned to me and said "this is so much fun, I should have done this sooner",' says Natalie. 'My girlfriends were queuing up to hit him.'

It wasn't entirely painless, though. Family politics reared its head when some relatives who had been invited by Mike's mother had to be uninvited by Natalie, but she maintains that it was worth it because they had the wedding they wanted.

'We've only had one fight since we got married, because [previously] we only ever thought about one thing, and that was when we were going to get married,' says Natalie. 'Isn't that strange? It's only one day but it made an enormous difference. We're happier than when we first met, and that is true love.'

A wedding survival guide from our celebrant
Manage your family relations.
Know that making up the guest list is always fraught with tension, especially when there are big families involved.
Keep a lid on the costs and plan well ahead.
Have attendants who will be helpful rather than theatrical.

Speaking from the heart

Back at the bridal expo, something else struck me. While there were hundreds of bridal variations when it came to the dress, the flowers, the cake, indeed all the frippery that surrounds a wedding, there was almost nothing there that catered to the actual 'getting married' bit—your vows—which, after all the intricate negotiation, colour coordinating and rehearsals, can easily become an afterthought.

Rob and I found this was the case with us. When we decided to get married we quickly picked the venue (an island in the harbour), the attendants (our two oldest friends) and the catering (cocktails and finger food with an Asian twist). No fights, no stress. But when it came to the ceremony, the actual heart of the wedding, we drew a blank. We weren't religious so a minister didn't make sense, but we didn't want something too quick and casual either. And knowing the law didn't help much either: all that's legally required for a wedding is for an exchange of vows to have taken place in front of a celebrant, as well as observing the requirements of the *Marriage Act*. In short, we hadn't a clue.

We started to realise that there's a reason tradition is popular. It provides a secure framework, a script that everyone understands and meanings that can be repeated by heart—'as long as you both shall live', 'you may now kiss the bride', 'I now present Mr and Mrs Married'—so everyone's comfortable and knows what's coming next. But we didn't quite want that, and we didn't know where to start.

Fortunately, our celebrant did. Meeting in the lunch canteen where she works her day job, the Bacall-voiced and elegant Kay Linton-Mann, handed over a folder with examples of different vows and ceremonies for us to take away and look through before our next meeting. Finally, we had something to think about. In the end we kept it simple—a few words from Kay, vows we'd adapted from some of the examples she'd given us, and the all-important signing.

Kay has been a celebrant for nearly twenty years. 'The first wedding I did, I was three days away from having my son, so I was huge,' she recalls with a soft, deep-throated laugh. 'I don't know who was more nervous, me, the guests or the wedding couple.' In her time she has conducted weddings pretty much everywhere—from gardens and reception halls to under waterfalls, atop cliffs and on the water's edge on beaches, the surf rushing around her ankles. It's a job she says she never tires of 'because you're there at all these incredibly happy days'. After witnessing hundreds of ceremonies, Kay says the biggest key to a successful wedding is good family relationships. She adds with a laugh, 'Or at least managing them.' She also believes the most important thing couples should think about is what they're actually going to say. 'It's important couples choose words they feel they can say comfortably to each other in front of all their family and friends. You're exposing a part of your personality and who you are by doing it.' This is the heart of the ceremony, but while you can get a wedding planner to organise the right invitations, toasts and ties, how do you choose what you're actually going to say?

'You get some men who are not prone to being emotional, but on the day their friends might see their softer side for the first time,' Kay observes. 'There's this big boofy bloke all of a sudden making these heartfelt statements. That's always interesting to me.'

Mark, 35, had done a lot of thinking about what to say in his marriage to Sally, 37, which took place in a white-roomed sandstone cottage one rainy Saturday afternoon in July 2002, just one month before their first child, Kate, was born. This was Mark's second wedding, coming just two years after his first. The two ceremonies could not have been more different. The first, the culmination of a ten-year relationship, was in a registry office with just two witnesses and a party the next day. That marriage ended a year later, shortly after Mark met Sally.

'I didn't actually think I was married before,' says Mark. 'I'd been though the ritual, but it was in private, in the basement at the registry office and lasted two and a half minutes. It wasn't a shared experience—more technical—which reflected the kind of relationship it was as well,' he elaborates. 'Then it was just the next logical step, the classic "let's get married because that's the next thing to do". With Sal I thought it was important to have a public show of commitment, to explain to our friends and the community at large that I'm with her and I'm going to spend my life with her.'

Kicking the 'we just want a party' trend, Mark and Sally resolved that it was the ceremony itself, not the soiree that was important. While neither is devoutly religious, they'd both had religious upbringings, so they decided on a Christian ceremony conducted by a minister Sally had known since her college days.

'It was the public affirmation we wanted,' says Sally. 'The traditional way of doing it. We thought the best way to do that was with a minister.'

Keeping with their make-it-personal philosophy, they also restricted themselves to fifty guests. 'We wanted to keep it small,' says Sally. 'We didn't want anyone there who the other hadn't met. We also only invited people we thought we'd know for the rest of our lives.'

The reception, held in the same room as the ceremony, was low-key. 'I didn't want to get hung up on tiny details like cars, flowers and getting my hair done, which I think really causes stress, not the wedding itself,' says Sally. And with two ticking deadlines—a baby due soon, a divorce not finalised until two days before the ceremony—they didn't want to go too over the top and then have to cancel.

The end result was a simple, personal ceremony. When Sally, wearing a white Indian-style pants-suit set off with a tangerine scarf, entered to the sound of a solo cello, both she and Mark cried. The unborn Kate—already named—was included as part of the ceremony. It was an emotional time at the end of an emotional roller-coaster of a year.

'There's something transcendent about marriage,' says Mark. 'It has legal status, but the ceremony wasn't so much about the legal tradition, but about representing our relationship. It was important it was done in an intimate way. We were sharing an intimate moment rather than demonstrating something.'

'I still get teary when I think about it', says Sally. 'There was just overwhelming happiness.'

> **The real traditions**
> 40 per cent of couples will pay for their own wedding.
> 27.3 per cent will share the cost with both sets of parents.
> 18.4 per cent will get the bride's parents to pay.
> 97 per cent of engagement rings will have a diamond.
> 97 per cent of men choose to wear a wedding band.
> 86 per cent of brides will take their partner's surname.
> 3 out of 5 women will wear a traditional, white, full-length gown.
> 4 per cent will sign a prenuptial agreement.[2]

It's finding a way to distil what matters, a way of saying to each other 'this is us' that is the biggest emblem of a wedding. It's laying down a template for how you'll really live your lives, rather than just the pretty photos and white-dove fantasy that wraps a wedding's memories so indelibly.

Jacqueline, 36, is a rabbi, one of only three female rabbis in Australia. When she married actor and writer Adam, 36, there was a bit of negotiating to do about what their wedding would be like. For a start, the couple came from rather different perspectives. For Adam, raised in a secular family, ceremony wasn't something he had thought about much.

'Growing up I never actually attended any weddings or funerals, or rituals of any kind,' he says. 'It wasn't until I went to university and attended my own graduation ceremony and went "wow, that was kind of important" that it hit me that rituals are significant.' Which was also when he first considered his own marriage ceremony.

'I imagined it would be some kind of ritual that we made up together,' he says, 'as opposed to following a strict formula or pre-constructed ceremony.'

For Jacki, on the other hand, a Jewish ceremony was fundamental.

'It was important that our commitment happened in a formal way in front of my family and friends and that God played a part in it,' she says. 'It's a traditional formula and it's significant that it happens that way.' And, she admits, she'd always dreamed of a full white wedding. So, like many a groom before him, Adam conceded.

'It was important to Jacki to have a full-on Jewish ceremony,' he says, 'more important for her to have that than for me not to have it.' A big fat Jewish wedding it would be, but that wasn't quite the end of it.

When they married on a sunny Sunday afternoon in June, Adam, dressed in a black suit, mauve shirt, silver and violet *kippah* (a cap), met Jacki, wearing a crystal and tulle fairy gown, her red hair tumbling over her shoulders, beneath a traditional hand-sewn *chuppah* (a traditional canopy). A *ketubah* (traditional marriage contract) was read, several rabbis spoke and the groom stomped on a wine glass with conviction at the end. It did look for all the world like a traditional Jewish ceremony. But still, they found ways to make it personal. For a start, much of the music wasn't traditional (unless you count *Fiddler on the Roof*, played before the ceremony). And under the *chuppah* the bride and groom circled each other seven times, rather than just the bride circling as tradition dictates. When it came to the vows, Jacki and Adam were anything but conservative. Each had their own promises. Adam vowed he loved Jacki more than computer games and that he would always sit beside her as she watched bad television and read trashy magazines. Jacki promised to always respect Adam's freedom and celebrate the freedom he gave her. Both agreed it was here they were able to say exactly what was most important to them.

'You know who I am and you know who you are and that's why I choose you and am letting you choose me,' sums up Adam.

'God is important,' says Jacki. 'My theory on love and partnership is one of the Jewish perspectives, that soulmates are two halves of one soul who find each other.' It was a ceremony that symbolised the marriage of two strong individuals.

'My mother pointed out, when we were planning the wedding, that if anything was important to me, I just went ahead and did it and if anything was important to Jacki, she went and did it too,' says Adam. 'That's how we are, anyway.'

'We got a really beautiful letter after the wedding from one of the congregants who said "thank you so much for including us",' recounts Jacki. 'They said "it felt like you let us in on a really intimate and beautiful moment". A lot of people said it was one of the most beautiful wedding ceremonies they'd been to. And that's why. It was traditional but it was also us within the tradition that really personalised it.'

Despite himself, Adam admits that the ceremony was transcendent. 'When Jacki walked into the room and when we circled and got dizzy, the ritual swept me up and carried me away,' he says. 'I think it's important to have that, not just in front of the person you're marrying but in front of a whole bunch of people who can hold you to it.'

The supporting players

The most popular months for getting married are October and February.

50 per cent of couples will invite between 50 and 100 guests. 4 per cent will invite over 300 guests.

75 per cent will have a full sit-down dinner at an evening reception.

12 per cent will have a cocktail party.

2 out of 3 couples will spend their honeymoon relaxing on a beach.[3]

A wedding is a rite of passage that each generation makes its own, each finding a way to be part of something that is an ancient institution. It does come loaded with expectations—it will be the 'happiest day of your life' for a start—but then, marriage itself comes with a truckload of history and expectations, too. These sneak up on you and chances are some part of your wedding day won't live up to the hype. Most people I know has a horror story about their wedding: the uninvited relative demanding a place, the drunken uncle making an awful speech, a rained out venue, a dress that didn't fit.

Does any of that matter? Probably, but in a way the bridal magazines don't tell you about. It matters only in how you make it through. That's your rite of passage. It's about how the two of you find a way to carve out your own space within a ritual that only pretends to be about you, in an event loaded with family expectation, cultural customs and drunken friends; all these factors will conspire to push their way into the intimate world you are creating. The rite is finding a way to say 'this is us, this is what really matters and the rest can go to hell.'

By the numbers
Average age at marriage   *2001*   *1981*
Brides   29   23
Grooms   31   26

Marriages performed by a celebrant
2001   53 per cent
1981   38 per cent[4]

To sum it up

- While you think your wedding is about the two of you, your families think it's about them. But remember, it is your wedding.
- A bad wedding doesn't mean a bad marriage.
- Your wedding will reveal the underlying tensions in your relationship. Negotiating all those tensions is a part of setting down the rules and limits of your own marriage.

- The ceremony *does* matter.
- Keep to a budget.
- You'll regret the friends you didn't invite more than the family you've offended by not inviting them.
- Regardless of all this tension, there is something transcendent about marriage.
- Your wedding is your rite of passage.

3

The Honeymoon is Over

Sire, I relate with a degree of pleasure of my experience of married life. I was married exactly three years ago. Since that time I have enjoyed a period of two years and nine months of uninterrupted bliss.

I am, yours truly, Gipp

PS: I may mention that I was separated from my wife three months after marriage.
—Letter to London *Daily Telegraph*, in 1888, in response to an article called, 'Marriage is a failure'[1]

For all the trouble it is, does getting married—or, at least, surviving the wedding—really make a difference? The good news is, nearly everyone I spoke with said getting married had made a difference to their relationship, and in a positive way.

'The thing that surprised me was the warm inner glow just being married brings,' says Chris. 'I thought that we'd made the commitment anyway, and the wedding would be just a nice party to have with our friends, but the morning after when you get up, being married actually feels nice. Maybe it's like a security blanket knowing someone else is prepared to commit to you legally and openly.'

'After you get married there's this real security, maybe for a year, where you think "you're my husband, you're my wife",' agrees Anne. 'It's a bit like the *Bridget Jones* smug club.'

After your honeymoon, the next few months can be a love bubble of marital bliss. The world is cast in a soft, warm glow and everything seems, well, happier. The house is fun! Your work is fun! Your spouse is fun! You giggle together like you've got a special little secret.

'It's like we're a little team, a secret team,' says Emma. 'If you're having a bad day, or somebody pisses you off, we know we can just lean on each other. It's like our marriage is a special secret we've got.'

It seems simply getting married has, somehow, made the two of you better. And it's true—according to research, simply marrying can induce a love fever that infects you for up to two years.[2] Counsellors see it too. Marie Burrows is a psychotherapist who conducts family and individual counselling. She says, on balance, when she's working with a couple in crisis she does see a difference between those who are married and those who aren't.

'When a couple makes a statement of marriage, it's quite conscious and deep,' she says. 'There is a transformation when the commitment is made to a life together, a consciousness of that commitment.'

At their wedding, a couple has a moment where all the ingredients come together. It's a moment, however, that doesn't last forever. One morning that big happy love bubble bursts and you may wake up with a very bad case of retrospective cold feet. The world looks different. Your spouse has morphed from a prince of comfort, wit and charm (or princess of grace, light and beauty) into a bad-breathed monster of *Alien* proportions. 'Oh my God', you think. 'What have I done? I'm stuck with him/her for life.' Which is what it was like for Emma and Barry. Their nuptial bliss lasted about six months.

It all started when they rushed into getting married. Barry, originally from Dundee, Scotland, met Emma in Adelaide on his first day in Australia, out on a twelve-month working holiday. After six months of boozing and flirting they got together. Emma then moved to Sydney and Barry followed. But when his twelve months were nearly up they got stuck, and there was no way for Barry to stay in the country unless they got married. Immigration made it clear that even if they were engaged, Barry would still have to go home and there were no guarantees as to when he would be able to return. So Emma and Barry decided that if they were going to stay together, they would have to wed, and quickly. It was, both agree, the last resort.

'We had talked about getting married before,' says Emma. 'We were in love. We felt like we would have [got married] anyway, but we did feel our hand was forced.'

'It was a couple of years early,' agrees Barry. With days to spare, they married in a botanic garden, the bride in white, Barry and his father wearing kilts.

'The first few months were magic,' says Barry, before a pause. 'But then I panicked.' From a big, close Scottish family, and still only 22, he started having doubts. 'I thought "shit I've moved away to Australia and the only person I've got here is Emma. I have no family and not a lot of friends".' He was miserable, working twelve-hour days and thinking 'What have I done? Gone and got married.' It wasn't that he didn't love Emma, Barry says, 'It's just that I went into a kind of shell. And when I go like that I just can't talk or discuss my problems.'

They hit crisis point and Emma left to stay with her aunt for a few days. 'I basically cried and drank loads of beer,' she says, laughing in retrospect. 'We got smashed, smoked cigarettes and bitched about men.'

'I couldn't handle her being gone. It was horrible,' says Barry. 'That's when I realised "shit, what have I done now?" I was on the phone to her in tears every night.' They were, he adds, the worst four days he'd ever had.

'I went to work and then sat in the pub most nights because I was miserable. I realised then that I couldn't live without her.'

Emma came back. 'He was forced into talking about his problems,' says Emma, adding with dry bemusement, 'Scottish men aren't noted for their communication skills—Barry's dad's a man of very few words too.'

'She really wanted to talk about our marriage trouble,' concedes Barry. 'I just wanted to move on. I like to forget about things and start again.' They did talk and now, says Barry, 'I still feel awful for what I put her through. I hate what I did.'

'He did make it up to me though,' says Emma. 'He was very affectionate after that.' Now awaiting the birth of their first child (and already fond parents to Wee Jock the dog) they can laugh about what was shaping up to be a marital disaster.

'I was young and stupid,' says Barry. 'It wasn't great immediately, but we got there. And after that first year passed we were just wonderful.' They had had to find some ground rules for the relationship and then act on them. In this case it was talk it out, never let a problem lie. But while this might have been brought on by a rushed wedding, what Barry and Emma experienced isn't that different from what many couples go through.

The morning after

It appears to me, Sir, that one of the chief causes of unhappiness in married life is that men look for their life partners in the ranks of the lady-clerks, who, while understanding perfectly well how to balance a ledger or keep a cashbook in order, are quite at a loss when called upon to assume the place for which women are better fitted, the 'drudgery', as they would doubtless term it, the true domain of woman—home duties.

Yours, Clericus

—Letter to London *Daily Telegraph*, in 1888, in response to an article called, 'Marriage is a failure'[1]

Whether you've lived together or not, married quickly or slowly, some time after the honeymoon tan has faded, the wedding presents have been unwrapped and the glamour photos have been put into albums, everyone is confronted by what they've done. This is often accompanied by a sinking sense of dread, and there's a name for it: Post-Nuptial Depression—PND. According to British psychologists, the start of married life marks the beginning of a deep depression for as many as one in ten brides.

'It's a very modern phenomenon that is very widespread and it ranges from a vague feeling of discontent to full-scale depression,' Philip Hodson, a fellow of the British Association for Counselling and Psychotherapy, is reported as saying. Both brides and grooms can suffer PND, though it's more severe in women,[3] perhaps because many brides invest so much in having the best and brightest wedding-to-rule-them-all. But while Hodson-the-romantic attributes PND to 'the realisation of the boring side of marriage' he has a point. If your wedding day is the happiest day of your life, doesn't that mean it's all downhill from there?

Greg and Catherine, now married for five years, live in a sprawling suburban, Cape Cod-style house with their three young sons and three dogs. After a rocky courtship, they had a fiery first year of marriage.

'Once you get married the fights become really intense,' says Greg, 'because you realise that if something gives you the shits you'd better fix it or you're going to have to live with it for forty years. The first year of our marriage we fought like cats and dogs because all the trivial stuff—like toilet seats and washing up—suddenly seemed important.'

'I vividly remember walking home one day thinking, "I can't believe it. I want to leave you and now I can't do it",' says Cathy, who was by then pregnant with their first child. But somehow they lived through these tough times and after that first year they found they fitted each other better.

'We just don't seem to fight about that stuff now,' says Greg.

Reflecting on this on a rare night out for their fourth wedding anniversary, Greg and Cathy asked themselves the question: 'If we met now, would we get married?'

'We decided we would,' says Greg, 'because the reason we had married in the first place was that we decided we were both capable of changing. I've always thought there's no point in meeting the right person who, there and then, is 100 per cent perfect, because you might grow apart. So it's better to meet someone who's 60 per cent right . . .'

'. . . and then just renovate,' finishes Cath, laughing. 'You need a project.'

'We asked ourselves, "why did it seem to make sense?"' muses Greg. 'And it was actually that we had had enough fights and run-ins before we got married, and had managed to work them out, so we thought we could probably work our way through most things.' Again, the couple were laying down the ground rules and learning to act on them.

'I've done a lot of work with engaged couples and one of the comments I often hear after they're married is "it's just so different from living together",' says Dr Michelle Simons from the Australian Institute of Family Studies in Melbourne. 'It's like they've got this internal switch and what's acceptable in a partner is not acceptable in a husband [or wife]—"Now that we're married this has to change or that has to change". I also think the social expectations change when a couple actually marry,' she adds. 'Mothers and fathers who didn't know what to call their son or daughter's live-in partner now have a son- or daughter-in-law and that tag comes with a whole lot of associated baggage about how they fit into and relate to the family. All those subtle changes impact on the couple.'

These experiences bring most married couples back down to earth, so nearly all experience a gradual but steady decline in their 'marital quality' for the first four years of their marriage.[4] Don't fool yourself that this time isn't important. Separations within the first four years of marriage account for about one-third of all divorces.[5] Even Andrew and Eleanor, despite having premarital counselling, had a bumpy first year.

'We both came into it as very independent people,' says Eleanor. 'I spent the first year fighting for my independence. We'd both been living out of home for some time so we were setting up house with two of everything. Something as simple as a drying rack could cause a problem. Andrew would say "We don't need this second one" and I'd be like "Oh right, that's just because it's mine". I was thinking, "I don't want anyone controlling me".' They squabbled a lot. A truce was finally called after Andrew sat Eleanor down and said, 'We have to work on the basis that we're here to help each other.' After that, they were at least on the same side. 'I always tell people getting married not to worry if the first year is really tough because you're still finding things out and working out all the little things,' she says now.

It's a tricky thing, finding a way to be married. Today we don't buy into that two-into-one sentimentality for a good reason. We are two strong individuals and we don't expect marriage to change that for a moment. Negotiating that, as Andrew and Eleanor found, is not something that's simply solved once and for all—it's more like developing a blueprint for action that is constantly revisited.

'We still have to work on it,' says Eleanor. 'We are very different. We had to agree to accept that the other person has our best interests at heart. You can't be thinking that the other person is out to get you or doesn't want you to be happy, or wants you to be tired. Letting your defence down is a big step. And that happens daily.'

Research shows that learning how to negotiate this conflict early in your marriage is important. One bunch of psychologists measuring the stress hormones of newlyweds while arguing found, when they followed them up ten years later, the ones who'd had the highest levels of hormones during their monitored arguments were the ones most likely to be divorced or unhappily married.[6]

Your new family

> If any new laws are to be passed for the better regulation of married life let them be for the limiting of the power and abolishing the evil influence of mothers-in-law, for this is the rock on which so many couples are shipwrecked, their lives blighted and their happiness blasted.
> I remain, Sir, yours truly, A VICTIM TO A MOTHER-IN-LAW.
> **—Letter to London *Daily Telegraph*, in 1888, in response to an article called, 'Marriage is a failure'**[1]

William Doherty, an American marriage therapist and former president of the National Council of Family Relationships, was recently in Australia giving lectures and promoting two of his books, *A Strong Marriage* and *Confident Parenting*. He agreed to meet me in the midst of a busy schedule to discuss what his two decades of relationship work have taught him. So, squeezed into the counter at Pelligrinis, a formica-topped and checked-floored Melbourne coffee institution, I asked him, 'What is it about marriage that makes it different, especially if you have already lived together?'

'Being married is a huge change from living together. You have in-laws for a start,' he chuckles, adding, 'The world treats you differently. It holds higher expectations. You are part of an ancient social institution, which is precisely what bothers some people. I think it's like the difference between being a foster parent and a biological parent—marriage comes with the cultural expectation of permanence in a way that cohabitation does not.' This is something I remember Suzanne, a community worker, commenting on after having married her long-term partner three years ago.

'That probably surprised me the most when we got married. All of a sudden I was expected to be there for all these family events.

This was after years of my husband's family being very clearly uncomfortable with me because we weren't married—some of his relations even refused to talk to me our first Christmas together. Then all of a sudden,' she continues, 'they were welcoming me with open arms expecting me to always attend family functions. I actually resented it because I hadn't changed, but their attitude towards me had.'

To Doherty, it's learning to deal assertively with these new realities and tensions that is exactly what a marriage needs. In his book, *A Strong Marriage*, he documents the case of Kate and Lonnie. Lonnie's mother insisted all major family events occurred at her house, including Kate's birthday celebrations. Kate put up with this for years, but when she and Lonnie had their own kids she wanted the celebrations to be shared between her family and their own place as well. It was only after doing a workshop on family rituals that Kate was able to deal with the situation, first by insisting her birthday be at her house and then by talking with Lonnie and gaining his support in spending some holidays at her parents' home also.

'Unless loyalty issues between the spouse and parents are dealt with early in a marriage, parents and other family members can undercut a marriage over the long haul,' writes Doherty. 'When that occurs, you have to fight for your marriage or you will lose it to your extended family.'[7] Research backs this up, noting that even in long-term marriages, conflicts with your extended family will erode your marital stability, satisfaction and commitment over time.[8] Studies also consistently find that approval of your spouse by friends and extended family is a very good predictor of how happy and stable a marriage will be.[9] In fact, in another study researchers asked two groups of people, one married, one divorced, what the most difficult issues they had faced in their time together were. Topping the list for married couples were child rearing (22 per cent), financial issues (20 per cent), parental/family interference (15 per cent) and death in the family (11 per cent). For the separated or divorced couples, the results were more scattered with financial issues (23 per cent) followed by a swag of almost equal problems including personality differences (10 per cent), child-rearing differences (10 per cent), work-related issues (9 per cent), parental/family interference (9 per cent) and alcohol/drugs (9 per cent).[10]

If family interference is a problem, Doherty recommends setting some ground rules for the family, including no unsolicited criticism of your spouse and no discussion about whether or not you should have gotten married.

'If you feel caught in the middle between your spouse and your family, get out of the middle by seeking an understanding with your spouse, then having a united front with your family,' he writes. 'Staying in the middle means being disloyal to your spouse. Battle it out first with your spouse until you reach a solution you both can live with.'

Unpacking the family baggage

> I am only recently married (last June), and already have doubts as to the propriety of the step I then took. My husband belongs to a cricket club, which seems to engross a great deal of his time and energies, and he also dabbles in amateur operatic singing, and returns home at all hours of the night, not always sober. Altogether my life is a most weary one, and he seems unwilling to relinquish any or either of these 'recreations' as he terms them, in order to give a little attention to his home and encouragement to me . . . J.T.
> **—Letter to London *Daily Telegraph*, in 1888, in response to an article called, 'Marriage is a failure'**[1]

It isn't just active family interference that can cast a shadow over a marriage. Working out your differences also means sorting out the baggage you've brought from your family. Take Carrie and Alan. Now married for eight years, their early married years were spent negotiating Carrie's Anglo–Australian Protestantism and Alan's Maltese Catholicism.

'Our upbringings were so different,' says Alan, as we sit around the kitchen table at their neat weatherboard home. 'Importance was placed on different things. From the basics—if you go to an Australian's house, the first thing you do is you go into the lounge room where the TV is on. In a Maltese house, the first place you go is the kitchen, where there's food. Everyone expects that.'

There's also the way family decisions are made. 'I see it in Alan's dad,' says Carrie. 'He'll say to Alan "Your mother wants to do this, this is what we're going to do". It doesn't matter if he wants to do it or not. Alan's the same,' she adds. 'He'll say, "If you want to do this, then that is what we're going to do", which is different from my Anglo–Australian upbringing, where I'll be asking questions like "Is this the right thing to do, or is this the wrong thing to do?" or, "Is this how this is supposed to be done?"'

Meeting when Carrie was 21 and Alan 23, and marrying around eighteen months later, both say one of their biggest advantages was marrying young, as they learned to compromise before they were too set in their ways.

'The good thing for us is we try and take the best out of both cultures for our own kids,' says Alan, 'and get rid of the things we don't agree with.'

> **Self-delusion is good for marriage**
> In a study of several hundred married couples, those couples who said that they were satisfied seemed to remember the past as worse than it was. This made the present seem better by comparison. The researchers noted that self-delusion may actually be a more accurate indicator of a successful marriage than good communication and openness in the relationship.[11]

That is precisely the thing. We pick and choose what we want to take from our own families and what we want to leave behind. So even negative experiences can be useful.

'I have some anti-models based on when I was a kid,' notes Stephen, 38, a technical writer. 'Men went out to work and women were at home and the men had an attitude of a polite, sometimes humorous, condescension to their wives—they weren't to be taken seriously. It was like the fathers had a pact with their children and they would laugh together at the things that women do. I thought that was very unsatisfactory.'

So Stephen and wife Shannon are doing things differently. Both work part-time and share care of their son Gabrielle, and both give each other time out to study languages. 'It's giving each other the opportunities to realise our dreams or impulses,' says Shannon.

The edges of our marriages can push out against family customs, religious differences and social expectations. We battle these out when deciding to get married, before the wedding and in the months after. Deciding to get married sets up a framework. All the negotiations over the wedding—its size, shape, and meaning—are about laying down the rules. The question is, is there a right, or wrong way to do this? Well, most of us have a ready answer for that one, but are we really right?

The biggest thing is the littlest things

> Manners are the chief ingredient of married happiness and the closer the relation, the more they are needed
> **—Nathalie Sedgwick Colby, 'Marriage'**, *Atlantic Monthly*, **May 1924**

What is the most basic rule, the real secret to a happy relationship?

'Communication,' says Eleanor. 'I have such a strong sense of, "My God, we just need time to talk".'

'I think it's communication,' agrees Andrew. 'I think it's important to spend time together just being silly.'

What's the secret to your relationship? I asked Anna, a 36-year-old doctor, and Jack, 37, a businessman.

'Communication,' says Anna.

'Communication,' nods Jack in agreement.

If ever there was an affirmation mantra for our generation it is this. Communication skills have been noted on our school reports and on every job application. They're what we say we want in our friends, work colleagues and partners, which would all be terrific if we could just nail down what the hell this actually means. Is it talking? Negotiating? Chatting on the phone for hours? Arguing dispassionately?

As it turns out we often get it wrong when discussing which communication skills are important, and assuming the wrong skills can send us off in a bad direction. Take 'active listening', which is at the core of most marriage intervention programs, particularly those that address conflict–resolution. The idea of active listening is that one person is supposed to truly listen to what their partner has to say, non-defensively, without arguing their own point of view. The listener then paraphrases what the speaker has said, considers it and then genuinely and empathically validates the speaker's feelings. It sounds terrific. The problem is it doesn't work.

One study of newlyweds found that those with active listening skills weren't any more likely to have successful marriages than those without such skills. Follow-up studies of couples who'd learned active listening as part of marriage therapy found that while it may have decreased their negativity in the short term, it did nothing to promote positive interactions, and they tended to slip back into old habits rapidly after therapy had finished.[12]

What's the problem? Well, for many couples the other's point of view isn't the problem, it's that they don't like what they're hearing.

I press Anna and Jack as they wheel four-month-old Luke across a dew-laden field, dodging divets and dog poo, to a car show that Jack's keen to see and Anna's well, seeing. What are they really talking about when they say 'communication skills'? As Anna concedes, it may have more to with exactly what they're doing now, learning how to negotiate different interests and points of view.

'I think I've probably learnt more about communicating in my life than Jack,' she says. 'Mum's not very good at communicating. She's the one who picks a fight and storms out of the room and doesn't stay around to discuss the problem. I used to do that as well. But now I think I've learnt to be more reasonable, more rational than I used to be.' Now we're getting somewhere. A great deal of what we mean by 'communication skills' is really 'negotiating skills'.

Negotiation is called for when the issue is less 'we don't communicate' and more 'I don't like what you're saying'. When Australian researchers compared two groups of couples—those in relationships for more than six years and those who were divorced—and asked them how they would advise other couples to communicate more effectively, they found something really interesting. Although both the married and divorced groups said that communication was the key and that it was important to deal with issues immediately, only the still-together couples also suggested that compromise and consensus were important skills too.[13]

For Anna and Jack, who started dating in high school and have been married for eleven years, learning how to argue has been a long process. With notably different personalities—Anna's studious, methodical and reserved while Jack's gregarious and laid back—they've negotiated Anna's medical studies, Jack starting his own business in the notoriously fickle film industry and then this year all the challenges that come with having a newborn. Anna admits ruefully that her fighting technique is still, 'lay a landmine, wait for it to explode and then reason it out'.

'I cry, he comforts,' she laughs. 'Or I kick and scream and throw a tantrum and he comforts.' However, they both agree it helps that they both work in industries where good service is a key, so they share an interest in learning to communicate better.

'We're both interested in striving to improve ourselves,' says Anna. 'Whatever you do on one day, you re-evaluate and ask, "How can I have done that differently?", "How could I have done that better?"' And with a new baby, while they may be bickering more, they say their problem solving is better too.

'It's not that we're signing up to any self-improvement course,' says Jack. 'But we probably analyse things a bit more now, especially now Luke's come along, because we think, okay, at the end of that day, what has worked with him and what hasn't? And we're probably applying those things to other parts of our relationship as well.'

Anna and Jack make it sound simple, but maybe this comes down to the fact that both are blessed with easygoing, good natures. But it got me thinking, while there might be something to those general communication skills like talking it out, maybe the secret lies in exactly what is being communicated. So my next stop was with John Gottman.

John Gottman is the guru of marriage research. He's been studying relationships for twenty years in his 'love lab', where he does diabolical things like wire couples up to monitors to check their heart rate, sweating and metabolism when they fight, or moving them into a special love flat to record all their interactions across a weekend, *Big Brother*-style. He tracks his couples over time too, monitoring changes in their relationship. These research results are changing the way we think of marriage.

Marriage maintenance

Talking down the line from his Seattle-based institute, Gottman says good marriages do stand out from the pack for one main reason.

'Basically there's a very rich climate of positive interaction, rather than negative. There's a lot more kindness and affection and interest in one another—humour, wit, silliness, all those kinds of qualities.' In other words, there's more of positive communication than negative.

According to Gottman, having a good marriage is actually easier than people think. He says one of the biggest mistakes couples make is thinking that positive communication is all about nutting out the big issues, while in fact it's the opposite. With happy couples, affection and respect—the important keys here—are communicated in small ways that are often easy to dismiss.

'Saying things like "I like the way you were playing with the baby last night, it was really beautiful" or, "I enjoyed our conversation at dinner" or, "That dish you served, it was delicious", that's what the masters of relationships are doing,' he says, adding, 'A lot of the time, the people whose relationships fail are having those same thoughts, but they're not voicing them.' He points out that it only takes fifteen minutes a day to keep up this good marriage maintenance, and that it comes down to saying 'hello' and 'goodbye' and finding some time to sit down and chat. In other words, treating your spouse like you would anyone else you're interested in.

William Doherty puts it another way: the biggest threat to good marriages is everyday living. That is, getting lost in the logistics of everyday life rather than truly communicating. He's a big advocate of finding rituals in daily life that put the relationship to the fore. 'Most of us greet our co-workers more personally and with more enthusiasm than we greet our spouses,' he says. 'And our pets are more excited to see our partners come home than we are.'

In short, creating a happy marriage simply adds up to treating your spouse like a human being: saying goodbye when they leave, hello when they come in the door and spending time being interested in how they've lived their life for the day.

While it's easy to say in theory, in our busy lives it's exactly these little habits of courtesy that we let slip. The trick is to make time for these small rituals in order to stay connected. For Carrie and Alan, who don't get much time in the morning as Alan is out the door for work at 6.30 a.m. while Carrie gets their three preschoolers up, it's the mid-morning phone call that makes the difference.

> **Adventure is good for marriage**
>
> Researchers have discovered that not only are shared activities good for a marriage, but that shared adventurous activities are particularly good. Their experiment compared couples who had been tied up together then made to negotiate a gym maze with couples who simply had to roll a ball around a gym mat. The couples who completed the more challenging activity scored much higher afterwards when asked about relationship satisfaction and romantic love than those rolling the ball.
>
> To test this in the real world, over a period of weeks some couples were sent on 'exciting' activities like attending music concerts, plays and lectures, skiing, hiking and going dancing. They were then compared with couples who went on 'pleasant' activities such as going to dinner or a movie, or attending church. A control group were put on a going-nowhere 'waiting list'. The couples who undertook the exciting activities showed a significantly greater increase in relationship quality over the ten weeks of the experiment than the other two groups.[14]

'Alan will ring me and say "How did everyone go this morning, did they get off to preschool alright? Has everyone been good, or are they throwing temper tantrums?"' says Carrie. 'So then I'll say "So and so's killing so and so".'

'And when I first get home from work, probably the first ten minutes is us talking,' says Alan. 'We're pushing the kids away, because they're in our faces, explaining to them, "don't interrupt, we're talking".'

For Sanjeev, a 38-year-old public servant, and Annabelle, a 36-year-old marketing manager, breakfast together is important— a ritual that was born of necessity. 'At one point Annabelle had classes on Monday and Tuesday nights, and I had classes on

Wednesday and Thursday nights,' says Sanjeev. 'We never saw each other. The only meal we'd get to have together on weekdays was breakfast so that's become a habit. We get to sit down and talk about things in the morning before our days start.'

For Tiffany and Andrew it's emails throughout the day keep them connected, followed by time after dinner planning their future.

'I sent Andrew an email this morning bitching about someone who was planning a trip to Europe,' recounts Tiffany. 'And Andrew replied "Well, I can't afford to send you to Europe right now, but we will go together and we'll work for it together and it will be more fun." So we have little conferences sometimes. You've always got to have something to look forward to. We've even been known to sit down with a pen and paper and go, "Well, what are we going to plan for?"'

While none of these things sound like much, what's interesting is the effect that these happy exchanges have when a marriage isn't going so well. Research shows that happy couples are more likely to respond positively even when one partner is being negative.[15] Why? It's all about deposits in the bank. Over time positive exchanges build up a line of emotional credit. There's even a magic ratio: in happy marriages, there are five positive interactions to every negative one. These happy interactions mean that if someone does have a bad hair day and is being snippy, their partner is less likely to escalate this into marital war because the relationship is in credit. In unhappy couples, with fewer positive exchanges and nothing left in their relationship account, partners tend to reciprocate negativity with more negativity. They also tend to habitually think of each other in negative ways, selectively concentrating on bad behaviour and attributing this to character flaws. For instance, if a husband arrives home late his wife may see him as 'a generally selfish person who doesn't care about the family', while in a happier relationship the same behaviour might be viewed as 'someone struggling to keep up with the heavy load at work'.[16]

Agreeing to disagree

In his book with Nan Silver, *The Seven Principles for Making Marriage Work*, John Gottman claims to be able to predict within just five minutes which newlyweds will succeed and which will fail, simply by observing how the couples initiate these discussions. While women initiate discussions about problems eighty per cent of the time, in couples headed for divorce a wife's opening statement is usually a criticism—'you're lazy and you never do any housework'—rather than a specific complaint—'you didn't take the garbage out last night'. Husbands aren't off the hook, though. Defensive reactions to discussions on their part show that they could be heading for divorce, while in stable marriages, he doesn't usually escalate the negativity.[17] In short, happy couples also choose their fights, and they keep them specific. Like Daniel and Monica, whose big difference is religious beliefs.

Dan's a devout Anglican, Monica an atheist. Both have firm views and robust personalities, so the combination has been combustible at times.

'I'm not just a non-believer,' says Monica. 'When we first married I was an outspoken atheist.' She's since learned not to pick a fight she won't win. 'I don't have those same discussions with Dan anymore,' she says, 'because it's not worth my breath.' Dan nods as he holds their squirming two-year-old son. Mostly they agreed to disagree, but when it came to religion and the children, they had to find a compromise. Now religion is delegated as Dan's responsibility, and their two sons have been baptised because Dan insisted. Over time their relationship has settled into an easier give and take.

'We kind of call favours on each other,' Monica points out. She adds that while Daniel's non-negotiable issue is religion, hers is career. 'I'm working full-time because we agreed on that, as a family,' she says.

'All couples have approximately ten issues they will never resolve,' writes Diane Sollee, founder of the Coalition for Marriage,

Family and Couples Education in the United States. 'And if you switch partners you'll just get ten new issues, and they are likely to be more complicated the second time around.' Instead, what's important, says Sollee, is developing a dialogue or 'dance' with your particular set of issues, just as you would with a chronic back problem or trick knee. 'You don't like problems, you wish they weren't there, but you keep talking about them and learn how to live with and accommodate them.' For some issues, the perpetually unsolvable ones, you will just have to agree to disagree.

To sum it up
- Don't kid yourself—being married will change things.
- It's not unusual to have a bad first year.
- Families will treat your differently.
- Don't let your families capture your marriage. You are a family too and it's up to you to make the rules.
- Communication is the key but be sure to practise the right kind of communication skills.
- The little interactions can mean more than the big ones.
- Find fifteen minutes a day to spend with each other.
- Treat your spouse like a human being.
- Have five positive interactions for every negative one.
- Some differences you'll never resolve, so learn to live with them.

4

The Art of Marital Warfare

> One hundred victories in one hundred battles is not the most skilful. Subduing the other's military without battle is the most skilful.
> **—Sun Tzu,** *The Art of War*

While good daily communication keeps a marriage humming along, let's not kid ourselves—it doesn't prevent us from having a barney. All couples, sooner or later, fight. After all, have a look at what a ridiculous proposition contemporary marriage is. Take two adults with minds of their own, in a world that values individualism, in a generation that is confronted with constant choices, who live in an era that is defined, then redefined, by psychotherapy. Then ask these adults to live together, buy property, have a family, have separate careers, develop their potential and do it all without disadvantaging the other. Let's face it, while regular doses of communication are important for maintaining healthy relationships, two organisms can only expand their territories so much before something gives.

Many couples interpret fighting as a sign that their marriage is in real trouble. 'We're always fighting,' they say. 'There must be something wrong with us.' In fact, some research shows that fighting is good for a marriage. Take heart especially if you've had an awful first year: one study found newlyweds who started their marriage harmoniously were initially happier than volatile couples but they were less happy than the fighters three years down the track. What might make you unhappy at first—the fights, the anger—may be healthier for the relationship in the long run.[1]

Now married for three years, Audrey, a 32-year-old government adviser, and Rudolph, 36, a political consultant, had to learn how to fight with each other. At the start each was taking a familiar family-patented approach—Audrey's lot avoided conflict at all costs, preferring arguments that were 'dry and sarcastic', while Rudy came from a bunch of table-thumping yellers. It's when you're at this pointy end of negotiations that you see how much baggage you've brought to your marriage. And it wasn't long after the first rumblings sounded that everything exploded.

'We didn't argue until after we got married,' says Audrey. 'Then when we first started arguing it was awful.' They settled into a pattern: Rudy would yell and Audrey would start weeping inconsolably and shut down, making Rudy even angrier.

'A couple of times he stopped the car and started walking down the road and I was hysterical,' Audrey says, wiping away a flood of pretend tears. 'I thought he wasn't going to come back and I'd never see him again.'

It was, as psychologists like to term it, a classic demand–withdraw cycle. Left to spin, this can easily turn into a marriage-ending cycle, though unlike Audrey and Rudy, usually it's the woman who demands and the man who withdraws. In the end, Rudy insisted on a circuit-breaker.

'Just yell back at me,' he told Audrey. 'This is not going to work if you're going to clam up every time you get frustrated.'

So Audrey started dipping her toes in the arguing waters. 'Little by little,' she says. 'I started arguing back to see how it went.' When that worked fine and she saw Rudy wasn't going to leave, she started yelling. 'One day Rudy was off ranting and raving and I was sobbing as usual. I could think of all these things in my head that I wanted to say that I wasn't saying,' she recalls. 'I thought "this is ridiculous" and went charging into his office and spat it all out. He was kind of taken aback.' Now, three years later, Audrey says, 'I yell back, I stand up to him. If he walks out, I follow.'

Rudy has moderated his style too, toning his anger down a few notches. Not particularly fond of being stroppy, he's learned to take a deep breath and chill out. And he's got a lot at stake. Rudy was beaten from when he was eight until he was twenty-two by his father, who was, in turn, from an abusive background. 'I've got a cycle to break,' Rudy says, with a bitter half-laugh.

Audrey and Rudy have found a mostly happy medium.

'I was coming from one side of the spectrum, she was coming from completely the other, so the only way to deal with it was to meet in the middle,' says Rudy.

Learning to express herself in a forthright manner also paid off at work for Audrey. 'There was a woman at work who was being a complete bitch,' she says. 'One afternoon she actually slapped me across the knuckles with a pencil because I had my wrists on the desk as I was typing. Having learned these new confrontation skills at home I told her, "Your behaviour is completely unacceptable and I won't tolerate it".'

But how much fighting is good for a marriage? Have Audrey and Rudy really found a happy medium here or have they set themselves up for never-ending crisis? Should they be more like Joanne and Luke, for example, who don't pull on the boxing gloves nearly as regularly as Audrey and Rudy? Though, like Audrey, Joanne says she also doesn't really know how to fight.

'I was an only child until I was thirteen,' she explains. 'I bottle it up. If there is a fight, I get really stressed and I always take it the wrong way.' But they have a different model. Instead of setting off the fireworks, Joanne and Luke like to talk their problems through and regularly check each other's mood as a barometer of their relationship.

'If you're bottling something up, or if I've upset you in some kind of way I can usually tell,' says Luke to Joanne, as he wrangles son Lachlan off the couch. 'The atmosphere is completely different— I can feel it because you're wound up.' So then they talk. This is helped, they say, because they are very compatible.

'We don't actually have many disagreements,' says Joanne. 'In my first marriage we always fought about his family because I married into a Dutch family with a different culture, and more conservative values. I become a narky person. Luke and I have been very lucky, our parents brought us up in a very similar way so I think that we have similar values.' It's a different, less combative style, but is it any better?

Then there's Sanjeev and Annabelle, who say they never fight. Is their marriage in the best shape or are they in denial? Visit them and you're struck by the harmonious, easygoing nature of the household, all the way down to their indolent Burmese cats. It's not like they don't have things they could fight about—managing two careers, dropping daughter Amelia off at school, picking her up, cooking, cleaning. There's plenty of material, but instead of fighting, they say they simply negotiate.

'Work comes up and one of us can't stick to the schedule,' says Sanjeev, 'so you have to be flexible.' It's all very reasonable. Each listens to what the other needs, and makes allowances. In fact, in over twelve years of marriage, they've had precisely one fight. And what was it about?

'Well, this is the thing,' says Annabelle, the corners of her mouth twitching as she struggles to hide a grin. 'The fight was about the question, "Is there an objective reality?" We must have been not speaking to each other for a week over that one.'

'We agreed to disagree,' says Sanjeev with a don't-open-that-can-of-worms look.

'Your one fight was over philosophy?'

'I know, I shouldn't have mentioned it,' says Annabelle, cheekily baiting as Sanjeev squirms on the couch. 'It's still a sore point. Sanjeev feels that it's valid to measure an objective reality, and I think that's crap.'

'That's right,' says Sanjeev starting to giggle. 'Who gives a toss who does the cleaning when you can argue about the nature of reality?'

So which one out of the three couples has the best model? You might be tempted to pick the negotiators, but interestingly, it wouldn't matter if you picked volatile Audrey and Rudy, validating Luke and Joanne, or the virtuoso-negotiating Sanjeev and Annabelle, you'd be right each time. All three have happy marriages and all have a good chance at succeeding because, according to John Gottman's research, how much or how little you fight has no bearing on how happy you are or how likely your marriage is to succeed. Instead, what matters is how you fight, and then how you make up.[2]

Breaking cycles

> Knowing the other and knowing oneself
> In one hundred battles, no danger
> Not knowing the other and knowing oneself
> Once victory for one loss
> Not knowing the other and not knowing oneself
> In every battle, certain defeat
> **—Sun Tzu, *The Art of War***

How do you actually learn to fight fair and make up properly? One wet, cold July weekend, Rob and I attempted to find out, along with six other couples huddled into psychologist Hilary Tupling's consulting rooms. Ostensibly a relationship-building weekend, we were there mostly as a premarriage experiment, but for some couples in the room this was clearly about trying to break a marriage crisis. Straightaway, everyone started arguing about where they fitted on a triangular personality map. There was one person disputing it particularly strongly. Naturally, it was my beloved. Rob insisted he didn't belong as a 'hub', the personality type he'd been assigned in the first test.

'Most hubs say that,' said Tupling dryly, as she pencilled him dead centre on the map.

The two-day workshop was called Understanding Relationships and it was based on the Relationship Awareness SDI (strength deployment inventory) model. It's a program designed to unpick people's value systems, give insights into underlying motivations and see how those values may clash. 'The basic premise of the model is that everyone has one thing in common,' Tupling says. 'That is, everyone wants to feel good about themselves.'

The system maps your motivations via questions that tease out in what ways, through being what kind of person, you feel good about yourself. Tupling was kept busy helping us map the strategies and behaviours we each employ to give ourselves that satisfied inner glow. The model she used describes three core values that are each assigned a colour: altruistic/nurturing (blue), assertive/directing (red), and autonomising/analysing (green). Pictured as a triangle, each of these is placed in a corner. Then there is a middle group, the hubs, people who draw from each area. No group is any better than any other and each comes loaded with strengths that can also become weaknesses.

Few couples are in the same corner on the triangle, though as it turned out, Rob and I are both hubs (though now, embracing the whole idea, he insists he's more hub-like than me). 'Each of these groups has very characteristic ways of approaching problem-solving,' Tupling explained later. 'At a simplistic level you are more likely to see a sportsperson coming from the directing/asserting motivational style because that's generally associated with competing. On the other side, the nurturing/altruism types are, you've guessed it, likely to be carers and therapists. Teachers often come between the two groups.'

And what about Rob insisting that he doesn't belong in the centre? 'Many people who fall into that middle group really resist being pigeon-holed,' said Tupling with a bemused expression. 'They don't notice that the red group don't give a stuff, because they know who they are, or that blues are asking, "You're not happy?" and the greens are saying, "Well it's just mathematical". The hubs just say, "Nup, I'm not going to be pinned down" because of their incredible desire to preserve their options.'

All afternoon we spent time mapping our responses to problems, sticking tabs on charts that noted our priorities, discussing what we think matters most. Occasionally a lightbulb lit up—'that's why you don't think this is a problem!'—or a time bomb was triggered. One couple—he was a take-charge red, she was an empathic blue—seemed to struggle to find any common ground at all.

'But how I feel and how you feel has to be the most important,' she said. 'No,' he shook his head, not if you're in the red.

'These core values determine how a couple are going to approach almost anything,' explained Tupling 'from planning a holiday, buying a house and their style of child-rearing, to managing the in-laws. All tap into "how does this person generally view the world?". They have different value systems, which lead to different approaches, different problem-solving styles, different emphasis, different interpretations. When you start to see the differences between the way people operate, you start to understand why certain things don't get done together,' she pointed out. 'Why it's easy for him to stay up watching TV because he doesn't mind being on his own, whereas, if she's a hub, she's going to feel really left out if she goes to bed on her own, even if she's dog tired.'

'How did you know?' I ask, hubbishly. Tupling smiles.

It was on day two that the fun really began: the topic was styles in conflict. The idea is that if you put anyone into crisis they retreat from being able to appreciate the other's view, defending their own patch. Really push it and we all mainline straight into the reptilian part of our brains, which is blind to everything except survival. So it can be a rather useful exercise to understand what you and your partner look like at each stage of a crisis.

'At the simplest level, conflicts need to be approached from the position of understanding the other guy's point of view,' Tupling told the group. 'Seeing that their view has validity, even if you don't agree with it.' People started mapping their conflict cycles though a blue-red-green sequence—even the hubs, who in conflict revert to predictable types.

'It never dawned on me until I did this, that not being able to make firm, instant decisions—a characteristic of hubs—and, instead, constantly looking for other options might really give someone else the shits,' said Tupling of her own hub-like journey. 'I couldn't see why someone else wouldn't want to reopen a discussion and look at it another way. And it never occurred to me that someone else might be really focused on "getting it right", because for me there wasn't a right. Or that somebody might see my behaviour and judge it as being wishy-washy and lacking backbone. It helps you not only understand your partner but also yourself. And,' she added, 'It allows you to laugh at it a bit too, because it's really quite funny.'

Tupling pointed out that when faced with a partner who doesn't think or react like you do many people become anxious and enter the first stage of conflict. 'Then we start to get different behaviours again, which can send people further apart because now not only is he different to me, I don't even recognise him anymore. He's not the person I married. Then you start to get this exponential experience of distance and stress that tests whether the person can self-soothe, whether they can validate themselves, whether they can stay solid in the face of this very different person. So it's not about communication, it's more about interpretation.'

Knowing yourself and being able to hold on to who you are when you're both in this cycle, along with acknowledging where your partner is coming from, is the main point of the exercise.

While Tupling doesn't credit the program alone with the power to save relationships, she does say it's a very useful tool to open up understanding. 'Apart from being able to see your partner from a different viewpoint, you see yourself as well,' she said.

But did it work for Rob and me? Well, it certainly explained why it took us two years to agree on the paint colour for the living room, and why when we're arguing it takes us so long to reach a consensus because, while I head into make-a-decision red, Rob goes off to let's-be-logical green. We weren't in crisis when we went to the workshop, but we haven't really had a door-slamming barney since.

'Ironically,' observes Rob, 'what probably brought us the closest was seeing couples who were in real crisis and thinking "we don't want to end up like that".'

In fact, at the end of the workshop, one of the older men—who was there because his retirement clearly triggered a relationship crisis—took Rob aside. 'It's so good you're doing this when you're young, before you're in trouble,' he said. 'Wish we had.'

The rules of engagement
>One who takes position first at the battleground
>And awaits the enemy is at ease
>One who takes position at the battleground
>And hastens to do battle is at labour
>Thus one skilled at battle summons others
>And is not summoned by them
>**—Sun Tzu,** *The Art of War*

You don't have to do a workshop like we did to start thinking about how to fight fair. After all, the first biggest secret in the art of any war—including marital warfare—is simply a good intelligence assessment. Understanding (and acknowledging) where your partner is coming from is something that simply takes practise. The real trick, of course, is learning how to do this in the heat of battle. And that's where it sometimes helps to draw up some rules.

Audrey and Rudy, after learning to battle on middle ground, sat down and drew up their exact rules of engagement. Their first rule was to actually listen to the other person.

'Listen and see whether they have a grievance,' says Rudy, conceding that, 'nine times out of ten Audrey has got a grievance'.

Second was to keep on talking. 'We've got a basic rule, which we've really only broken once,' says Rudy. 'Don't go to bed without coming to a conclusion.' The one time this didn't happen was when Audrey stayed out late and didn't tell Rudy where she was. 'I turfed a pillow out of the bedroom with a set of pyjamas and she had to go and sleep in another room,' he says. They made up in the morning.

Then there is the need to accept that there is drama in fighting. 'You need to be able to express yourselves,' says Rudy. 'Desk thumping, growling, staring, dramatic pauses,' he says, waving his hands about, 'they're all good because they give you a vent for your emotions. You can get it out, express it and demonstrate how frustrated you are.'

Finally, concedes Rudy, sometimes it's just that kind of ridiculousness that breaks the cycle. 'I've had tantys and Audrey's just looked at me and gone "What are you doing?" Half an hour later when you've calmed down you look back and go "That was really stupid, wasn't it?"'

So that's their final rule—put it into perspective.

And they're not the only ones I found who had done this. Newlyweds David and Jennie like to keep their rules simple—they only fight about the issue at hand.

'Never say "never" and never say "always",' says Jennie. 'As in "you always do so-and-so", or "you never do so-and-so".'

'Those words are *banned*,' says Dave with a flourish. 'And if Jen does something that upsets me, I try to keep it very specific when I tell her "when you did X, it made me feel Y"—that's my strategy when we have some kind of friction.'

This strategy of not making personal accusations has already helped them cope with family stress. Last year tragedy struck David's family when his stepfather was diagnosed with cancer, as had his biological father previously.

'David was very angry about Des being sick, and it was coming out in very strange ways,' says Jennie. His temper was on a hair-trigger and it seemed to be directed at Jennie. 'I worked out pretty quickly that it was misdirected anger,' she says. 'Not long before Des died I asked him, "Are you angry at Des for being sick?" At first he denied he was angry, then two seconds later he admitted, "I'm really angry that Mum has to go through this again." And that was actually all he needed to stop expressing his anger in bizarre ways.'

Learning to take a step back and not take anger or other emotions personally, especially if your partner is under stress, is also important. You might feel like the target when your partner is lashing out, but being able to recognise the actual problem—and voice it—can help you reach a resolution. But rules for fighting aren't just about finding ways to empathise with your partner. They can also be about taking responsibility for yourself.

Matt, a public sector senior manager, 44, and Sarah, 47, managing director of a children's book publishing house, agree they have a direct approach when it comes to communicating.

'Matt will turn around and say "that's bullshit" and I'm quite a direct person too,' says Sarah, who laughs when she tells me Matt's nickname for her is 'streetfighter'. 'I am quite combative,' she admits. 'I knew that Matt was the one for me when we had an argument and he told me to "get fucked". I thought, "Yeah, this

The rules of engagement
Rule 1: Fight
Couples who fight can have stronger relationships and marriages, but it's how you fight that makes the difference. If you avoid conflict and skirt issues that need airing, ultimately you may damage the relationship.

Rule 2: No one wins
If one spouse 'wins', both lose. Nothing chips at a marriage more than the feeling that you're always giving in. You're solving a problem, not winning a war. And sometimes you will have to agree to disagree.

Rule 3: Fight fair
Maintain some respect for your partner: no name calling, no contempt, no hitting below the belt, no throwing your partner's weaknesses in their face.

Rule 4: Don't bring in the cavalry
Adding friends or family to the debate will only make it worse. They will meddle. They will remember. They will remind you.

Rule 5: No past history
If it's settled, don't bring it up again, especially if it's just to sledge your partner. We've all done dumb things, made mistakes and acted badly.

Rule 6: Stick to the subject
'Never' and 'always' are banned during arguments, as in 'you never' or 'you always'. Stick to the specific problem rather than making things global—you don't want to escalate the problem into World War III.

> ### Rule 7: Maintain a sense of humour
> Fighting is the most fabulous, theatrical, over the top, yelling, screaming, chest-beating good fun, right? Have you seen yourself? You look ridiculous. Enjoy the moment and then move on.
>
> ### Rule 8: Don't go to bed angry
> Finish the fight. If you or your partner get too upset, take time out for thirty minutes or so until you've both calmed down, then sit down quietly and try to resolve it.
>
> ### Rule 9: Don't slide down the slippery slope
> Stonewalling, avoidance, disengagement, contempt, criticism or the silent treatment all lead nowhere good.
>
> ### Rule 10: Keep talking
> You might want to kill your spouse but you love them as well. Don't shut them out during or after the fight, or punish them for having the argument. Work on maintaining that magic five-to-one ratio—for every one negative make up with five positives.

is someone who's not going to stand for any nonsense." I really liked that.'

While not every marriage might flourish with such a direct approach, the real point, Matt and Sarah say, is that their communication is deliberate, a pattern they consciously set up together after participating in a transformational course.

'We promised to do certain things,' says Sarah. 'It is quite empowering to think I can make a promise and have the strength of mind to stick to it.'

Part of their promise was agreeing to take responsibility for the message they were trying to get across to the other.

'It's easy to find excuses for misunderstandings,' says Matt. 'You can say "oh well, it was the circumstances", or "she didn't understand me" rather than taking responsibility for being understood.'

If you boil down what all these couples are saying, fighting fair and fighting well isn't all that complicated: be willing to listen; take responsibility for expressing your views; be willing to talk about a problem; find a way of expressing your frustration; look for compromise; and don't turn a battle over one problem into a war on everything. Of course, you have to learn to do all this when you are feeling angry, frustrated and happier to kill than kiss your partner, which is easier said than done. But it's important, because if those negative emotions run over you, you can end up in a destructive cycle.

Four easy steps to divorce

All happy families are alike but an unhappy family is unhappy after its own fashion.
—Leo Tolstoy, Anna Karenina, 1877

John Gottman disagrees with Tolstoy. He says unhappy families look remarkably alike and he has compiled a set of anti-rules, if you like, that show there are really only four easy steps to take when it comes to setting your marriage on the road to divorce. And they pretty much all occur when you fight. Outlined in his book, *Why Marriages Succeed or Fail*, Gottman calls them the 'four horsemen of the apocalypse'—criticism, contempt, defensiveness and stonewalling.[3]

Step 1: Criticism

Criticism is a negative comment about something you wish were otherwise, unlike complaining, which can be good for a marriage as it ensures gripes aren't left to fester. Criticism adds *blame*, turning the problem into a personal attack or accusation, rather than being about specific behaviour. A quick and easy way to discern criticism is to use the very sentences Dave and Jennie banished—'you *always* do selfish things like that', or 'you *never* listen'.

Step 2: Contempt

This readily follows criticism. This is all about not showing respect and intending to cause hurt—'Lobbing insults right into the heart of your partner's sense of self', as Gottman puts it. Making negative character judgements—she's stupid, he's incompetent—ensures that you fail to see your partner's good points and ride roughshod over any positive aspects of your relationship. Contempt neatly erodes admiration and nothing signals this like using insults, name-calling and mockery when you fight, especially if you're with company, as that is publicly humiliating your partner.

Step 3: Defensiveness

This feels like the natural response to contempt and criticism. This useful tool for escalating your quarrel also muddies the marital waters, so that specific grievances are now well and truly forgotten. Defensiveness lets you paint yourself as the innocent victim. If your spouse complains the house is dirty, tell them it's not your fault, that you can't do everything. If you are late home without calling, it's because circumstances are beyond your control and you certainly don't have to explain yourself. Defensiveness takes no responsibility and answers complaints with counter-complaints, thus ignoring the issue your partner is raising. Defensiveness is all about capturing high moral ground.

Step 4: Stonewalling

All three tactics neatly lead to stonewalling, or putting up an emotional wall, which is the final and most effective defence of all. Stonewalling can be used at any stage of an argument and is easily spotted by tell-tale glazed eyes and stony silence. Other stonewalling tactics include switching to monosyllabic responses and changing the topic as soon as possible. Reading the paper when you've said your piece or are finished with the argument is also useful. Best still, just leave the room—a particularly useful technique for men, as their wife's heart will quickly race to panic.

Gottman offers a caveat on stonewalling. He says men are particularly vulnerable to their emotions when arguing and stonewalling can be a way for them to shut down their panic. When monitoring couples' heart rates during tense discussions Gottman found that their hearts often sped up past 100 beats per minute, compared to an average of 76 beats per minute for men, and 82 for women. When this happens hormones like adrenaline start surging, kicking in the 'fight or flight' response, and blood pressure rises. This leads to 'flooding' and once you reach this stage you can't fight rationally—you're now just fighting for survival and stonewalling is a common coping response. And men are more likely to become 'flooded' than women, generally taking longer to calm down. Gottman is at pains to point out that it's not an excuse to completely stop the argument, but that

---

Domestic violence

There is one caveat in this how-to-argue chapter: if your fighting includes physical or emotional violence the best advice is get out and get help—separately. Staying and trying to sort out the issue yourself will probably make the relationship worse rather than better.

When it comes to getting help there is emerging evidence that group programs for men who are violent are more effective than individual or couples counselling. The most effective of these programs run a substantial period of time and focus on educational, attitudinal and behavioural change, rather than on therapy, support or counselling.[5] Research also suggests that a woman's behaviour has little influence on the level of aggression in a violent relationship and consequently, any work the woman does to improve the relationship may make little difference.[6]

Relationships Australia provides counselling and support services for individuals, couples and families where family violence or sexual abuse of children has occurred.

taking a break can be useful and the best response is to agree to resume the discussion in twenty minutes, once you're both able to think rationally again.[4]

When is enough?

> There is no instance of a country having benefited from prolonged warfare.
> **—Sun Tzu**, *The Art of War*

What do you do if you find yourself having destructive fights? Tracy, 44, 'mother, wife, radio presenter, comedian, singer, actress' and David, 62, lighting designer and architect, have been married for ten years. It is, they say, a passionate relationship and both add that for them passion involves fighting.

'We love passionately and hate passionately,' says Tracy. 'There are times I hate him and I tell him—"I hate you." I'm really vicious.' And it's never about big things, she adds, rather it's the little things. 'Like David not putting his socks in the washing basket or finding out we're out of yoghurt. We do sleep apart quite a bit,' she admits. 'I think it's important not to feel like a failure if you can't stand to look at each other.'

Rather than letting the fighting defeat them, Tracy and David decided to break the cycle. 'Tracy is a lot more open and verbal than I am,' says David. 'I tend towards retraction. When we were bitching I was carrying it inside. She said, "If we don't talk to someone, we'll break up" and I thought "I don't want that".' So they signed up for what is now regular counselling. 'One of the best pieces of advice our counsellor gave us is so simple,' explains Tracy. 'When you start to hate each other, sit on the couch and hold each other's hand.' And while admitting she's likely not to want to do that, Tracey says, 'it works pretty much every time'. For David the counselling opened up a whole pathway to understanding himself and now he sometimes checks in with the therapist on his own.

'You maintain a car by taking it to a bloke who fixes it, so you may as well get a marriage tuned as well,' he says and, drawing on his thrice-married experience, adds 'The people you learn from are your parents. Unless you make a conscious decision to change your own behaviour, you'll repeat it.' Now they still bicker, but after the fight they sit down and talk it through.

'We're always better after we've talked,' she says.

Which is also exactly what Gottman advocates. 'One of the most important techniques a couple can try and develop is to have a good recovery conversation after an argument, which is very different from saying you should fight in a constructive way.' This means, he says, that when things are calm you need to talk about the last fight and, rather than arguing your own point of view again, try to understand your partner's position. 'Understand that both positions have validity,' he says. 'Get some emotional distance and then figure out one way to make the next conversation about that issue better.' If a couple always fights about his mother, for example, 'If they have good recovery conversations, gradually they'll stop fighting about his mother.'

But Gottman warns there isn't any such thing as having one good big fight that will settle everything once and for all. Nor is it the case that once you've settled one area of disagreement, all others will magically fall into line. 'If the same couple fighting about his mother also fights about money, well, you've got to go over all that again,' he says. 'You've got to cycle through all of the issues, and for some people, there are three or four issues, for some people there's only one, for some people there are fifteen. It's just a matter of really going through it. It is a slow process and it takes some commitment.'

Extreme marriage solutions

Even if you are fighting so much you think your relationship can't be saved, it almost always can. A recent study shows that two-thirds of people who told researchers that they were unhappily married but

> **Bad couple therapy and how to avoid it**
> When it comes to getting professional help one of the biggest problems can be finding an effective therapist. The dirty little secret of the relationships therapy industry is that while some couples (between a third and a half) find marriage therapy helps them in the short term, research shows only a small percentage see any lasting change in their relationship.[7] What is more, anyone can call themselves a 'therapist' so it is worth looking to registered organisations like Relationships Australia for someone who you know is actually qualified to counsel couples.

stayed together, said that their marriages were happy when researchers followed them up five years later.[8] When William Doherty and his colleagues set out to find out why, they again found it was the simple things that had made the difference.

'Put one foot ahead of the other day after day,' Doherty says. 'The surviving couples talked about their problems and things got better. Often the stress that they were under went away—the husband got a job, the mother-in-law died, the kid left home.' Even seemingly intractable problems, 'like husbands acting badly', says Doherty, were outlasted. He offers as an example a wife who says 'I love you and I want to be married to you but I can't keep doing this anymore. You have to start coming home, you can't go out the pub every night.' The husband, says Doherty, will finally wake up and say, 'I don't want to lose my wife and child' and shape up. 'I think that even when marriages go bad they can be good again.'

Liz and Brian came perilously close to losing their fourteen-year marriage. Married at twenty and nineteen respectively, the early years, says Liz, were an adventure. Both teachers, they spent their first three years together in country New South Wales, and the second three in Canada, where they had their two sons, Ben and Joe. Back home again, when the children were young, Liz stayed home, studying part-time at night for a diploma in art. Once the kids were in school, she went back to work but somehow, Liz says, by then their lives were going in two different directions. Each partner had their own interests and both were busy running the house. And they were not getting along at all.

'We were stuck in a rut, the wheels kept spinning and we kept trying to do the same thing to get it to work,' says Liz. 'You can talk until you're blue in the face. Talk, talk, talk, and not get anywhere. Finally it got to the point where I said, "I cannot live like this." Something had to happen, either one of us left—and I didn't want the kids to go through that—or we'd have to do something drastic.' So they did. They bought a boat to sail away in.

'What did I have to lose?' says Liz. 'I kept thinking, "Live in the house and lose the marriage, or sell the house?".' Not that it was a magic solution at first. 'Instantly, we had awful fights,' she recalls. 'We were fighting continuously. I think it was just the enormity of our decision.' It didn't bode well for their future plan to sail all the way to Canada. Once they were on the boat, everything fell into place.

'The kids fitted in perfectly and we had to get on. We were together, and had to do things together,' Liz says. 'When we were in a house, we each had a career and there were distractions and diversions. On a boat, with the focus just on the four of us, there was no arguing.'

On a boat, she says, you find out what has to be done and you just do it. 'There are no dilemmas. No, "I should have said that, I shouldn't have said that." You find each other's rough edges and you have to accommodate them. You want to make it work. 'It was raw living, there was no protection. Beautiful sunsets and sunrises, the smell of the sea. The boys fitted in and loved not going to school—they rowed the dingy, read charts, had real hands-on experience—we didn't have tantrums. The four of us had to work with each other. We did it before when they were babies and we bonded again on the boat.'

After a year of meandering up along the coast they finally made it as far north as Brisbane. Canada, as it turned out, was not going to happen. Liz never quite got comfortable on the open sea, and they were ready to stop.

'We got off the boat and we were good friends,' she says. 'The marriage was definitely saved and it was worth saving. I think the way we both changed was the unity, realising we were on the same team, and what our priorities were, us and the kids. The kids don't need Nike™ shoes on the boat, you don't need a dishwasher. It was realising normal life is too much about money and status symbols—and they're not what's important.'

Two weeks later the boat was sold, and Liz and Brian have now been married for thirty-four years.

To sum it up

- Fighting can be good.
- Learn how to fight fair.
- There's no one right way to fight.
- Understand what values are driving you.
- Try to see where your partner is coming from.
- Take responsibility for how you react in a fight.
- No criticism, contempt, defensiveness or stonewalling allowed.
- Be specific when you argue—fight each fight on its own merits and don't turn it into a war about everything.
- If you're having a big problem, get some proper help through counselling—don't leave it until you really hate each other.
- Set your own rules of engagement.
- Even a bad marriage can come good again.

5

Men v. Women: can we be on the same side?

> That every normal woman has the maternal instinct, and a desire for a home and family, is probably true; that every woman has the cooking and cleaning and nursing instincts is neither true nor desirable. There is no more reason that marriage and the parental function should involve the utter renunciation of a professional, artistic, or business career for the many women naturally adapted to such careers, than that it should do so for their husbands. But as we keep house at present, it does and must mean such renunciation in most cases, because it is not humanly possible for a woman to do exactly double the work of a man.
> —**Mary Leal Harkness,** *Atlantic Monthly,* **October 1911**

As I sat scanning the pages of yellowed, sweet-smelling 100-year-old marriage manuals in the stained glass light of the Mitchell reading room at the State Library of New South Wales, something started to bother me. I was meant to be here looking for some humour—arcane quotes, advice and aphorisms for the modern turn-of-the-century young lady or gent contemplating marriage to lighten the tone of this book. While I did find plenty of the ridiculous, along with a surprising amount of anti-marriage sentiment, there was something even more startling.

At first I thought it was a lucky strike on the part of one prescient author, who outlined the conundrum of women who want a career and kids. Then I kept finding the same set of questions repeated over and over. And they sounded, well, darn familiar: do women get a raw deal from marriage? If looking after a home is a full-time job, how come only one of you is doing it? Why should women have to choose between an intellectually satisfying life and having children? How could a husband and wife do anything but grow apart if his world was all about work and money and hers was about home, kids and servants?

How is it that more than a century after women first began fighting to be freed of just home and hearth—and for their husbands to be more than just walking wallets, do we still seem to be grappling with many of the same problems today? (Well, with the exception of issues relating to servants, that is.)

Don't get me wrong. Things have changed—women do have substantially more rights than they did 100 years ago; and husbands are no longer as likely to spend more time at the club (or pub) than at home. Nor is having a career something women have to actively fight for. But still, the questions do have a spookily familiar feel to them.

In short, the question still being asked 100 years later is: can a man and a woman have an equally satisfying marriage?

If you believe the barn-load of modern titles bowing the shelves of any self-respecting bookstore, the answer seems to be no. Wives, we are still being told, get a raw deal out of marriage. For instance, there's Susan Maushart's somewhat depressing 2001 title, *Wifework*, where she asserts, 'Women who tell themselves that marriage is "just a piece of paper", that "it won't make a difference to our relationship at all", are kidding themselves. If you are female, marriage will make a huge difference—and most of it will be negative.' This is really just an extension of Jessie Bernard's influential 1972 book, *The Future of Marriage*, where she states, 'there are two marriages . . . in every marital union, his and hers. And his . . . is better than hers."[1]

The male point of view is ostensibly provided by John Gray in his barnstorming series, which began with the book, *Men Are From Mars, Women Are From Venus*. In the original blockbuster he writes, 'The most frequently expressed complaint women have about men is that men don't listen . . . The most frequently expressed complaint men have about women is that women are always trying to change them.'

What's the common theme that links the two views? While they would probably agree on little else, both sides seem to be saying the same thing: men and women want different things from a marriage—and it's implied the other is getting the better deal. Is that really true? Certainly there are differences. Studies consistently show that, in general, male and female brains look and work differently: men are more aggressive and competitive and better at skills that require spatial ability and mathematical reasoning; women are more sensitive to nuances of expression and gesture, more adept at judging character.[2] Men are more open to sex with strangers, more likely to commit adultery, less insistent on emotional intimacy as the foundation of a relationship—and less likely to talk about their feelings.[3] When arguing, men clam up and women talk more. When courting, women value financial prospects around twice as highly as men[4] and when it comes to ending it, women initiate two-thirds of divorces.[5] And these are differences which show in our marriages in ways big and small.

'Females and males are very different,' agrees Alan sitting around the dinner table after helping pack his three kids off to bed.

'He's very much a "tell me when it's that time of the month" guy, before he beats a retreat,' laughs his wife Carrie.

'The female psyche is so hard to understand at times,' says Alan, shaking his head. 'You're better off not challenging some things because guys are not going to win. If you have an idea of how to do something and your wife has a different idea of how to do it, instead of showing them how to do it, you're better off letting them do it, even if they make a mistake.'

Would it be a mistake to think this couple is tied into unchanging gender roles courtesy of their biology or community. For instance, while Carrie is currently staying at home with the kids and Alan is the breadwinner, they don't entirely fit the stereotype. Alan is an involved parent, starting his work day early so he can be home by 4 p.m. to help with the kids' afternoon routine and with preparing dinner. Carrie, for her part, is back studying at college. What's more significant is that for all the 'we're from different planets' banter, Carrie and Alan do agree on the bigger picture. Like pretty much every couple I asked about how they saw their marriages, two words kept coming up again and again: 'partnership' and 'equal'.

It's no great stretch to say that this is our modern ideal of marriage—a partnership between equals. It's what we consistently say we want and because of that, it is the thing most likely to cause us stress if things do go off kilter in the equality department. However, on the one hand we have this equal partner ideal while on the other hand the complaints. How do we negotiate the differences between what we see and the ideals we hold?

Who cleans the toilet?

Things Women Forget
That there is a limit to every banking account
The precise hour of any appointment
That a man is still a man even if he happens to be their husband
That the most trivial unkindness is capable of immense hurt and a
    man has no power of retaliation
Last they do not remember that they are generally loved vastly
    more than ever they love
—Rose Henniker Heaton, *The Perfect Hostess,* **1931**

How do we test if we're living up to our own ideals? There's one pretty straightforward litmus test and it's exactly the battleground identified by all those old—and new—relationship manuals: housework. Marriage research makes it clear that there is a significant relationship between how happy a marriage is and the couple's perception about how fairly the housework and childcare is distributed. What's more, this applies to women *and* men: both are happier when they perceive their spouse is sharing equitably or, in some cases, doing more than their fair share.[6] Studies also show that egalitarian-orientated men (those who believe in sharing family responsibilities equally) have higher levels of 'marital quality' than non-egalitarian men,[7] and wives who work have greater satisfaction within their marriage if the division of housework is fairer.[8] But here's the rub. The figures on who's actually doing what don't add up to reflect those egalitarian values. The picture, instead of showing tasks split equally, looks more like that described in those nineteenth-century marriage manuals. According to the Australian Bureau of Statistics, unpaid work consumes almost one third of women's waking hours while only one fifth of men's.[9] On average, women spend twice as much time on domestic labour as men.[10]

It's stats like these that fuel a lot of the women-lose-from-marriage hype. But is it that simple?

Husbands cause housework
De facto couples have a more equitable split in the housework than married couples, though women do more in both. But couples who lived together before marriage carry a more egalitarian relationship over the threshold post nuptials. Remarried couples also have more equal arrangements than first marrieds.[11]

Michael Bittman, from the Social Policy Research Centre at the University of New South Wales, has devoted his academic career to studying time—how we use it, how we divide it and who does what. Over lunch in the college cafeteria, he confirms the housework problem for women starts as soon as they simply walk down the aisle. When they wed, women who previously lived alone will more than double the time they spend on laundry (from two to over four hours per week) while men get to halve their washing time from less than an hour to less than half an hour each week. She increases by 40 per cent the time she spends on the cleaning, he decreases his cleaning time by about 40 per cent.

Even the good news is a little misleading, says Bittman. 'If you look at the share of household tasks, men's share is increasing. But this is mostly because women's share is decreasing—they're doing less.' So while men might be doing a little bit more (particularly when it comes to childcare)[12] what is really changing is women's standards. Left with 70 per cent of the unpaid household work[13] they have simply become less houseproud.[14] No matter which way you slice it, women do a whole lot more unpaid work in the home. And this is something that's seen worldwide.

Women's share of total unpaid hours worked ranges from 70 per cent in egalitarian Sweden to 88 per cent in patriarchal Italy, with Australia landing smack in the middle on 77 per cent.[15] What's more, the move towards a 50/50 split has seemingly stopped improving—the number of hours men devote to housework has barely shifted in over a decade.[16] While women have more free time than men (when the number of hours worked—paid and unpaid—are added together) but free time for men (around 60 per cent of their leisure time) is spent in uninterrupted activities. That's not the case for women, who have less uninterrupted leisure time, and the time they do have is more fragmented. Unsurprisingly, the people with the lowest levels of leisure time are mothers whose youngest child is under two years old. They have a grand total of 2 hours, 38 minutes a week. How on earth did we come to this? Why is the gap still so wide? And how does this look to your average equality-loving, its-a-partnership couple?

'Housework?' sighs Audrey. '"Women's work", you mean.'

While Audrey and Rudy have a lot in common—a keen interest in politics, a biting wit and the ability to hang tough when toughness is needed—they don't, it seems, share an interest in a well-maintained house.

'The problem', says Audrey, 'isn't so much that Rudy doesn't think it's his job—he's all for the egalitarian sharing of tasks—somehow he just doesn't notice that the housework needs to get done.' He does try, of course.

'He bought a dishwasher because he doesn't like doing dishes,' says Audrey.

Did that solve the arguments?

'No, because someone has to unload it now. He leaves old dishes in the sink piled twelve-foot high and leaves the dishwasher full,' says Audrey. 'After the weekend, with only two of us home, I put twelve cups into the dishwasher on Monday morning. I clean up at night, and clean up in the morning before I go to work. And when I get home—Rudy works from home—all the breakfast dishes are out, scraps are just sitting there on the bench when the bin is just three feet away, and the milk's been out for eight hours.'

So the million-dollar question is, how do you live with it?

'Well, every so often I'll have a complete nervous breakdown and throw a crying, squealing, hissy fit and he'll feel bad and clean up for about two days,' she says. 'Then we'll go back to how we were.' And while she concedes Rudy does a cleaning spree every so often, 'The problem is that he's not doing the simple daily maintenance of actually noticing a mess and then cleaning it up.'

David and Jennie had similar issues, albeit for slightly different reasons. David grew up in South Africa and moved to Australia when he was eighteen.

'I hadn't even made my own bed until I came to live in Sydney,' he says. 'So I've had to learn to do a lot of things that Jennie has been

> **Housework causes depression**
>
> Women who do most of the household tasks are more likely to be depressed than those whose husbands shoulder some of the burden. Women are also likely to become depressed if they feel the division of labour that would suit them—one that included more time to themselves, or more help with childcare from their husbands—would not be best for the family. Men, on the other hand, get depressed when their estimates of how much housework they do are greater than what their spouse thinks they do. Men and women both get depressed when their expectations about the division of labour before the wedding are proved wrong by married life.[17]

doing since she was six.' He admits to taking a slapdash approach: 'I shove things in draws and under carpets.'

'Literally,' adds Jennie. 'He hides things. I'll come home and say, "Wow, this looks amazing, the whole room has been de-cluttered," and then find everything in the shower recess in the spare bathroom.'

'There were some negotiations,' concedes Dave. 'Jennie's quite a particular person and likes things done a certain way.'

Like Rudy, it's not that David thinks he shouldn't do housework. He's as egalitarian as they come and task sharing is practically part of his DNA, it's just that he feels he doesn't have the same expertise as Jennie. Not having grown up doing these tasks, he doesn't know the basic rules, such as 'if you tidy up, put things away where they properly belong'.

Both these couples are typical and there's a whole list of reasons that men and women give that shows they don't seem to see eye to eye on the domestic job front, including:
- ignorance: 'I didn't know we made the bed every day'
- selective blindness: 'I didn't see the dirty dishes'

- incompetence: 'What do you mean you have to separate the whites?'
- dismissal: 'I'll pick the clothes up on the weekend'.

In short, couples will fight over housework. The question is, will this become a marriage breaker, or are couples finding a way to negotiate this. And if men are generally slouches at the kitchen sink, are they making up for this in other ways?

Things a husband ought to know

> How to repair the electric light when it fuses
> How to put a washer on a tap
> How to mend the electric bells
> How to mark out the tennis-court
> How to find your keys when you lose them
> How to mend things
> How to make excuses for you over the telephone
> How to garden
> How to be nice when you have made a perfect fool of yourself
> **—Rose Henniker Heaton,** *The Perfect Hostess***, 1931**

When talking with couples about the nitty-gritty of their cleaning domestics, I noticed that something else very interesting was going on. When I spoke with the women, while I could see how they might get angry about this extra work they were doing, they didn't seem to be angry. Somehow their anger was quarantined. It wasn't spilling across to the rest of the relationship in the way you might expect it would. This puzzled me. It wasn't until I talked with plaintiff lawyer Kate and cardiac surgeon Julian that I started to understand what might be going on.

Both Kate and Julian agreed that finding a balance with the housework has been a struggle and they've had a few tough times getting that balance to where both feel happy.

'I'm probably the tardiest on the domestic front,' concedes Julian. 'It was a sticking point early in our relationship.' But it wasn't that admission that was the most interesting. It was what Kate said next.

'I've come to realise he's not trying to subjugate me,' says Kate.

'I'm just lazy,' adds Julian.

'It does still piss me off,' Kate admits, 'but in the end, practice makes perfect.' Nor does she simply ascribe the problem to male blindness. 'I've lived with female housemates who are more untidy.'

It's telling that when Kate says that Julian is not actively trying to pull her down, she's voicing what a lot of the housework tension is about. Because not folding the socks says a lot to women. Housework gets value-added. Women don't just see it as separating the whites from the coloureds, they see it as respect. The issue is being seen as an equal, not a servant. It's about *what's fair*. It's a dialogue in women's heads that men don't always get to hear.

Instead of calling in the gender police, Kate simply decided she was fighting a bigger battle than she needed to, that it could be just about the cooking or the socks or a clean bathroom. So she persists with making sure these chores get done. Which is just what Gottman advises—tackle each issue on its merits and don't turn it into something about bigger values.

From his point of view, Julian is consciously trying to avoid slipping into the conventional roles, even when he can see his contemporaries taking that path.

'I don't want to see us falling into the roles of "husband" or "wife",' says Julian. 'I see it with the consultants I work for—their wives are there to support them by cleaning or getting dinner on the table, even ones of my generation. When Kate calls and says it's my turn to cook, they're going "what are you cooking for?"'

For couples like Kate and Julian, the housework problem is just the housework problem. They don't let it become a problem of universal female suffrage, even if that could be justified, as it doesn't help. Kate knows Julian is consciously bucking the not-my-job mentality. So they treat it just like any other problem to be solved rather than turning the argument global.

This made me start thinking that maybe this is why, even though there are plenty of books that might say differently, the couples I was talking to just didn't seem angry with the other's gender anymore. Husbands weren't a pain because they were men, they were a pain when they didn't clean the toilet. Wives weren't simply irrational women because they had higher standards of cleanliness, they were just the neat freaks of the house. It all comes down to how the problem was framed. As sociologist Arlie Hochschild has noted, how wives *perceive* the amount of support and help they receive from their husband is more important than the actual division of labour when it comes to determining their marital happiness.[18]

This doesn't mean it's all rosy and perfect, of course. Housework can still lead to resentments and fights that, if unresolved, will eat away at your marriage as effectively as any of the big issues like family interference or money problems. But talking with these couples I didn't get the sense that solving this was different to anything else they dealt with. Maybe they'd get in a cleaner, maybe each got defined jobs to do. And that started me thinking that maybe men and women didn't see marriage so differently after all.

Still, I had to be sure. It's easy to put up a 'we're a team' front if you're sitting next to your spouse talking to a journo, but what would those same people say if I talked with them separately, in their peer groups? Surely if anything was going to flush out a gender divide it would be that. And to do that, I decided to observe each in their natural habitat. For women, I picked the natural environment of a girly book club, while for the guys, I convinced a male friend to let me into his regular boozy, 'hold 'em don't fold 'em' poker night.

What women want

> If women are to effect a significant amelioration in their condition, it seems obvious that they must refuse to marry.
> —**Germaine Greer,** *The Female Eunuch,* **1970**

It's a rainy evening in late November and the book club is meeting for the last time this year. When the group started seven years ago they met at each other's houses and gourmet home-cooked meals garnished the literary erudition. Busy careers and even busier motherhood has put the kybosh on that, and now the group meets in restaurants. Tonight, they're gathering at a cheery Lebanese eatery set in a cluster of similar restaurants downtown. The red, green and gold place has the comfy, peeling feel of a reliable old standard, an oasis of constancy in an area better known for the sharp design stores that punctuate the strip of ever opening and closing cafes du jour.

As a gust of music blares out onto the street and swooshes me in I find the group is already assembled around a table high on a landing that overlooks the rest of the diners. They're chatting in twos and threes and fielding calls from the stragglers who phone in updates on their progress. Around the table are three long-term marrieds, three long-term de factos, one double divorcee and a single. All are in their thirties. Half are mothers. Danni, a film-maker and first-time mother, is excited to be here on her first night out in the three months since she had Ellery.

But first things first. While tonight's book is *Holy Cow*, by journalist Sarah McDonald about her time in India, right now the group is preoccupied with ordering baba ghanoug, fried cauliflower, meatballs, felafel and the house lemon drink that everyone is addicted to. As the first plates of dip arrive I begin.

'What I want to know,' I ask as the eyes turn grudgingly away from the goodies, 'is whether men have a different marriage to women?'

The table falls silent.

'You have to say yes,' says Lauren, 30, a communications specialist, after a pause.

'You do have to say yes,' agrees Georgina, 33, a union organiser.

'I think men and women enter the marriage for different reasons,' begins Kate, 33, a magazine editor.

So things are different. We're getting somewhere already. Just then Danni's phone rings. It's her husband. The baby is crying and won't stop.

'I'm sorry everyone,' Danni says as she scoops up her bag. 'I'm going to have to go.'

'Hasn't he been left with the baby before?' says Georgina to Danni's retreating figure as the others roll their eyes. Apparently not! By consensus, he'll soon learn. Still, despite what's just happened, the men v. women discussion now stalls as the group struggles to come up with actual examples that show men are from another planet.

'My dad doesn't understand why women would live with men without being married,' says Georgina. He says men just want regular sex, basically, and if women live with them they get that. Women—his view—want the security thing.' She adds that he still believes this, even though both his daughters have lived with their boyfriends, which they've subsequently married.

'So do you think that stereotype holds up?' I ask.

'No,' she says.

'I think that devalues men's contribution to the relationship to say it's as simple as that,' says Lauren. It appears I won't be hearing from the right-on sisterhood tonight. So I change tack.

'What about emotional housekeeping—the hard work in making sure you're maintaining the communication in a relationship? Is that women's work?'

'It's usually me who will say let's sit down and talk if things are a bit unsettled or grumpy,' agrees Kate. 'I probably do the majority of the social planning and arranging for us.'

'Yes,' goes round the table.

'It's the complete opposite with us,' says Miranda.

Miranda has lived with James nigh on ten years and for that period James has been the social and emotional secretary for the two of them.

'He's the one who will say "why have you been so vile for the past week—you have to tell me,"' she says. 'He's the one who does all the work in our relationship, and,' she adds with a laugh, 'he does the tax returns.'

'Who does the cooking and cleaning?' demands Lauren.

'I do more of the cooking than he does, but he cleans the bathroom,' says Miranda.

'Good lord,' says Samantha, 36, twice divorced.

'Wow,' says Georgina.

'You've trained him well,' says Lauren.

'I think it's his mother actually,' says Miranda. 'Strong, feminist mother.'

Those feminist mothers again. I'd been hearing quite a bit about them. It's a quiet revolution on the domestic front: trickle-down feminism. I first heard about them when talking with Sanjeev and Annabelle, who look for all the world like the poster-children for egalitarian relationships. Drop around to their house for dinner and one will be chopping while the other is putting on the pasta. Annabelle puts Sanjeev's willingness to do his share down to one simple factor—his mother. Sanjeev's parents separated when he was twelve, after which his mother taught him how to cook. So for him, practical help is the norm.

And for all his gloomy statistics even Michael Bittman agrees that change is happening but, he states, it's at a generational level. According to him this is largely because husbands and wives still unconsciously replicate the housework their fathers and mothers did. So change is a series of slow, intricate generational steps.

Firstly, there are old habits to break. Bittman says, 'If the husband has an habitual route to the living room from the front door, and the wife to the kitchen, varying these routines requires, at least initially, a continuous minute-by-minute awareness of the implications of the agreed change.'

Secondly, domestic skills take time to learn and time to teach. 'The husband may not know how to operate the washing machine, or hasn't developed the ability to sort the clothing for the best results in the wash.' Add to that the need to confront expectations about what is manly, or what a good house looks like, and it's less surprising that even if both partners agree to a change in theory it seems difficult to manage in practice.[19]

But Bittman says that the biggest factor effecting this change is the social shift that has occurred over the past decade. In 1987, the most common type of family had a husband working full-time with a wife at home. By 1997, the most common family was made up of a husband working full-time, with a wife working part-time. In the same period the working day has become longer—ten plus hours a day is becoming more frequent—so time is getting squeezed every direction. Something, Bittman says, has to give.

Back at the book club, Miranda has now started the ball rolling.

'Tom cooks and cleans like an angel,' adds Kate to another round of 'wows' around the table.

'It's the cooking thing I can't break,' says Georgina. 'He's getting a Christmas present to help him along with that. But then he is pretty good with cleaning. I had to train him. I thought it would never happen, and then he kind of did it.'

'Did that take lots of arguments?' I ask.

'I think, um, well actually, we do have a cleaner now,' says Georgina. 'Which he always wanted. I didn't want to spend the money but I finally gave in and it was just the best decision we ever made. It just stopped a lot of the arguments. And weekend time, you actually use it. It's definitely the best marriage counselling.'

'My man is really anally retentive,' says Kate. 'He's a real neat freak, whereas I struggle with mess. I actually have little piles of things around the house, envelopes I haven't quite opened. He's like, "clean it!" It's a source of frustration for him.'

Again, it's what is missing that is most striking. It's the absence of raw anger, the sort of anger you sometimes hear in older women, the resentment that fuelled a hundred 'mere male' columns in women's magazines for decades. The anger of women whose partners just won't see, won't do and won't change. But while these busy women—with plenty of kids and careers between then—do still sometimes fight with their spouses over the housekeeping, the problem seems to eventually get resolved. They don't expect or accept incompetence from their partners, or vice versa. And while we could keep looking for the difference between men and women, what all these women seem to be saying is that they don't think the men versus women thing is really much of a problem.

In a fitting final act, just as the plates are being cleared and the talk can turn to the book, the group breaks into spontaneous cheers. Danni has walked back into the room.

'She was asleep by the time I got home,' she says. 'And she stayed asleep.' Satisfied her husband was fine on the home front, Danni turned around and came back out.

'He'll learn,' says Georgina confidently. 'He knows now.'

Rob Marjenberg is the research director for Heartbeat, a qualitative market research company. He says there has been a massive shift in men's attitude to housework, but only among the younger generation.

'There is a fault line between under-forties and over-forties,' he says. 'It's like a generation gap. In general, men in their forties haven't got the idea this is all about a partnership. They're more likely to

> **Housework prevents divorce**
>
> Married men who are more involved in household work considerably increase their chances of staying married. In one study of newlywed couples, marriages where men were actively involved in housework were 81 per cent less likely to end in divorce than other marriages.[20]

support strict gender roles. But women and men in their twenties take equality for granted.' As an example, Marjenberg points to a recent television advertising campaign. A man is drinking at the pub with his mates, but has told his wife he's working back. When his wife calls on his mobile, all his mates make office noises to cover for him.

'The guys over forty loved it,' says Marjenberg. 'The guys in their thirties say, "That's something my dad would have done". They don't want to be at the pub with their mates, they want to be at home with their family.' Given Heartbeat researches across the entire city of Sydney, it's a telling insight. 'With guys who are younger, it's no big deal. It's a practical egalitarianism,' he says. 'These guys aren't SNAGs. Their attitude is more "You pitch in, you do your bit, and you do what's fair." They've turned the gender tunnel vision off. It's all about what needs to be done.'

Indeed, says Marjenberg, many domestic images are being turned on their head, and these days having a messy house is 'almost a badge of honour'.

'The mentality is more "coping is achieving",' he says. 'If someone goes into a perfect house the thought is, "What are your priorities?" People say "The clothes aren't ironed but I'm helping kids with their homework or playing with them".' And, he adds, it's often women who are proudest of the shortcuts. 'One woman said "I love it when it's Winter and I only have to iron my daughter's sleeves, the rest is covered by her jumper".' Women are finally leaving behind the

> **Housework builds better children**
> Children who do their share of domestic cleaning alongside their fathers are likely to be better adjusted, get along better with their peers and have more friends. They are also less likely to disobey teachers or make trouble at school and are less depressed and withdrawn.[21]

expectation that a good wife is one with an immaculate house. But if this is how women see things (or rationalise, depending on who you talk to) what do the men say?

The poker night

> Another thing the tactful husband does is to let his wife cry . . . He does not get up and rage about and kick footstools out of the way and say, 'Oh, for Heaven's sake! Stop crying, or you'll drive me to drink!'
> No! He goes and pats her shoulder soothingly and says:
> 'There little woman! I'm sorry the cook has left and your new gown hooks up on the bias but cheer up! Let's go out and have a jolly little dinner and tomorrow I'll write that tailor a letter that will make his hair curl.'
> **—Lilian Bell, *Why Men Remain Bachelors and Other Luxuries*, 1906**

One week after my visit to the book club I gain entry to the boys' poker night. The deal is, I can ask questions so long as I'm prepared to be the sacrificial novice—the poker bunny—and lose all my cash to a group who have been playing together for ten years and mount regular raids on Las Vegas. Armed with $50 and one hour's worth of poker tuition I arrive at the poker den, Dave's city apartment. Situated just up from tattoo parlours and 24-hour bars, the modern, sparse space is also a short stroll from Dave's work, where he gives policy advice to the state government. Dave's married, but his Brazilian wife, Leticia, who is pregnant with their first child, is sensibly absent.

They game is already set up around the kitchen table when I arrive.

'Give me your money,' greets Dave as I walk in. I'm handed a pile of chips with instructions to count them for myself. Craig, 34, a single insurance manager, and Michael, 35, a married investment manager, are busy tallying their stacks. We'll soon be joined by Matt, 31, single, a student and paramedic; Dave, 36, married with a child on the way, senior policy adviser; Adam, 36, actor, married; Evan, 36, married with two kids, aspiring politician and full-time father; and, later in the evening, Kahl, 33, a long-term de facto with two kids, a professional punter who works from home. Later still will be Paul, a banker, popping up for a drink before going back to work.

The game is seven-card stud and dinner is packet crisps and beer pulled from a shiny red fridge. Idle chatter is quickly called to order when it interferes with the game. On the second hand, a rush of testosterone fuels a betting spree between Adam and Dave, which sees Dave lose $66. The guys look at me with eyebrows raised.

'The chick factor?' I ask as they nod solemnly in agreement. It seems a good place to start as any.

So do men have a different marriage to women? I ask.

'How the fuck would we know?' whoops Dave to loud guffaws.

'That's fair,' says Adam.

'Yep, that about covers it,' says Evan.

Fantastic. Three sentences for my $50. This had better not be the end of it.

'Anyone seek to digress from that position?' I ask desperately.

'We're different types of people, men and women are different,' says Dave in an isn't-it-obvious voice.

'Our reality of the world is different, it has to be,' agrees Evan.

In what way? I ask.

'In almost every way,' continues Evan. 'You have a male perspective, you have a female perspective in almost everything you do. Marriage is a small part of that.' Another hand is dealt.

'A lot of women think of marriage from an earlier age, and there's a weight of expectations that goes with that, a weight of history,' says Evan at last. 'For men, it's generally something you come to later in life. You don't play at getting married or have this expectation—reinforced by your parents—that at some point they're going to pay for your wedding and walk you down the aisle. I think your idea of wedding and what flows from that is different, because the starting point is different.'

The girls said something similar—different starting points mean different expectations, at least in the beginning.

'I assumed that most of my friends would just live together forever,' says Craig. 'It wasn't until one of my really close friends got married and watching it hit me quite hard. I realised it's something quite more than just going "Yeah, this is who I'm going to spend the rest of my life with." It's that public declaration, whether it's religious or not.'

'It wasn't until you guys started getting married I really started appreciating it a lot more,' agrees Michael.

'My conception of what marriage was definitely changed after I got married,' says Dave. 'Before I got married it was just "I want to be with her" and it was a mechanism to prove to governments when we travelled that we're related. But after I got married I completely revelled in saying "this is my wife"—I loved it.'

'And it gives him another excuse down the pub,' says Craig. 'When he says, "I've got to go home, I want to see my wife,"' imitating Dave's drunken slur. 'Before we'd be "what are yah?" but if he mentions "wife" it's like, "well, go on . . ."'

What's going on here? A generation ago men were running to the pub to escape their wives and kids. Now they're escaping the pub for their families. I'm reminded of the Heartbeat research—maybe the under-forties men *are* different. Though, of course, not too different—this conversation was, after all, taking place at an all-boy play-past-midnight poker game that, like the girls' book club, happens once a month or so. Still, I wondered, if men are putting in more time at home, are they doing this grudgingly or willingly?

> **Men, listen to your wives**
> A husband's willingness to accept influence from his spouse is a significant predictor of a happy marriage. The only reason the reverse doesn't hold true is that research shows women already accept such an influence.[22] This is the same even in a conservative African country like Ghana, which is patriarchal and has traditional gender roles. Less traditional decision-making and more open communication are equally important in predicting how happy a marriage is.[23]

'Do you have any nostalgia for the kind of marriage your fathers had?' I ask. 'The traditional he-goes-out-to-work, she-stays-at-home?'

'I think of my grandparents and I just see that being completely disempowering to my grandmother,' says Dave. 'I can't see why anyone would want to have that kind of marriage.'

'When we were both working,' says Evan, 'Jennifer and I used to say we needed a wife. Someone to do all the stuff. At that moment what happens is you get a really crap division of labour, which often the woman's doing all that stuff whilst going out to work. Or both of you are doing all the stuff and going to work, so perhaps it was easier in some ways.'

'The flip side ought to be you have a better relationship with your partner,' says Dave.

'I guess we're living in an age where all that stuff is more negotiable than it was,' says Adam. 'Every couple is making up their own rules.'

There it is again. Negotiate. Work out the rules between you. Maybe my generation's choice is different after all.

'But we're living in the elite here,' says Evan, who currently stays at home with the kids while his wife works. 'At home we're in a fortunate position, we both could earn the same amount and I wasn't happy in my job. I don't know how many mothers' groups and play groups I go to where I'm the only male. They're talking about their husbands and the frustrations are still there. There's such a gulf between the person who is the breadwinner, and the person who stays at home. There is no equality in the relationship. That's the fundamental problem, the power issue. I don't think you can say it's moved forward in those circumstances.'

It's a fair point. Around the table everyone has a university degree and along with Evan there's another dad working a part-time business at home so he can be near his kids. Maybe I am finding what I want to by talking to a small group of sensitive new-agers. But I put this question to Heartbeat as well and their focus groups crossed all class lines and still turned up the same changed attitude.

'My parents are very interesting as they have what I would call a very workmanlike relationship,' says Adam. 'I'm sure they love each other, but when they met in their mid to late twenties both of them were social workers, so they were aware of all that power play. So they negotiate, and have always negotiated and that's what I grew up with. They've been comfortable taking turns with who was the primary breadwinner.'

'My dad is the primary cooker at home,' says Craig. 'Mum hates it, he's been the primary cook for years.'

'My dad does more housework now than he did previously, now he's retired,' says Evan.

Again, what they're describing is what Bittman talked about earlier—generational change. Grow up in an equality-operated household and equality will seem normal. However, this attitude change hasn't entirely solved the housework dilemma. Women still do a lot more. So what other solutions do couples come up with? Sanjeev and Annabelle may have divided the housework, before kids, but once they had daughter Amelia they decided they were simply both doing too much.

Their solution? 'We've outsourced it,' says Annabelle. 'After Amelia was born I was sitting there one weekend, I was working full-time, I had this small child and I had my hand down the toilet and I said "no".' The cleaner was booked the next week.

Surprisingly, this is a solution that only four per cent of Australian couples adopt, a figure that hasn't changed in over a decade. But while outsourcing house cleaning isn't yet a tidal wave, outsourcing of other domestic arts is, such as cooking. Today we are more likely to go out regularly to restaurants or get takeaway than previous generations, and this holds true whether you are in the poorest ten per cent or richest ten per cent of the population. We're buying more prepared foods and less raw foods, and are spending a lot more on reduced preparation and high-convenience foods[24] particularly if we're in a dual-income household. We are beginning to outsource more laundry and gardening. Maybe outsourcing the cleaning will achieve the popularity it deserves.

Most surprisingly in talking with these guys, however, was the number who seemed willing to go the whole hog.

'I could easily be a house husband, I'd love it,' says Kahl, who already works from home. 'I'd be the primary carer and in the house face to face with the kids. At home right now Sarah does do more of the cleaning and washing but I would love to be Mr Mum, full time. But financial constraints stop that happening. '

'I'm likely to be in that position,' says Adam. 'Jacki is earning heaps more than me. In fact, she might love to stay home and look after the kids, and might be resentful that I've since given up this IT career to go be an actor and not earn any money, that I get to stay home with the kids and have fun.'

'I know one couple who I think have it best—they're job sharing the same job,' says Evan, 'which I think is the perfect solution. Each works three days.'

In short, if there's nostalgia, it's not for the dinner-on-the-table-when-you-walk-in-the-door role that dads played in the previous generation. If anything, the guys sometimes feel a mild resentment that being a breadwinner narrows your options, particularly when it comes to time with your kids. Men, just like women, are also feeling the strain of the burden of balancing life, work and family.

But does this new egalitarianism translate into a new sensitivity?

'Do you talk about your wives or your partners to each other?' I try.

'I often get jealous when I hear Sarah talking to her friends,' says Kahl.

Is that because she's got confidantes? 'Yeah.'

'I certainly would only talk about my relationship with my wife, with my wife,' says Evan.

'I agree,' says Kahl. 'There's heaps of stuff I wouldn't talk to anyone about.'

'I think there would be different groups of my friends who I would talk to,' says Dave, 'and it would depend on how drunk I was when they were around. If we were at the pub, and the lights were low . . . Craig and I always talk at the pub.'

'If I was having really bad problems or something, I'd probably talk to my mum,' says Evan, 'but it hasn't come up.'

'I don't talk about my wife, other than her successes,' says Paul suddenly. 'I promote my wife, 'cos that's indirectly promoting myself. There's a pecking order, "look what I've got".'

'That's why he never talks about any of us to anyone he knows,' jokes Dave.

'But that's okay too,' says Paul, 'having separate compartments in your life.'

'That's the stereotype about men,' I say.

'As soon as it starts overlapping, that's when problems arise,' says Dave.

'Like George in *Seinfeld*,' shoots back Craig.

'The wives and girlfriends, may never meet,' says Dave, miming George's toast.

'You're killing independent George,' says Craig, delivering the punchline to chuckles all round.

Back on safe male ground we call it a night for the tape recorder. Two hours later I walk out $30 poorer than when I walked in.

As I walk to my car, well past midnight, I conclude that in the end, the sum total of the great divide is this: maybe the guys envied the girls their confidantes (a little) even as they acknowledged they liked the compartments, and they envied women a little their greater degree of choice—stay home or work—without being so readily yoked into the breadwinner plough.

They're really thinking more along the lines of how Dave Smeidt, who specialises in writing about relationships, put it when we chatted. 'Working in an office full of women and being the only boy, you get an insight into the mistakes other guys make. That's been a real education process for me. I don't want to be in a relationship with a girl who goes to work and bitches about what an inconsiderate tool her boyfriend is. I don't want to be that guy.'

How do you feel loved?

When couples were asked by researchers the type of things their partner did to make them feel loved, women most often mentioned shows of affection—hugs, kisses, touch and the giving of small gifts and their partner saying he loved them. Men gave similar responses but also suggested having their meals cooked for them, their house cleaned and their children cared for as being equally important.

After talking to all these couples and then talking to men and women separately, I couldn't help thinking that the men versus women pundits were getting it fundamentally wrong. Men and women do want very much the same thing out of marriage and what's more they are willing to work on solving the problems that stand between them and their ideal. So simply looking at the raw data doesn't give us much of a clue at all as to how couples creatively work to realise their own ideals of partnership and equality.

Sociologist Linda Waite has a similar view. She describes how marriage works just like a business, the two dynamic drivers being good old-fashioned specialisation and bargaining. 'The basic purpose of any contract is to allow partners in a productive enterprise to specialise and exchange goods over time,' she writes in her book, *The Case for Marriage*. 'What economists call specialisation, spouses call fighting about who-does-what.' Each partner plays to their strengths and does what they're good at, then trades this skill off with the other.

Couples like Emma and Barry, who admit to having had the odd barney over how to keep their flat neat, are willing to acknowledge their differences then work through these towards something that works for them. Like many couples, while they have different starting points—Emma grew up with a feminist mother who taught her to sort her laundry, while Barry grew up with a house-proud mother who did pretty much everything—Emma's seen past that to the real problem. 'It's wasn't so much that he didn't feel he should have to do the work,' she says. 'It was more he didn't know *how* to do it and he wasn't used to having to do it because it just got done around him.'

Instead of splitting every single task 50/50, Emma and Barry have split up the jobs into his and her specialities that fall along pretty conventional gender lines: she's the cook who enjoys pottering around in the kitchen preparing all the meals, except for when it's time for Barry's special tacos or barbecue; Barry washes the dishes, cleans up after the dog and takes care of the rubbish. Emma does the dusting, vacuuming and putting things away, and Barry does the laundry, pays the bills and takes care of the paperwork. Some tasks get value-added in the tally.

'As far as I'm concerned, taking the dog shit out three times a week, which is only a five-minute chore, is worth me cooking for half an hour or an hour every night,' says Emma. Barry's out-clause is cleaning the bathroom. 'I just can't do the toilet,' he says.

'It's about respect for each other,' says Emma of their horse-trading. 'It's not about "who's getting away with more". We try to make it as fair as possible.'

To Waite, it is negotiations like these that make a couple productive, as each specialises in what they're best at.[25] And that's also why in apparently traditional families, where she stays home and manages the household while he goes out to work, they can still consider their marriage an equal partnership. They're each doing what they think is fair.

It is the idea of specialising that is the dirty little secret of the domestic goddess revolution. Which is to say, if it's a scummy job and you're the one to do it, you might as well make it applause-worthy. Take Catherine. Previously a sub-editor, these days she is mostly at home with her and Greg's three young children. During the week the domestic load falls largely to her, though she confesses, 'The weekends really tip me over the edge when I have to get up and clean up again.' She also has a cleaner, so she's outsourcing some of the drudge, but she's also picking up her expertise by throwing herself into cooking and parenting courses.

'In a way it's making my home a job,' she says. 'I've got to treat it like a job. You've got to take pride in what you do even if you're hanging out the washing, otherwise you'd just go crazy.'

Men and women want remarkably similar things from their relationships. Indeed, after two decades of research John Gottman has concluded that what is fundamentally important to men and women in a marriage is exactly the same—friendship. 'All the masters of marriage talk about friendship in marriage and how lovemaking is an extension of that friendship,' he says. 'Seventy percent of the passion, romance and sex for men stems from friendship and the

> **The ultimate incentive scheme**
>
> There has already been a shift in the amount of housework men are doing over the past twenty years, and researchers have found that when the change happens, despite men being initially unhappy, the extra housework is something that just becomes normal.[26] But beyond that, there's the best incentive of all: sex. John Gottman discovered in his research that wives interpret husbands' domestic contributions as a sign of love and caring—and they are more sexually attracted to helpful mates. Or, on the flip side, if she has no time left on her to-do list, you'll be the first to go.

percentage is even higher for women. Men aren't from Mars, nor are women from Venus. At the end of a hard day, men and women want the same thing.' Other research has shown that, contrary to popular belief, men are more likely to believe their relationships could be improved than are women.[27]

As far as Gottman is concerned, the gender differences that do crop up—men tend to be compulsive problem-solvers, women emotional facilitators—are stylistic differences. They have to be tuned and negotiated, but they're not really standing in the way of communication. In fact, if there is a real key it is that power is shared in relationships, and men in particular are willing to share power with their wives.

'Only about one-third of American husbands accept the influence of their wives,' says Gottman. 'But a good marriage needs give and take. A man can't be powerful unless he allows himself to be influenced.' It's a life-long battle for men, he jokes, citing Stamford University research on three-year-olds. 'Little boys,' he says, 'when little girls suggest some kind of play activity are more likely to say "no" than if a boy suggests it. Girls are as likely to accept suggestions from boys or girls when they are three and that continues through to adulthood. The boys that are willing to accept influence from their women when they grow up are in much better shape.'

Gottman's personal best story to illustrate this occurred when he was publishing his book *The Seven Principles for Making Marriage Work*. 'I went to New York to my publishers to convince them to spend a lot of money marketing the book,' he tells. 'And the head of marketing was this really arrogant guy. He said to me, "In thirty seconds tell me one thing I could do to improve my marriage." He had his chin jutting forward and tipped back in the chair. And I said, "If I had to pick one thing, it would be to honour your wife's dreams." This guy's mouth dropped open and he got up and left the room. It turned out he left the building and went home. He later told me, "I was horrified when you said that because I thought, 'what are my wife's dreams?'" He went home and she said, "What are you doing home?" And he said, "What are your dreams?" "What are you talking about?" "Well, this guy was chasing me with a book and I asked him 'what is the one thing I could do to improve my marriage?' and he said 'honour your wife's dreams' and I realised I didn't have a clue what your dreams were." And she said "No, you don't. You don't have a clue," and they had this great conversation. And then they made love. So, you know, it did improve his marriage.'

To sum it up

o There's nothing new in the practical problems of marriage.
o Men and women want the same thing in a modern marriage: partnership and equality.
o All couples will fight about housework.
o When reasoning it out, it helps to not turn the discussion into a lecture on women's oppression.
o Don't assume you both have the same skill base—housework, like anything else, has to be learned and practiced.
o Doing different jobs doesn't make you unequal.
o Thank our feminist mothers—this generation of men is different.

- Practical egalitarianism is the name of the game.
- You both come into marriage with a different set of expectations; these will take time to sort through.
- Men aren't nostalgic for the good old days—they prefer contemporary partnerships.
- Don't waste time on the theory, look for the practical solution.
- When negotiating the housework, play to your strengths and find the right balance for the two of you.
- If it's a dirty job, outsource it—or do it so well you get the applause.
- To women, a man doing housework is sexy.

6

SEX: ARE WE HAVING FUN YET?

I would warn husbands not to recklessly habituate their wives to a degree of sexual frequency and intensity which they (the husbands) may be quite unable to keep up for any length of time . . . [or else] he has the painful choice between chronic 'nerves' on his wife's part, which destroys marital peace and happiness, and equally chronic sexual overstrain and fatigue on his own.
—**Dr Th Van De Velde, *Ideal Marriage*, 1926**

Is married sex still fun? If you believe the jokes married sex is either bad, boring or absent. But what really goes on behind our bedroom doors? Certainly we know things change in the bedroom—they have already. At the start of a relationship you're on 24 hours a day and you can party all night, but sooner or later that stops and chances are it's not going to come back. Much as you think you'd like to return to that sex-every-night time, there is no substitute for that hormone and adrenaline-fuelled thrill of the new. It can't last and it doesn't. The question, which feeds the sex-groaning shelves of every bookstore, is does this really matter? The answer is almost invariably yes.

'Naively in the first year of marriage I thought, "This is crazy, these people having sex once a week". We were doing it four and five times a week,' says Audrey one Friday afternoon over a long-lunch. 'Then by the end of the year you're going "We haven't done it for a couple of weeks?" "You sure? I don't think it's been that long."' She shrugs. All her girlfriends say the same.

Then there's an old story when it comes to sex in marriage. Put a jellybean in a jar for every time you have sex in the first year, and take a jellybean out for every time you have sex thereafter. By the end of the marriage, there will still be jellybeans left in that jar. The moral is simple: sex in marriage gets boring. But let's face it, married sex mostly gets bad press. Married sex is the best sex you've had.

Researchers have found that married people have better, more emotionally satisfying sex than singles or couples living together[1] and the happier they are, the more sex they have.[2] In fact, a full two-thirds of women in one United Kingdom survey said the best sex they ever had was within wedlock and 76 per cent said their partner was a 'great lover'.[3] But if married sex is so good why do we worry we're not having such a great time? Well, time, it seems, is the operative word.

Jennie, 36, and David, 34, may only have been married a few of months, but like most busy professionals—she's in advertising, he's a writer—they're worried about whether they're getting enough. 'We'd both like to have sex more,' says Jennie, 'but I find that I get home at the end of the day and I'm really tired.'

'So basically, she couldn't be fucked,' says David with perfect comic timing.

Then there's the regular tussle between the night owl and the early bird. 'I am a morning person and David is a night person,' explains Jennie. 'In the beginning it was a real frustration. I'd be saying, "I'm going to bed now" and he'd say, "I really want to watch the end of this show". So then I'd be saying, "Well, you can watch the end of that show, but I'm going to bed now and I'll be asleep." He'd say, "stay awake" but I can't, you can't physically make someone stay awake. I'm an early-to-bed person.'

'And she wishes I was an early-to-rise person,' shoots back Dave, with a Groucho-Marx eyebrow wiggle.

'The first few months of living together we'd have this circular discussion: just as he can't wake up at 6 o'clock and be on, I cannot stay awake past 10 o'clock and be totally in the mood,' says Jennie. 'We've got a routine now.'

They make a good double-act, but underneath the banter was a set of common insecurities playing out. 'If we stop having sex the first thought is "is it because I'm not sexy enough?"' explains Jennie. 'I'd be saying "I'm tired"—David was taking that personally. He'd say "Is it me? Am I not turning you on?"' Now they talk, and say that weekends are important.

Perhaps Dave and Jennie are more attuned because David writes about relationships for a living, so for him discussing sex is an almost daily occurrence. But what he and Jennie are talking about here could pretty much be recorded in thousands of marital bedrooms across the country any night of the week. Why? 'Sex is our bellweather for our relationship: if it's not going right in the bedroom, we tell ourselves, something is fundamentally wrong in the marriage. And, broadly, there's something to that. Generally couples who say they have a high overall satisfaction in their relationship do have more frequent and more satisfying sexual relationships. Similarly, a high proportion of couples seeking help for marital problems say they are dissatisfied with their sex lives—in one study it was as high as fifty per cent.'[4]

It's not hard to see how easily we become so hot and bothered by it all. We cast sex as both the problem and the solution. Getting better at sex, we hope, will improve the relationship. Or will working on the relationship make the sex better? It's a classic chicken-and-egg scenario. No matter which way we look at it, we place a lot of responsibility on rubbing wiggly bits.

Are you getting enough?

A newly married couple are liable to err on the side of frequency, but they can soon adjust to each other... As a general rule I should say that if a couple have a connection once or twice a week and make it last for half an hour they would be doing well.
—Edward F. Griffith, *Modern Marriage and Birth Control*, 1935

For a generation bombarded by choice and intent on making up its own rules, when it comes to sex what we are really worrying about deep down is, 'Are we normal?' and, 'Are we getting enough?' In other words, is it true what they say about the jellybean jar?

Georgina and Martin, married for two years and together nearly a decade, live in London, within a crowds' roar of Arsenal stadium. Both have busy careers, in media and design respectively.

'We have argued in the past and it was because we were comparing ourselves to other couples,' says Georgina. 'Someone would say "we're having sex five times a week". We'd be lucky to have it once a week.' So what is normal?

Gabrielle Morrissey is a sex therapist, sexology lecturer, president of the Australian Society for Sex Educators, Researchers and Therapists, and author of *Urge*, an 'infotainment sex manual'. Want to drive her crazy? Ask her 'what's normal?'

'I have a huge problem with that question,' she sighs. 'It's the most common question I'm asked.' Morrissey reels off the research. Globally, around 1.8 to 2 times a week is average, 'but you never know if sex research is completely reliable.' She also points out that marriages go through both wild and heavy periods and periods of no sex.

'I tell people not to stress,' says Morrissey. 'Libidos fluctuate and it's an average over years and years, and some years might be good

> **The honeymoon effect**
> Most married couples do have more sex in the first two years of their marriage than after. One survey found nearly half of newlyweds had sex three times a week or more and another four in ten had sex between one and three times per week. But when it came to couples married two to ten years, only around a quarter had sex three or more times a week, with half reporting having had sex between one and three times per week.[5] But the good news is contrary to habituation theory—the idea that the more you get to know each other's bodies, the more bored you'll get—sex doesn't keep tapering off after that second year, which it would if boredom were the problem. So, if there's a problem in the bedroom, it's not that familiarity is breeding contempt.[6]

yet another year you might have a drought. But if you're still feeling intimately connected, don't worry. Are you still pillow talking, body hugging and kissing? Then there's still desire.'

There also is another big clue to why we care so much about sex. It isn't just doing it we're worried about, it's the connecting—the intimacy—that goes with it. Sex is a big part of the intimacy that is the glue we use to stay connected that keeps our marital ecosystem healthy. It's a good question, though—if sex drops off, does that mean the connections in the relationship have dropped off too? And if it has, what can one of you do to turn that around?

For Georgina and Martin the solution was not complicated. They stopped comparing. 'We don't have those fights anymore,' says Georgina, 'probably because we're more confident in ourselves. We have sex when we want. It could be once a week, once a fortnight or whatever—we don't count anymore. We go through phases. We've been together nine years and I'd say it's only got better and it's changed a lot. We might go through a period of going at it like rabbits, or maybe we'll be like last year, when our sex life wasn't so good because Martin—when he was unemployed—wasn't feeling so good about himself. It's an important part of our relationship,' she concludes. 'Sex is definitely something we enjoy—kind of like time out. You can get really, really busy and I think it's important for a marriage to allow time for that. But I think being best friends is more important than being wild sex fiends.'

What's normal? It depends who you ask:
One study found your average married couple under sixty did it seven times a month—or 1.6 times a week.[7]
Another study found that 20 per cent of married couples have sex less than ten times a year.[8]
Yet another study found that 16 per cent of couples had no sex in the month prior to the survey.[9]

Boosting desire

> ... above all, I would impress on all married men: every considerable erotic stimulation of their wives that does not terminate in orgasm, on the woman's part, represents an injury, and repeated injuries of this kind lead to permanent—or very obstinate—damage to both body and soul.
> **—Dr Th Van De Velde, *Ideal Marriage*, 1926**

Sexpo is an annual 'heath, sexuality and lifestyle' exposition held (most appropriately) in the same film studio venue as the Sydney Bridal Show. It is a giant sex-mart; anyone with a sex-related product or service can pitch their tent and wait for the punters to roll in. I'm here trying to uncover what might turn us on again if our sex lives are, well, a little limp. According to the press release more than 50 000 people are expected to crowd through the doors of the four-day event and four in ten of them will be women. Today, on ladies' day, childcare is offered as a bonus and looking at the crowds they have indeed been successful—there are more than a few ladies and while some seem to be here for a snicker, just as many have come armed with a shopping list. Still, the industry's mainstay remains the roving packs of young males, here for the sly thrill of it all.

Despite it being cold and rainy there are also plenty of couples here, ranging in age from just-past teens to late middle-age. Some are giggling, clutching hands tightly, while others breeze by with such businesslike expressions they could be house hunting. I try asking them what they're looking for.

'We're here for the fun,' squirms one pair before running away. Another likely looking middle-aged pair—they were on stage earlier participating in the pick-a-bum competition—turn out not to be married, or at least, not to each other.

'Oh, we always come together to this,' she says. 'My husband certainly wouldn't.' Then I spot newlyweds 'Princess Gibbons' and 'Tony Bathurst'—we agree to use their porn names (the name of your first pet, then your first street)—stepping breezily out of a swingers stall, having just booked their first post-nuptial swing set.

'Why are you here?' I ask.

'I've always been very open minded,' says Princess, 'willing to try anything.' They swung before their wedding. 'I like women, and I have fun sharing him,' says Princess, the real enthusiast, while Tony Bathurst looks on with can't-believe-his-luck bemusement. 'We've always been honest with each other about what can turn us on,' he says.

So others are here seeking like-minded folk. But while swinging works for some, if the sex research—rather than volume of enthusiastic magazine stories—is to be believed, they are in a small minority. Maybe the stall-holders will be more enlightening.

The biggest display here is the Adultshop store, done out, in almost staid woman-appealing white and purple in an attempt to take some of the sleaze out of sex—'the Granny Mays of Sex Shops,' says manager Ruth Bamford, who is down from Darwin, where, like Canberra, the X-business is legal. Because I'm here with my friend Danni, who's pregnant, she first mistakes us for a lesbian couple and we're hustled over to the girl-friendly wall of dildos, massage oil, collars, cuffs and games. After a swift demo of the functions and operating instructions we set them straight that we're straight, so Bamford swiftly recommends a marital aid called the rabbit—a curious egg-shaped strap-on his 'n' hers vibrator that's apparently a popular gift at Easter.

'I've heard it wrecks your sex life,' says Bamford (*sotto voce*) in an instant review. 'Apparently regular sex just isn't as much fun.' And while the lurid, pearl-embedded dildos catch the eye, judging by what's being tucked into the takeaway bags the hit of this year's festival is the less threatening yellow rubber duckie—just like your old bath toy with an added vibrator built in.

Bamford does a brisk trade catering for hen's parties, buck's nights, 18th and 21st parties, 'but what I really love is seeing older people,' she says. 'They're coming in for penis extenders or erection help—and they're usually embarrassed. We tell them we have a seniors' card.' It breaks the ice.

Further insights come from porn star Serenity who, along with fellow star Jewel De Nyle, is manning a busy booth with the prize performer of Serenity's company, Ron Jeremy, aka the Hedgehog. Jeremy is famously short, hairy and well-endowed and is, in his industry, as big as Bono. Right now he's getting chatted up by one of his biggest fans, a rock popette from a band that's currently charting. Serenity says she sees more and more married couples coming to these conventions, testament to the growing popularity of porn films. And when they approach her, coyness is definitely out.

'They ask for advice on titles,' she says, 'and then about products, "How do I use it?" "How do I clean it?"' Today, in between dispensing advice—to buy good porn, find a reputable dealer; if you're buying over the Internet, order something inexpensive first as a test run—

she's posing for photos with her adoring fans, who pay for the privilege. For extra she'll go topless and give you a photo you can't show Mum.

Serenity is married and her husband also works in the industry, behind the camera. So do they have issues with sex?

'Work is work,' she says. 'There's a lot to be said for trust.' And while she adds, 'Sex is fun, it's our play'—a play that extends to the odd orgy—she does admit that when it comes to her work, 'I've learned not to bring the job home and compare. No details on how the day was. I keep the relationship inside the relationship.' Somehow it's reassuring that even porn stars have to watch out for sexual jealousy.

Still, even though there are stalls offering everything from tantric sex to rubber fetish to a peculiar high-tech bidet, along with a less-patronised aisle offering medical advice and support groups, something is missing. Maybe making sex 'couple friendly' tames it of its illicit danger—though the swingers and bondage enthusiasts do their best to keep up the salacious quotient—or maybe the sheer

---

Problems? Are you sure you're having them?

A telephone survey of 20 000 Australians found the most common sexual difficulties were:

- lack of interest in sex (24.9 per cent of men; 54.8 per cent of women)
- coming to orgasm too quickly (23.8 per cent of men; 11.7 per cent of women)
- not having an orgasm (6.3 per cent of men; 28.6 per cent of women)
- not enjoying sex (5.6 per cent of men; 27.3 per cent of women)
- physical pain (2.4 per cent of men; 20.3 per cent of women).

The study also found that 48 per cent of men and 72 per cent of women experienced some kind of 'sexual difficulty' in the last year, which suggests that having problems with sex is natural.[10]

volume is desensitising. The whole experience of walking through Sexpo feels like rolling though a giant sex K-mart, where there is everything you could conceivably want and nothing that really stands out. Sex from the lolly shop seems, ultimately, a curiously asexual affair. Yes the toys are fun and can pep up your sex life, but if you're really having difficulties, will buying one solve anything?

Let's (not) talk about sex, baby

> . . . the man who neglects the love-play is guilty not only of coarseness, but of positive brutality; and his omission can not only offend and disgust a woman, but also injure her on the purely physical plane. And this sin of omission is unpardonably stupid.
> —**Dr Th Van De Velde, *Ideal Marriage*, 1926**

Here's our guiltiest sex secret: we still can't talk to each other about sex and we aren't terribly honest about what we really want in bed. When sociologist Peggy Orenstein travelled across the United States talking to professional women about their lives and aspirations she discovered that honesty about sex in relationships was still one of the biggest no-go areas. Most of the women she talked to sheepishly admitted to not really being able to ask for what they want.

'It's the dirty little secret of a generation,' she writes. 'They had sex earlier than their mothers did, have had more partners and are more likely to initiate encounters, yet more experience and freer licence haven't necessarily translated into greater enjoyment.'[11]

It's something Nikki Gemmell picked up on when she wrote her book *The Bride Stripped Bare*, which purportedly tells the truth about sex in marriage. She told interviewer Andrew Denton of emailing twenty of her girlfriends and asking them to tell her one thing they absolutely loved and one thing they absolutely hated in bed. One third said, 'I do not like the breast stuff.' (And before any readers vow never to touch a breast again, that means two-thirds probably do like it. The important point here, girls, is to speak up.)

'Why don't we ever talk about this and say it to our partners?' asked Gemmell. 'Why is it so hard for women to be really honest when it comes to sex and why are we often so subservient to the men and kind of so intent on their pleasure and forgetting about our own.'[12] It certainly resonated: *The Bride Stripped Bare* was one of Australia's biggest selling books of 2004.

Gemmell is right too. Finding a way to talk about it does matter: a survey of over 100 000 women in the United States found that the strongest indicator of sexual and marital satisfaction among the women was 'the ability to express sexual feelings to their husbands'. Furthermore, the more they talked, the better they rated their sex lives, marriages and overall happiness.[13] Another study found that over half the women who 'always' talked about sex rated their sex lives as being very good, but only one in ten women who 'never' talked about sex said the same.[14]

As with all other disagreements, arguing, rather than letting the problem fester, can be good. An American survey found couples who argued about sex were more likely to be having some sex, while the sexually inactive couples had just given up and stopped talking.[15]

'... One of the most destructive patterns I've seen in marriages is when people become extremely bothered by things their spouses do or say but keep their feelings to themselves,' writes Michele Weiner Davies in her book, *The Sex-Starved Marriage*. 'They might try to tell their spouses about their annoyances early on, but if their spouses don't acknowledge their feelings, agree, or change their behaviours, they basically give up. Giving up is not to be confused with accepting. Giving up means taking their angry feelings and storing them inside.'

Solving the number one problem

Shrink: How often do you sleep together?
Alvy: Hardly ever! Maybe three times a week.
Annie: Constantly! I'd say three times a week.
—Woody Allen, *Annie Hall*, 1977

So what is the biggest problem couples have with sex? Easy: he wants it, she doesn't or when she does, he says no. Desire discrepancy is so common that 'in horniness and lack of horniness' should probably be in most people's wedding vows. Low desire is, in fact, the number one problem brought to sex therapists.[16] For many couples it's simple—one partner wants sex more than the other. But they compromise.

'He wants it more than I do, of course,' says Audrey, married for three years. 'I could take it or leave it more often that not. I'm conscious I should probably offer it to him. Because I think it's important for their esteem occasionally.' So Audrey and Rudy have learned to compromise. But for others, this becomes a niggling sore that eats away at the rest of the relationship. So what are the dynamics here?

It's true that on average women are the ones with the lower desire in any heterosexual couple. In fact, around 16 per cent of men and 25 per cent of women report that disinterest in sex constitutes a problem for them.[17] Though a different study of people in sexually inactive marriages found that in 60 per cent of the cases it was the man who had stopped the sex, for reasons ranging from extramarital affairs to demanding jobs, or problems with drugs, alcohol or finances.[18]

There are plenty of theories as to why it's mostly women who have lower sex drives. Some look at how women are less likely to experience orgasm during sex and therefore don't think their sex lives are so great. Most, however, point to what Morrissey was talking about earlier—different ideas on closeness.

There's a lot of research that suggests men and women experience intimacy quite differently in relationships. For men, just being together, or sharing an activity, is enough to feel close. But women rate their happiness and relationship satisfaction in proportion to how much emotional support, and how much sharing of feelings, they're getting.[19] In other words, women mostly need to feel close to someone to want to have sex with them, so that means spending some time together just talking. Men, on the other hand, feel close by doing, so sex *is* their way of being intimate.

Take Matt and Sarah, who say that although they have a good sex life, they aren't necessarily in tune. 'Though Matt complains all the time we don't do it enough,' says Sarah.

'I can't help it,' protests Matt before conceding, 'I think it's that when a bloke wants it, he wants it now, whereas for women it isn't that straightforward.'

'The only issue we have about sex,' says Sarah, 'is that I think marriage gets like a business and a lot of our conversations are like with my marketing manager at work. When we ring each other during the day we might say "How are you feeling?" but it's more likely "Are you going to buy the vegetables?" or "How much did they say was in the bank account?" Just the perfunctory stuff.' In short, this doesn't get Sarah in the mood.

'Matt will be like that with me all evening then expect me to be cuddly and sexy when we get into bed,' she says. 'To me, it doesn't work like that. You have to be wooed a bit.'

Or there's Andrew and Brigid who say that sex has been a source of conflict for them, mainly because they have different ideas of what intimacy and sex actually mean.

'I think it's less important to me whereas with Andrew, I think I underestimate the importance that it has for him,' admits Brigid.

'You'd just be happy if we both sat in the bedroom puffing pillows behind us, watching TV,' says Andrew, who points out he has something rather more physical in mind. 'I hate sitting in bed watching TV.'

'But that's what I do, that is intimacy,' says Brigid. 'Just being with someone.' She adds that having had an accidental pregnancy with their first son 'changed a whole range of things about sex too, because you know pregnancy can happen in an instant.'

Michele Weiner Davis describes the 'go nowhere game' that happens if these differences aren't resolved: men wait for their wives to become sexier and more receptive to their sexual advances before putting energy into their relationships. And if this doesn't happen, they shut down emotionally. This in turn makes women feel starved of communication. And because disconnected women tend to feel depressed, short-changed and resentful, they lose their desire. This sets up a vicious cycle, so that 'when men tune out, women turn off. And when women turn off, men tune out.' So women can't understand why their husbands are interested in sex when they're not feeling emotionally close, while men may only give themselves permission to feel tender emotions during sex.[20]

It's something the Viagra experiment shows. In the United States, five years after Viagra's release, more than half of the repeat prescriptions for the drug weren't filled. Why? Because, according to Dr Abraham Morgentaler in his book, *The Viagra Myth*, 'Viagra cannot create love, intimacy or desire. Yet many men turn to Viagra to help them solve complex problems . . . Many of my male patients, together with their partners, have come to realise that finally achieving a great erection doesn't solve their relationship problems. In fact, it has frequently made them worse.'[21]

When women fake it

Women do lie about how much they liked it. A study has found that women underestimate their number of partners, the age they lost their virginity and whether they masturbate and use porn. They were caught out when they were hooked up to a dummy polygraph and told the device would know if they were lying.[22]

In the mood

The art of sex is the harmonious blending of the physical, emotional and aesthetic qualities of the sexual relationship. The sexual embrace should become neither a duty nor a routine of marriage. It should be a shared experience, with the husband and wife each attempting to make the relationship mutually pleasing.
—**Hannah M. Stone MD and Abraham Stone MD,** *A Marriage Manual,* **1939**

So what can you do when one of you wants it and the other doesn't? Sometimes the solution can be simple. For Suzanne, a community worker who (bucking the trend) found she was the hornier one, it simply came down to setting a deadline.

'It got worse after we had our child,' she says. 'For the first six months I was like "go away" but after that I'm the one going "why don't we do it any more?"' This is a complaint, she adds, shared by a few women in her mother's group. 'In the end,' she says. 'I started

> **Slow sex solutions**
>
> In *The Sex Starved Marriage*, Michele Weiner Davies offers some simple solutions to steering your sex life out of the skids.
>
> *Do what works.* Think specifically about what you need in order to feel intimate and ask for it. A call home once a day while travelling? Call home. Need time to sort out your day before being confronted with home dramas? Say so.
>
> *Trust the intimacy cycle.* 'When you show your love for your spouse by placing more importance on your sexual relationship—even if you're out of practice—you trigger a solution cycle: your spouse becomes happier and more loving in return.' And quid pro quo, 'you start liking your spouse more and feeling more attracted to him or her, which inspires your spouse to be even nicer back, and so on.'
>
> *The Nike™ Solution—just do it.* 'Push yourself on a more regular basis to ignore your little inner voice that says, "Oh, no, not now, I'm too tired." Or "Again? We just made love two nights ago." Or, "I've got a million things to do". Why not just assume that your inner voice is misguiding you? If you enjoy sex once you get started, I really believe that you've unconsciously trained yourself to have "I'm not interested" thoughts every time your spouse touches you.'[23]

giving him sex-dates, "We should have sex tomorrow night," that kind of thing. If he has a day to think about, he's up for it by that evening.'

Tiffany and Andrew admit to having had some 'horrible times' on the sex communication front. Like most couples with young children—they have two—they've found sheer exhaustion and lack of opportunity have taken a toll.

'Before you have kids, weekends, what do you do? You stay in bed for an extra two hours in the morning,' says Tiffany. 'What happens when you have kids? You get up at 6 o'clock, and hope that they'll watch telly for five minutes.' Unsurprisingly, in a survey of American women nearly half said having a good night's sleep is better than sex.[24]

For Tiffany and Andrew, the workable solution came down to first talking honestly with each other, and then doing something. 'It's like any aspect of a relationship,' says Tiffany. 'It needs work. There are always going to be times where you have good sex, times you have bad sex and times where you have quite enough sex for you, thank you very much, but not enough for the other person. It's just another of those things where you have to try to sit down and talk about it rationally. And a good place is away from the bedroom. No alcohol in sight.'

Yet they don't pretend it's been easy. 'I don't know if it's possible to talk about it without getting emotional,' says Andrew. 'It's definitely been a source of tension between us. We do buy the books and try different things, but after a while the same old issues tend to arise.' So now they recognise it's probably going to be an ongoing negotiation.

'One person might have to accept that it's not going to be sex six times a night, seven days a week, and the other person may have to accept that once a month is not enough,' says Tiffany. 'You have to meet somewhere in the middle. There's the old cliché about the more you have the more you want. So if you actually make an effort, it can be worth it. But it's a hard one to negotiate.'

Getting your mojo back

> It is frequently suggested that sex union is bad because it leads to fatigue and the individual feels 'done up' as the result of the experience. This is quite wrong and merely indicates that the couple have not understood the underlying principle of sex activity. If sex energy is creative energy, its rightful use cannot lead to fatigue. On the contrary, it should provide a feeling of exhilaration and refreshment.
> —**Edward F. Griffith,** *Modern Marriage and Birth Control,* **1935**

Gabrielle Morrissey says one of the biggest problems with married sex is simply that couples let their priorities change.

'Before people get married, you have a selfish attitude to life. It's all you, you, you and sex is a first or second priority,' she says. 'When you are married it becomes us, us, us. You have gone from instant gratification to a future-looking model where you have investments, house, mortgage. And that can have an impact on your sex life. You turn your attention to other things. Your sex life drops down the list from priority number one or two, to eight or nine.' And that only gets worse when children enter the picture—fatigue, carpooling duties, an unequal distribution of labour, a busy lifestyle and stress can all put on the sexual brakes.

'The issue is really that you have to stop the slide of priority given to sex,' says Morrissey. 'A huge number of couples say "I want to get the passion back". We take our sex lives for granted until they're cold. The lucky thing is, we can turn it around and rejuvenate it.' Morrissey's first suggestion is turn off the television.

'People say to me "we don't have time",' she says. 'I always ask, "How much television did you watch last night?"'

Finding a way back to intimacy, particularly after having children, is something Steve, 38, and Shannon, 32, both technical writers and parents to four-year-old Gabriel, have had to think about.

For Shannon in particular, this meant confronting what actually made her want sex.

'It doesn't really matter how non-conformist you are, in a settled relationship sex occupies a space in a sequence of things,' she says. 'When you're courting someone you go to see a film or have dinner, go for a romantic walk, kiss by the river, then have sex in the car, or on the picnic blanket in the deserted park, or back at the house after coffee. There's a sequence of events. But when you have a baby', she continues, 'you don't get to leisurely move into sex, quietly, peacefully. It's interrupted. If you do get to have dinner together, you don't get to go for a walk.'

'You come home and talk to the babysitter,' agrees Steve.

'Unless you're really good at concentrating on the things that make you feel like sex—and doing something about them,' says Shannon, 'sex may never happen.'

It was a confronting thought.

'You expect men to be initiating sex,' she points out. 'The idea is still that you have to fend it off—even if you make an effort not to conform to social norms. So at some point you have to confront your sexuality and say "Actually, I do want some sex but I've never had to make that clear to someone before." Then,' she adds almost ruefully, 'it gets pragmatic. You say, "I need that and I've got to fit that in—just like I find the time for the washing." If you don't like the idea of it being less romantic, or less spontaneous, it's going to make it harder.'

It's the smartest thing I've heard anyone say. If you want to have sex, you have to figure out what turns you on and what you can do about it. Then just do it. Sex and marriage therapist David Schnarch has written an entire book on this topic called *Passionate Marriage*. His ideas centre around the importance of what he terms differentiation—finding ways to feel secure in yourself and your own sexuality, rather than depending on your partner for cues and reinforcement. And while he treats couples, he makes the point that even if only one partner is willing to embrace a change in attitude both partners will end up having to change, because when one changes, the equilibrium in a marriage shifts.

Making time to have sex can have other flow-on benefits. Audrey had already left the cafe after our interview but then she came rushing back.

'I had to tell you this,' she said with a wicked grin. 'Four of my girlfriends in Melbourne have a pact. They offer their husbands sex three times a week and they also have to drink two litres of water a day.'

'Why?' I ask.

'So their skin is better, they'll be healthier, and they get whatever they want,' she quips. 'It's amazing, their partners all of a sudden are offering to do housework, do dishes, buy flowers and they get whatever they want.'

'Do their partners know?'

'No,' she laughs. 'They just think all their Christmases have come at once.'

'How long have they been doing it?' I ask.

'It was a year ago they first mentioned it to me,' she says.

'Do you do it?

'I tried it for about a week,' she says, pausing for effect before laughing. 'But I don't like to drink that much water. It wore me out. It was too hard on both counts.'

Can you play away?

> If a man cannot afford distinct and different pleasures to the woman he has made his wife on two successive nights, he has married too soon.
> **—Honoré de Balzac**

Here's a question. What outsourcing is acceptable in a relationship? Cooking? Who doesn't get takeaway, at least occasionally? Housework?

Definitely, even if it's just in our fantasies. Childcare? Probably. But sex? Sex is something we still have very firm opinions about.

'I was talking to a friend of mine a couple of weeks ago,' recounts Rudy. 'And he said, "So are you having an affair?"' Rudy was indignant. 'I said, "No. What on earth made you think that?" He said, "You're the only other friend I know apart from myself in our circle that isn't—out of about ten blokes."' Rudy still doesn't understand it.

'Why get married? Why stay married?' he asks. 'If you want to go sport fucking, get yourself a red car and get divorced. You make a commitment to somebody, you expect them to hold up their side of the bargain so you have to hold up yours. Everybody looks around, everybody window shops, but I think you've got to have loyalty and commitment, if you don't have that, there's nothing left.'

Rudy's in the majority here. While almost everyone I talked to had no great hang-up about being attracted to someone else, the bottom line was always the same: look, but don't touch. Indeed, decades after the sexual revolution and forty years after the introduction of the pill, our attitudes to extramarital sex are barely unchanged from those of our parents.[25] One survey of 20 000 Australians found that three-quarters agreed that having an affair outside a committed relationship is wrong.[26] For Rudy, the answer to why he wouldn't was straightforward.

'First and foremost it would really hurt Audrey, and that would shatter me,' he says. 'Secondly, I would have let down my side of the bargain, and I know I'm better than that. I don't think the attraction to other people ever stops, but getting onto the sex side of it, you just have to make it really interesting—put your time and effort into it, surprise them, keep it spontaneous. If you have sex every Thursday night at seven-thirty and you do it the same way each time, well, it will get boring. So mix it up a bit. Be imaginative.'

In fact, most couples have very direct conversations about fidelity right from the start of their relationship, setting out the rules. 'Even before we talked about getting married, being faithful was just part of when we were seeing each other,' says Emma. 'There's just no excuse for infidelity for either of us. You're not allowed to be with anyone else in any way—no kissing, nothing. And we talked about that extensively, so we both knew that was the boundary.'

'And if anyone did cross the line, that's it,' agrees her husband Barry. 'We've sat and said, "If you put yourself in that position, you're probably going to be tempted and you're probably going to cheat".'

'Especially if there's alcohol involved,' adds Emma.

'So the trick of the whole marriage, the whole relationship, is not to put yourself in the position where you're going to be tempted,' says Barry.

'If you've got the type of marriage where you spend lots of time apart, especially if you've, say, got single girlfriends who are out on the pull and getting nice looking young blokes waved in your face a lot of the time, I think that's very hard to resist,' agrees Emma. 'You simply don't put yourself in that position.'

Sounds like a good set of rules and it's something most people stick to—but not all. Affairs do happen, though how frequently is the source of some debate: estimates for wives range anywhere from 20 to 40 per cent; for husbands it's somewhere between 35 and 60 per cent.[27] And as Barry and Emma point out above, an affair doesn't necessarily mean your relationship was in trouble in the first place. Sometimes it just means there was the opportunity, particularly through work.

As psychologist Shirley Glass, a doyenne of infidelity research, recently told *Psychology Today*, 'The work relationship becomes so rich and the stuff at home is pressurised and child-centered . . . People get involved insidiously without planning to betray.'[28]

Outsourcing sex

> I learned long ago that the only two people who count in any marriage are the two who are in it.
> **—Hilary Clinton**

Jennifer and Craig's marriage—'a pressure cooker', both admit—has survived hard financial times, children and this very question of fidelity. They live in red-dusted Alice Springs, their house a cheery chaos brought by kids, neighbours and boarders who trip in and out regularly. An audiologist and film-maker respectively, each gravitated here separately a decade ago after growing up in Melbourne. Their early days together were all sex, drugs and rock 'n' roll.

'When we teamed up it was fast and furious,' says Craig, 'a relationship born of real passion. Jen was a great drinking buddy and we've been allies, lovers and friends.' After Craig proposed 'in a lime green and brown caravan at Hepburn Springs', they married in a dry river bed. Then along came their first son, Michael, and Jennifer was soon pregnant with another. One night, shortly before she was due to give birth to their second child, Jen turned to Craig and said, 'You've had an affair.'

'I've no idea how I knew,' she says. 'I just knew.' Craig put her off.

'Lets not talk about this now,' he said, telling her a little, and then nothing more was said. Tim was born then they went away on holiday. Still nothing. Then came a gradual unfolding.

'It took Craig three or four weeks to come out with the whole truth,' says Jen. She points to a white mark carved in the wall on the other side of the living room. 'I picked up that white rocking chair and I threw it at Craig,' she says. 'That was my only violent act through the whole thing.'

Stuck with what to do next they decided to try couples counselling with Relationships Australia.

'At that stage I was in shock and awe,' says Craig. 'It was great to have somewhere to start from. I don't spend much time connected to feelings. I'm a bloke, not a woman.' In the process, some of the groundwork of the relationship changed, 'even if it didn't lead to many long discussions about the situation at home,' says Craig. They had a start.

They looked at how they came to be in this situation. Jen admits it wasn't entirely one-sided. When she's pregnant and breastfeeding, sex simply doesn't interest her.

'I get very asexual, which is still a really hard thing for him to understand,' she says. 'When I was going through that, I assumed he would live with my decision that we weren't going to have sex.' Craig didn't demure. He became silently frustrated. Then he outsourced.

Craig says, 'Jen's a hormone monster when she's pregnant and I went diving for cover. The affair was what I needed to keep my head together. I'm torn in my feelings about it. On the one hand I want to fall to pieces and demonstrate remorse, on the other hand it also sustained me so I don't know if I can really feel guilty.' Still, he's made an important change. 'I do choose very carefully now what I do with my dick,' he says.

'There were two sides to the story,' says Jen. 'I understand my part in it and I accept some responsibilities, though I don't necessarily accept he did the right thing.'

Having talked it through, they then had to choose what they were going to do. 'On the emotional level the easy way out was to separate,' says Jennifer. 'It wasn't going to be the easy way for the kids necessarily, but it might have been if it was going to be the easy way for me.' Months passed as Jennifer took her time deciding. The turning point was quiet and unexpected. Jennifer was having her star chart done and the astrologer said to her, 'two years ago, big shit happened'. Jennifer told her the story. The astrologer then said, 'The good thing is you've waited for two years because Mars has a two-year cycle and Mars is the ruler of relationships and it takes two years for a relationship to finish or to decide.'

Jennifer realised a month or so later that the two-year anniversary had ticked over and that she'd made the right decision. She was where she was meant to be.

'It's alright,' she says. 'I love being with Craig most of the time and I think it's good that he drives me mental. There's no pretence. But he makes me laugh, and I love his work as a dad. I made a commitment. Craig really pissed me off over this whole situation, but I'm a guilty party too, and there's a lesson to be learned in terms of relationships and to try and get over that hurdle and to learn something else about myself in terms of communicating.'

'It's absolutely permanent when there are kids involved,' says Craig. 'I couldn't think of moving out and not being with my kids every day. Our marriage survives because we're such a good working family unit. There's too much at stake. I don't think there's anything too terminally wrong that can't be fixed. The kids are the glue.'

An affair is the one marriage out-clause that no one would dispute, but, surprisingly, most marriages do survive affairs. A recent survey by British counselling service *Relate* found that despite what they say initially, two-thirds of couples stayed together following the disclosure of an affair.[29]

Not that it is easy. According to a United States online survey of more than 1000 spouses whose partners had been unfaithful, the key to getting past an affair is talking about it at length, over time. Couples who do so are 'more likely to stay married and more likely to recover personally,' writes Peggy Vaughan, author of *Beyond Affairs* and *The Monogamy Myth*. Vaughan, who has studied extramarital affairs for 25 years, says there is no such thing as just one discussion about the affair. 'There is no quick fix. It is a long-term process.' In fact, 86 per cent of the couples in Vaughan's survey who discussed the affair thoroughly were still married and living together, in contrast to the 55 per cent who talked very little about the affair and were no longer together. More than half (54 per cent) of those who talked a lot felt mostly healed; whereas only 35 per cent of those who did not talk much felt that way. And, Vaughan points out, partners do want to know everything—the more specifics that are discussed, the less the aggrieved partner imagines on his or her own. Only about one third of either sex wanted to discover only general information. Vaughan says there's no pain-free path out, however, and more than half of men and women said they still carry the pain daily.[30]

For Jennifer, the answer to why she stayed was to do with the challenge. 'It's a lesson in life to learn to be interdependent in a relationship,' she says. 'I don't necessarily want to be an independent person. I don't want to be dependent, but I'd like to learn interdependence, to learn to live alongside Craig, enjoy him, work with him, but not be his reflection. To separate would mean I would learn nothing about myself. It's nice to be able to share the journey with someone, watching three kids grow together, because there are only two people who think your kids are as good as they are, and that's you and your partner.'

Domesticate and die

> Normally, sexual communion has a most beneficent effect on mind and body of both partners. Especially when drowsy relaxation is followed by a short rest . . . there develops a sensation of profound gratification, of mental and physical peace, balance, self-confidence and power which is hardly attainable in such perfection through any other experience.
> **—Dr Th Van De Velde, *Ideal Marriage*, 1926**

Making passion, as well as love, last over time is a challenge for all marriages. Few couples I talked with said it always came easily. Life kept getting in the way, pushing it down the list of things that really mattered. Sooner or later, most realised that passion did matter and started doing the simple things like making time for sex, making it a bigger priority, because almost to a person they agreed it was vital for the relationship.

Although I spoke with many couples and experts about their tips and tricks for making passion last, it was in a book, *Can Love Last?*, by renowned psychoanalyst Stephen Mitchell, that I found what seemed the most enlightened approach. Mitchell concluded that couples don't lose their desire because they became bored; instead, he writes, they smother it in domesticity because they become scared. Because passion is scary—it's then we're most open and vulnerable. So we allow our passion to become routine, as a defence against the vulnerability of romantic love.

Human beings crave two things, says Mitchell, security and adventure, the familiar and the novel. Romantic love and desire are both of these. But, he concludes, 'Love, by its very nature, is not secure,' even though 'we keep wanting to make it so.' He dismisses easy magazine tips as missing the point. The aim isn't to try something new, he writes, it's to take a good look at what you are already doing. The easiest thing you can do to a relationship is make it domestic and harmonious.[31] Nothing is quite so efficient as the routine of everyday living—the year-in, year-out managing of children, jobs, money, house—to quell your passion, because then everything is made safe. Mitchell would have us pull down the barriers we're putting up that make sex and intimacy pedestrian, and love our spouses again like we would a lover, scary and vulnerable as this leaves us.

The marriage duty of maintaining your spouse's sexual interest, married to the more modern drive to keep your own desire sharp, might be desperately unfashionable, but sounds like pretty much the best advice on the subject. In the end, nothing is going to make you feel quite so warm towards your partner than some good old-fashioned sex.

To sum it up

- Everyone worries about sex.
- Sex is an important glue for relationships.
- There's no such thing as the right amount of sex.
- It's not the number of times you do it that counts, it's the everyday intimacy.
- If you're not doing it, you need to find ways to make sex a higher priority.
- Toys can be fun but they're not going to solve a problem.
- The list of common sex problems in a marriage can be summed up in three easy phrases: 'I want it, you don't', 'I'm bored' and 'this isn't fun anymore'.

- Yes, men and women are different.
- Don't get stuck in the 'go nowhere game'.
- Talking about it is important—no matter how difficult that is.
- Yes, kids make it harder.
- Be honest about what you need in order to feel sexy.
- If you're out of the habit, just do it.
- If you're having real problems, get a medical diagnosis and look at counselling.
- No one really thinks infidelity is okay.
- Marriages can survive affairs, but it's not easy.
- Real passion scares us because it leaves us vulnerable.

7

Show Me the Money

> It is a truth universally acknowledged that a single man in possession of a good fortune must be in want of a wife.
> —Jane Austen, *Pride and Prejudice,* 1813

While affairs are the stuff of drama and heartache, surprising as it may seem they're not the biggest killer of marriages. They're not even in the top three. And what are these top three? Well, they're more prosaic, more everyday, more common than you might imagine. And they're things dealt with routinely in most relationships.

In 1998, Relationships Australia commissioned a survey of 1400 Australians. It found the three factors that contributed most difficulty in relationships were 'financial difficulties' (29 per cent), 'work or study demands' (26 per cent) and 'having or bringing up children' (24 per cent).[1] Notice what came first?

This backs up other studies, like the one where researchers quizzed two groups of couples—one lot that were still together and one lot who had split—about the most difficult issues they had faced in their relationships. Again, the same list came up: finances, work and child rearing. Significantly, when it came to the couples who'd split, money matters was the number one problem by a country mile (23 per cent), followed by personality differences (10 per cent) and then child-rearing issues (10 per cent) and work issues (9 per cent). Those who stayed together put child rearing as their main concern (22 per cent) closely followed by finance (20 per cent).[2] What's more, these three issues have a way of cascading onto one another. For instance, when researchers looked at couples dealing with a gambling problem, they found—not surprisingly—that over half also said they were having financial difficulties, likewise eight in ten of those citing unemployment as a source of problems. And nearly half of those who said having children was a source of difficulty had financial problems as well.[3]

In a graphic example of how much money matters, a United Kingdom study found that the risk of becoming a lone parent through a marriage dissolving was a full 50 per cent higher if there was a deterioration in the couple's finances in any given year. For couples whose financial situation improved, however, the opposite was true—their risk of separation the following year was 50 per cent lower than for those who had no change.[4]

When I talked with couples these same three issues kept arising. But it was money that was the hardest of all for people to discuss. Indeed, they were more comfortable with me in their bedroom than in their wallets and would reveal far more about their sex lives than they'd ever confess about their finances. Simply put, more than any other factor, money problems will kill a marriage. It is money that cuts deepest into the heart of what marriage is, and has always been, about.

Before you choke on your St Valentine's Day chocolates, consider this: when 700 women, who were living with their boyfriends, were asked the question, 'Will you get married?' by social researchers, one in four said no. The reason? According to these researchers a big part of their response came down to the women wanting to marry for money. Specifically, eight out of ten educated women who lived with men of equally high socioeconomic status said they *would* marry. This dropped to just five in ten if the man had a lower socioeconomic status.[5] In short, women don't hesitate to marry someone who is likely to be a good provider, but they may think twice about someone who might not be.

Certainly the biggest losers in the marriage stakes are unemployed or underemployed Australian men. With around one in three unable to find full-time employment or earn an annual income of more than $20 000 in the prime of their working lives, demographers say this group are the least likely to wed.[6] Not that all workaday men need despair. Australian statistics show that more and more educated women are 'marrying down'. Census figures from 2001 show that more women aged 25 to 29 with degrees married less-educated men (12 per cent) than married their graduate peers (11 per cent)[7] though, of course, this doesn't say whether these men were earning more or less.

Lest you think marriage is all about female gold-digging, its worth noting that it's the men who reap financial benefit of tying the knot. This is known as the marriage effect and it's quite simple—married men earn more. To be exact, married men are more likely to be employed than single or cohabiting men; and if they are employed they are also more likely to work longer hours and to be in a management or supervisory position.[8]

There are three favoured explanations for this: marriage frees up men to do more paid work as women pick up the slack of the unpaid work in the home; women marry better earners; or there is something about marrying (and having children) that causes men to work harder. These arguments were mostly settled in a study comparing men who married because their partners were pregnant, with men who married for other reasons. It found that the shotgun guys didn't enjoy the same marriage advantages when it came to earnings, thereby suggesting that 'marriageable' men are the ones who marry, rather than it simply being marriage itself helping earning potential.[8]

This doesn't work for women, however. Marriage doesn't increase their individual earnings at all (although married women do work fewer paid hours on average). Instead, women's income and workforce status are determined by their level of education and whether or not they have children.[9] Indeed, for women the so-called mother effect is even more significant than the overall gender gap in wages.

In the United States the difference in hourly wages between women who are mothers and those who aren't rose from $0.42 in 1980 to $2.07 in 1990 and became larger than the overall difference between men and women. While this gap can partly be explained away by mothers, with their often interrupted work histories, having less job experience and undertaking more part-time (and less well-paid) work, researchers concluded there are only two real explanations: either mothers are less productive, or employers discriminate against them.[10]

Marriage makes you money
A United States survey of over 7000 households found that on retirement, people who had never married had only 14 per cent of the financial assets married people had accumulated. Divorcees who did not remarry had only 15 per cent, while those who had divorced and remarried had about 65 per cent more assets.[11] This is because married couples save significantly more than other households—an effect which isn't simply due to higher incomes nor to a simple aggregation of two individual's wealth.[12]

Money changes everything

> The obstacles to marriage are, generally speaking, few. The most serious is that of finance. Few young men can earn enough money to marry until they are thirty or thirty-five years of age . . . Frequently the girl herself will either have some money or her own of earn some, but usually she will keep this for her own expenses, relieving the husband of this item of the budget.
> —**Theodore Besterman,** *Men Against Women,* **1934**

So what is it about money that causes us so much stress? One big clue comes from what we actually fight about. Looking at our levels of household debt, you'd think most of the arguments would be over the big-ticket items. But when it comes down to it, you're far more likely to share the experience of dual career professionals Chris and Ann, a marketing manager and creative director, respectively.

'We really only argue about money at the periphery,' says Chris. 'It's the tiny little amounts. We've spent a lot of money over the last few years—buying houses, share investments, cars—and we never argue about that stuff. It's "why did you buy takeaway" or something like that. We'll argue about $15 or $20 for half an hour, but we have a very common view about what we need to do about big transactions.'

'It's more about personal attitudes to money,' agrees Ann. 'I'll get frustrated with Chris if he gets uptight about my spending a little bit. Then I'll find out how much he spent on another item he thought was essential. Sometimes it's like trying to redress that balance.'

In other words, fighting about money often isn't really just about the money, it's what the money stands for. Anne Hollands, past CEO of Relationships Australia, says many arguments about money are actually symbolic of something else, the argument itself masking our anxieties about deeper issues.

'Your capacity to discuss money reflects your background,' she says. 'In some families money was not openly discussed and was used as a tool of control between partners. We come to our partnerships now with all sorts of attitudes to money that we don't realise we have.' So money fights are an arena where you sort out other values that have come to you, you guessed it, courtesy of your family. Money is a stand-in, the metaphor for the other differences we don't quite know how to talk about.

Take Carrie and Alan, who from the beginning of their relationship found they were starting at rather different points, courtesy of cultural differences.

'Money is a big thing in a Maltese family,' says Alan. 'You learn how to treat it well and you try not to do the wrong thing.' In Alan's family, this included rules like not wasting money by borrowing it from a bank where you pay interest and fees when you can borrow it from within the family. This worked fine for him but it was an approach that was a little confronting if you come from a don't-talk-about-it Anglo background, as Carrie soon found out.

'The weekend after we got engaged I wanted to buy a car and I was $2000 short,' she says. 'I thought, "I'll go out and get a credit card and use the $2000 from the credit card and pay it back." Alan, on the other hand thought he'd fix the problem by sorting out a loan for her from his brother Steve. I was mortified,' says Carrie, who swiftly informed Alan, 'I'm not taking money off Steve. I don't know Steve. I'm only just engaged to you.' And the situation was only resolved when Alan ended up giving her the money.

'It was only a little bit,' concedes Alan.

'It was only $2000, but I wasn't taking it from your family then,' says Carrie resolutely.

These differences are compounded by another simple fact: most of us come into marriage already handicapped because we simply don't know a lot about handling money. In *Marriage Money*, an entire book on the subject, author Supriya Singh opens with a quote from 72-year-old Ian who notes that talking about money and banking, 'is a bit like talking to your children about where babies came from. We had to find that out for ourselves.' Which is to say, because money has always has been a very private matter, not discussed between friends and rarely talked about within families, particularly Anglo-Saxon families, we know very little about the practicalities of managing a household budget. Indeed, Singh notes that in Australia people are so reticent about the topic they often don't even know how their parents handled money.

'It's still private in other cultures,' she says down the phone. 'But in India, for example, your boundary of privacy is broader, and your network of support is broader.' In her book she cites, by way of contrast, a fishing community in Southern India, where information about loans and debts is shared among a woman's close relatives because there was a neighbourhood network of credit that cements the kinship and community ties.[13] In Australia, no such communal knowledge exists, and chances are you'd very much like to keep it that way, so it's a fair bet you don't know the size of the debts your cousins, siblings or parents are carrying.

While this privacy does have its advantages—chief of which is limiting the ability of outsiders to meddle in your financial concerns—it also means couples can end up endlessly reinventing the wheel as they learn financial competency. And it can mean that while you carry all your family's attitudes to money, you don't inherit any learned skills. And learning to run a budget today can throw up some very different outlooks about what money's for.

Who spends what?
Economists studying family spending have concluded that when men's income increases they're more likely to up their spending on tobacco, alcohol and men's clothing. When women's income increases they are significantly more likely to spend it on education, health and household services. Women are also more likely to spend money on children.[14]

Audrey and Rudy agree that they have very different approaches to saving and spending. 'He spends too much and I don't get to spend anything,' says Audrey, adding, 'Will we ever have a joint account? No way.'

Indeed, while they try to split expenses down the middle, it's really Audrey who controls the lot. But, she adds, eyebrows arching, this is the result of bitter experience. 'If I hand him the credit card it's going to be, "but honey, there was this great laser printer and I just bought our seventh computer and we needed another VCR and I've got a TV for the bedroom and a TV for the spare room now".' She staged her financial coup quite early in the relationship after she found bills weren't getting paid and reminders were arriving. So now, while she admits it might be a little demeaning, Rudy is given pocket money and that's it. But, she adds, when she did take over, he was jumping with glee. 'I tried to hand it back a few times, but he doesn't want to do it,' she says.

Rudy puts their differences down to coming from different socio-economic backgrounds, and the way this flavours how they measure success. 'Because my family never had much money you learn not to measure yourself by what you've got in the bank, or how much is coming in,' he says, adding that it's a common working-class mentality. 'I look at all my mates who I grew up with. Before having kids, probably nine out of ten of them used to drink most of their pay packet every Friday night. They'd never had money before and they were going to go out and live life like their parents told them they should.'

Audrey in turn comes from a more middle-class background. 'Savings are important and they've [Audrey's family] had the ability to save,' says Rudy. 'For her, my spendthriftness has had to be curtailed. I've now had to put money aside, learn how to save, all that kind of stuff. I think it's a cultural thing. It is important, but it's also something that gets negotiated.' He points out these negotiations aren't just about the money, but their plans for the future. 'We want to have kids and Audrey wants a house before we have kids, which is completely understandable, to get that stability.'

One of the biggest reasons money is so important (besides its obvious putting-roof-over-head, food-on-table uses) is that today it's our main measure of status. And it's almost our sole way of showing we're doing well. We use it to measure ourselves against our parents, our neighbours and our peers; the house we own, the toys we buy, the holiday we can afford to have, all demonstrate our worth. Reveal how much we earn, we think, and we risk revealing our true value. Many budgets get blown by people who can't get past this way of thinking.

> **Over-stretched and underpaid**
> As an age group, generation X owns significantly fewer assets than the generation before: in 2003, 25- to 39-year-olds controlled 19 per cent of Australia's cash, financial and property assets, down from 27 per cent for the same age group in 1986. Only 54 per cent of the group own their own home, compared with 64 per cent in 1989.[15] The average house price in Australia has risen 70 per cent in five years to $280 000, with the average cost of a Sydney home rising to $500 000 in December 2003. By contrast, the average full-time wage has risen only 26 per cent.[16] Just one in ten Sydney property purchases are made by first-home buyers, whose average age is now 33.

Good housekeeping

> Living within an income is an art and few young persons are trained in the scientific data underlying practical programs of spending wisely. Who shall hold the money gag or dole out allowances? Shall the wife receive a regular amount weekly? Or monthly? Shall it provide for the table only or include her personal needs? Shall the weekly wage or monthly check be turned over, in toto, to the wife, to be handled with her discretion, including an allowance for her husband needs? . . . They must depend on the personalities married.
> **—Ira S. Wile,** *The Man Takes A Wife,* **1938**

What's the easiest way to find the money attitudes each of you are carrying? Simple: just combine your household finances, like Dave and Jennie, who found in merging their accounts and expenses that they had brought along some very different family values around ready cash.

'David's upbringing was very much "my money's your money", there's one wallet and don't worry about anything,' says Jennie, who couldn't have come from a more different approach. 'My family's all about "have your own money", "have your own stash". My mum and dad always talk about "you pay that with your money" or "I'm going to pay that with my money".' So for Jennie, having her own money was all about independence, while for David sharing money was what families did. It took them a while to adjust to each other's point of view.

'I couldn't get my head around it, the I-feel-like-I've-paid-for-too-many-things-lately stuff,' admits Jennie, who has now mostly embraced David's approach. 'But over the last three years, I've learned to change my opinion on that. I've still got one account that's mine, but everything else is very much shared now.'

Joint finances, particularly the joint account, are the centre of money in marriage. And as Singh points out, it's unique to married relationships—you don't have a joint account with your parents and you won't have one with your grown children. In her survey of middle-class Melbournians, 88 per cent of married couples had joint accounts.

'It is taken for granted that the joint account follows marriage or the commitment to marry,' she says, contrasting this with de facto couples who rarely had joint accounts, or if they did, were mostly planning to marry. 'Couple after couple talked of it in ritualised terms, describing how, soon after marriage, they went together to the bank to change all or some of their separate accounts to joint accounts.'[17] So money, and sharing money, is also our way of symbolising commitment. In fact, according to Singh this symbolic act has become more pronounced in the past three decades.

Not that this means husbands and wives don't also have other accounts. Nearly half of those in Singh's survey also kept separate accounts in addition to the joint one. The most joint-finance gun-shy were, unsurprisingly, couples on their second marriages. Singh cites research that shows a trend to separate finances in remarriage, particularly if there are children from the first marriage involved. She also notes, just like Jennie's experience showed, for women especially, retaining some control over money remains a very big deal. And this is where some values around money get very tricky indeed.

There is no question that women today very much equate money with power. And that's also been a defining theme of feminism. Virginia Woolf famously declared that if a woman wished to be creative she 'must have money and a room of her own', a price she set at 500 pounds sterling a year (that was 1929—in today's terms we're talking around AU$60 000).

Another Wolf—Naomi—took up the same theme in her paean to female power, *Fire With Fire*, which in large discusses the joy of financial clout. 'Financial literacy is a goal as basic to women's empowerment as reproductive literacy,' she writes. 'When women have money, the opposition has no choice but to listen.'[18] Certainly, recent women's history justifies such interest in money. Our generation has been weaned on the horror stories of women suffering sexually-transmitted debt (as befalls women who sign up for joint loans with their husbands only to be saddled with the whole debt when their husband leaves). And it's not so long ago women that didn't have equal economic rights: in the United States before 1975, a woman could only get a credit card as a subsidiary card to the original belonging to her spouse or father. Also, today the gap between men and women's average weekly full-time earnings is in fact widening, from a gap of $163.20 in 1996 to $197.40 in May 2003.[19] So we still aren't financially equal.

If money is power, how do we square it in our equality-driven marriages? It's the million-dollar question as women do baulk at having to share their cash. As Peggy Orenstein puts it in *Flux*, her study of what drives American women: 'If for the previous generation the "feminine mystique" surrounding marriage and motherhood was the trap, the solution for today's young women and the object lesson drilled into their heads, is financial independence.' It's the golden rule, she says: 'Whoever has the gold, makes the rules.'[20] But, Orenstein notes, there's a catch. When women say they envisage being self-supporting, they only mean of themselves, not a family. From when women leave university, she argues, they choose jobs, based not on earning capacity and title, as men do, but on flexibility. In other words, from the start most women don't plan on being the main breadwinner—they assume they'll be in and out of the workforce.

This isn't a bad assumption if you want a family, but it's not the best if you want to have that independent financial clout. This may help explain why women are so choosy when it comes to marrying men with an income. Women still equate power with having their own money, yet if they are to have children, they also need a husband who has the earning power to support a family. At home that can sound like 'what's mine is mine and what's yours is ours'.

Mandy and Andrew, parents to Ruby, 3 years, and Harry, 4 months, are like most young parents. Mandy picks up some shift work with her journalism, but essentially, Andrew is the main breadwinner. Still, Mandy gets to keep her pay.

'I get my money for work and I can spend that how I like,' she explains, while the mortgage and expenses come out of Andrew's earnings. But lately she's started to see how that adds up. 'I actually said to Andrew a couple of days ago, "It suddenly dawned on me, you're not the only person responsible for our financial security",' she confesses. 'It's probably that I've also come out of this haze of second baby. Now I don't have to have any more kids it's like that path is clear. If we need more money, then I'll go and work.' It doesn't sound radical, but for a generation who looked to their own independence, sharing the family costs along with the family spoils is a leap forward. But then, as our marriages progress, it's also possible we're starting to realise that the simple 'money = power' equation isn't really how money works in marriage.

Who has control?

> The younger generation has appreciated the meaning and worth of sharing an income. Marriage at early ages is attended with participation in production. Many a young professional man has achieved his economic salvation, while a vigorous young woman with full faith in him, worked to pay their rent or more. This idea is rich in idealism and is founded upon a sense of parity in effort and mutual belief in the values inherent in constructive economic participation.
> —Ira S. Wile, *The Man Takes a Wife*, 1938

Simple question: does the person who contributes more money have more control? Or is it the one who controls the budget that calls the shots? Certainly many of the men I talked to mentioned the negative pressures of being the primary breadwinner. They were stoically sticking with jobs they disliked, or making pragmatic high-earner career choices rather than pursing more fulfilling employment.

'I'd love to quit my job,' said more than one, wistfully, 'but it just doesn't make financial sense.' That would suggest that earning more doesn't automatically make you feel more powerful. So who is really in control?

Ironically, in the couple who best illustrated what these pressures were and how they could play out, the woman was the primary breadwinner. Sarah, 47, a book publisher and Matthew, 44, a public sector manager, seem the very model of the new egalitarianism. She earns more than he does, though strictly speaking she doesn't support him, as he works too. This situation has never bothered Matt, particularly having observed how his mother—'a very strong and capable woman, but she didn't earn'—got depression once her children left home because she didn't feel she had a function anymore.

While Sarah may bring in the bigger bucks, Matt is the one who manages the family income. 'I'm very good at company finances,' says Sarah, with a laugh. 'I'm not so good with my own. I give him every docket, every receipt I get from the EFTPOS machine.'

Still, while she was peeling off the price tag from Matt's 40th birthday present—paid for from joint funds—Sarah realised she wanted her own account. 'If somebody's birthday came up, suddenly we'd be short of cash for that week,' explains Sarah. 'I didn't like that because we earn enough to be able to manage it. It wasn't so much a control thing, it was just I didn't like having to ask Matt for money.'

The household budget was rearranged. Matt worked out what they needed to keep for all the regular expenses and what would be left. They smoothed out the mortgage and household accounts and now Sarah has her own cash for extras like presents and kids' activities and she knows exactly how much is left over.

Economists, who get excited about this sort of thing, note there are two sorts of control when it comes to finances. There's the power to make big financial decisions—orchestration power—and then there's the day-to-day money management, or implementation power. Orchestration power is mainly about the fun stuff, like deciding which car to buy, and it's probably why so many of us still maintain separate accounts so we get to decide at least some of the spending. On the other hand, implementation power, which is nominally all about budget control, can be downright tedious and time-consuming. So who gets to do what and what are those powers really worth?

When they're asked, around half of all couples argue that they have equal orchestration power. But do they really? The answer depends on where you look. Research suggests that, for most couples in the United States, financial decision-making is shared equally. But other research from the United Kingdom indicates that the lower the household income, the more the wife controls the spending, while for those with higher incomes it's more likely to be the husband.[21]

> **Women's work**
> Women who earn more money than their husbands (as occurs in 30 per cent of marriages in America)[22] do more housework. When Michael Bittman and his team analysed the amount of housework done in relation to income earned he found a sliding scale: as women move from complete economic dependence to providing an equal income, their balance of the housework also progressively becomes more equal. But once they pass the halfway point and contribute more than half the household income, their housework increases in line with their contribution to income.[23] As researchers of female-financed households have observed, women can go to great lengths to emphasise this isn't normal and their husbands aren't deficient.

Still, how orchestration and implementation power is divided is only half of Matt and Sarah's story. We'd been chatting out back in the cheery family room of their recently renovated house. 'I love this house,' says Sarah. 'We bought it clearly thinking this is a house we can renovate and can stay in until the kids leave uni.' And near to the kids' schools and transport links, its position can't be beaten. But they came close to sacrificing all this recently because the money–child–career equation stopped adding up the way they wanted. Last year there was a crunch.

While two of their three children are in school, all three have special needs: the eldest has mild autism, the next is very gifted, while the third is asthmatic. All require extra support. And Sarah was becoming more and more unhappy with the lack of time she had for them because of her work.

'I was so worried about my children and I was feeling like I wasn't in control with them in a way a parent needs to be,' she says. 'I found it very, very frustrating. I think I was the unhappiest I had been ever in my life.' She and Matt were fighting and she was threatening to resign from her job.

'I felt really unsupported because Matt didn't understand how frustrated I was,' she says.

'And I felt really torn being the person who knew where the money comes and goes and you telling me effectively that you wanted to cut off our income by more than half,' counters Matt. 'I felt in a difficult position.'

'But to me, bugger income, somebody's happiness has got to be on top of that,' says Sarah.

It was, in fact, the classic breadwinner pinch. Money couldn't buy Sarah the one commodity she wanted most—time. While on the other side, controlling the household budget, Matt knew exactly what they stood to lose. They were stuck in a phenomenon social scientists have dubbed the two-income trap. The book, *The Two-Income Trap: why middle-class mothers and fathers are going broke*, spells it out. United States research indicates the cost of middle-class lifestyles has skyrocketed in recent years—particularly when it comes to big ticket items like housing, childcare and education. Today, in order to buy a house and get your kids a private education, both parents have to work. And a household economy set up this way is doubly insecure because if one loses a job, drops an income or wants to make changes, both are in trouble.

Fortunately for Matt and Sarah a solution presented itself. Sarah saw her overseas boss at a big book fair in Boston and told him she'd have to reduce her hours. The company supported her and now she works four days a week, spending Fridays with Felix, her youngest. She also plans to start early twice a week so she can be home when the kids arrive home from school. And while she and Matt still tussle over the finances ('I get cross with Sarah because she'd make a fuss about what seemed like very little things,' says Matt, 'where I'd see that she'd sacrificed twenty per cent of her salary and then not really get extra time because she would work half the weekend') they're finding the balance and Matt has rejigged their finances to compensate for the salary hit. 'I just needed to see an alternative,' he says.

Who was most in control—Matt, who organised the finances, or Sarah, who earned the bigger share? In the end, earning more money didn't mean Sarah had more control. But while Matt probably called most of the shots because he was controlling the family budget, Sarah also negotiated a no-questions-asked allowance and in the end was prepared to sacrifice her job if she had to, so he wasn't in total control either. So, let's call it equal. Most significant of all, what ended up really mattering to them wasn't control of the money at all. It was what money could and couldn't buy—a life.

The downshifting revolution

> When a woman marries, it's as if she entered a convent, except however that it is not taken ill that she have children, and even many of them. Otherwise, it's the life of a nun; no more balls; hardly any more society; a husband as estimable as cold for all company; and that to the life eternal. I ventured the other day to ask one of these charming recluses just how, exactly, a wife could pass her time in America. She answered me, with great sang-froid: in admiring her husband.
> **—Letter from Alexis de Tocqueville to his sister, 9 June 1831**

Escaping the two-income trap isn't easy. While some couples are able to negotiate a better balance at work, others take far more drastic action. Downshifting—voluntarily reducing your income and consumption—is a big trend: 23 per cent of Australians between the ages of 30 and 59 downshifted in the last decade, a number that increases to 30 per cent if you include those who have returned to study or have set up their own business. It's households with children that are most likely to downshift, as couples move to pursue more time with their families. Upper socioeconomic groups are leading the charge: around one in three female and one in five male executives who have downsized their aspirations, just like Matt and Sarah above, say it was mostly because they were tired of the sacrifices to family and personal life they were having to make.[24]

When Mark and Sally found their second child was on the way, city living finally stopped adding up. It wasn't that they weren't capable of bringing in a decent living—Mark's a senior public servant, Sally a solicitor—but they decided that if they wanted the option of having real time with their children and still affording time for each other along with some personal time out, there was only one thing for it. Leave the city. So in a swift lifestyle move they sold their house, packed up and moved to Sally's home town of Orange, four hours west of Sydney.

A few months down that track, Sally is currently staying home with six-month-old Will, while Mark commutes 40 minutes to Bathurst each day to his job at the local university. From the newly renovated warmth of their spacious house, which now includes three chooks and a rose garden, both agree it was a great decision—the move out west has resulted in more time together as well as with their children. They can afford a cleaner, and someone to come in most afternoons to help with the kids and they can still plan a night at a nice restaurant and to visit the local wineries. Neither can think of a downside. Sally hasn't experienced a career-deprivation crisis—'My role at work doesn't make a huge difference in how I see myself. It comes down to how Mark values me'—though she's managed to keep her hand in with some incidental lecturing at the College of Law and is investigating setting up a mortgage-brokering business.

Having also overseen the renovation of their new place, along with looking after a newborn, Sally has a new-found respect for the demands of home. 'Running the household, organising the mortgage, on top of the kids is a big job in itself,' she says. 'I think that's been something that's been devalued.'

Like most voluntary downshifters, they are overwhelmingly happy with their decision and are in the fortunate position of not yet missing the extra income (one sixth of downshifters, and particularly those with children, while still happy, also find the loss of income hard.)[25]

Broke

> If a woman wishes to earn, why should she not? If marriage is a partnership, why should she be barred from her desired contribution? Or is it merely a relic of the old idea that a woman's place is in the home, to administer creature comforts to the toiling man who works so hard to support her? Is it sheer selfishness, passing as morality?
> —Ira S. Wile, *The Man Takes a Wife*, 1938

Voluntarily forgoing money is one thing, but if you really want to see a marriage tested, try losing it. Kathy Garthe works at the Bush Connection, an agency based in Toowoomba, Queensland, that assists farmers who have had to leave the land. Its services are in high demand.

'It takes a very heavy toll on marriages,' says Kathy, who estimates that only one in two of the marriages coming to the service survive intact. 'It seems like there isn't a middle path. Either it strengthens their marriage or they break up. Often they've left the problem [to] go on too long.' Husbands especially, she says, tend to bury their heads in the sand. Then there is the rural ethic of not putting up your hand for help, and not wanting people to know your problems.

Kathy knows all this from first-hand experience. She and Lindsay, both 48, met 26 years ago. An only son, Lindsay was a second-generation farmer who had worked the family farm since he was sixteen. Kathy was a primary school teacher. When they married they moved onto the property and had their three children.

The first few years were easy. The farm was prospering and as well as their prize-winning wheat, they were having success with other grains. Then the weather changed. The years 1992, 1993, 1994 came and went and the rain hardly fell. They went into debt. They tried irrigating but couldn't find quite enough water. They kept going backwards. And while Lindsay was working the land by himself after his father died in 1985, they also had his mother to support.

'I felt a bit of a failure over the dry years suffering crop losses,' says Lindsay. 'Whatever I tried didn't work. I got despondent and downhearted. Lost a bit of direction.' He tried to stick it out. It was the family farm after all, there was a lot of sentimental value tied up in it, not just for him, but for his mother and sister too. Finally he hit the bottom. 'There were three weeks I really got bogged down. I actually felt ill. I knew I had to keep going. I'd talk to Kathy, then go out on the tractor. I knew I never wanted to feel that again. It was severe enough to shake me up.' He knew it wasn't a life he wanted for his kids and it wasn't a life he wanted for himself anymore either.

They decided to sell. Six months later they found a buyer and left with their teenaged children.

'When we sold it was a relief,' says Lindsay. 'I was excited about the future. Farming was all I had done.' Since then he's taken every opportunity that's come his way, working stints as a farming instructor at an agricultural college, a grain salesman and an insurance salesman, along with picking up some farm work. Kathy also found work and now devotes her days to the Bush Connection. They've had disagreements since but nothing like they had before.

When asked why they survived the experience when so many don't, they're at first stumped.

'We're good mates,' says Kathy, after a pause.

'I've always really respected Kathy,' says Lindsay. 'She's been my backbone.' They agree they're fortunate. When they sold they walked away with money in their pockets and were able to buy another block of land and set up Lindsay's mother as well. Most of all, says Lindsay finally, 'We agreed on the decision that had to be made and we made it at the right time.'

'I think it comes down to commitment and honesty and being up-front,' says Kathy. 'Our marriage is far from perfect but I think neither of us will bail out when times are tough.'

It seems, just like Matt and Sarah or Mark and Sally, Kathy and Lindsay could see past the money to what mattered most—them and their family. And in doing so, they took their finance problems seriously, but saw them as finance problems rather than "them" problems, and consequently set out to fix the money situation, without letting it become a relationship issue, or a metaphor for other things that may have been bugging them. In other words, sometimes the money problems are just about the money. Or, as discussed in chapter 4, successful couples solve the actual problem in front of them and don't let it escalate into a relationship-breaking issue.

> **Who wears the financial pants?**
> According to focus groups commissioned by Australian brokers Mortgage Choice, women make up 75 per cent of first-time callers to mortgage consultants, and about 60 per cent of final home loan decisions are made by women.[26]

To sum it up
- Money breaks up more marriages than any other factor.
- We bring into our marriages a lot of family assumptions about how we deal with money.

- Fighting about money isn't just about the money, it's what the money stands for.
- You go into marriage with many assumptions, but few skills, about how a household budget should work.
- The joint bank account is symbolic.
- The 'my money is my money, your money is ours' mentality is a trap.
- Whoever earns the most doesn't necessarily control the budget, and whoever controls the budget doesn't necessarily control the spending.
- It's not really about the money, its what the money can buy.
- Look for creative solutions to financial problems.
- Avoiding the money issue will only drag you further into debt.
- See past the dollars to what really matters.
- You might need a financial advisor, not a marriage counsellor.

8

All Work, No Play?

> Women are not what they were. The new woman is properly so-called. Her status has altered so that she dares to issue challenges, to doubt her husband, or to offer compromises for her own behaviour. Her place is no longer definitely fixed in terms of kitchen, church and children. She believes in her own capacity to meet life, even without a husband. She puts her belief to trial in a career that grants her freedom . . .
> —Ira S. Wile, *The Man Takes a Wife*, 1938

Be honest, how do we define ourselves? The answer is simple. It's by what we do. 'I'm a journalist,' I say. I don't say 'I'm a wife, a friend, a mother.' It's been going on all our lives. Children are constantly asked, 'What are you going to be when you grow up?' Today, it is the same for men and women. Indeed there's probably been no single greater change in marriage in the last hundred years than this: women now work. And just as it is for men, work is a very big part of a woman's identity. The dual-career marriage is now the norm. Since

1966, the proportion of women in the labour force has almost doubled (from 29 per cent of all wives to 57 per cent in 2001), and close to 60 per cent of couples with dependent children are now dual earners.

If working is so normal, why does it cause so many difficulties in relationships, ranking in those top three problems? For me and my husband, one of our most difficult times was when I was starting out in journalism, my second career. Rob had already been working in the field for several years and was by then editing a national magazine. So while I was begging people to return my phone calls, he was getting invited to all the cool events. At parties, people would schmooze him and then walk away from me. I began to feel like the junior partner at home because that's what I was at work. Of course, it was all about ego. I felt like we were competing and I was the one coming off second best. Dual-careers meant dual-career jealousy, at least until I got established.

Because our identities are so tied up in work, it's not hard to import work stress into a relationship when you are negotiating the edges between what's important for the individuals and what matters as a couple. But while that's easy to say, it's not always so easy to fix. Andrew, 38, a public servant with a career in youth advocacy, got what sounded like a dream job down in Tasmania. It involved a big move that would uproot his family from Sydney— where they'd been living next door to his wife Brigid's parents, who helped care for their two young sons on a daily basis. The opportunity was too good to miss, so the family moved to Launceston. With youngest son Joseph only months old, Brigid opted to stay home while Andrew worked. It was a very traditional arrangement that contrasted sharply with their experience with their first child, Patrick, where Brigid had taken the first year off, Andrew the second.

Once they arrived in their new home, however, things quickly turned sour. For a start, Andrew's job turned out to have very long hours so he was hardly getting to see the kids or Brigid.

'When Joseph was doing benchmark things—like talking in long sentences—Andrew wasn't there,' says Brigid. She also felt isolated in a city where she knew no one and far from her family to whom she was very close.

It wasn't just the work hours, though, it was also the job itself. Brought in to reform the organisation, Andrew found he'd been handed a poisoned chalice and was on the receiving end of death threats and a staff revolt.

'We felt the tension between us a lot,' says Andrew. 'It was a really tough time emotionally, personally and family-wise.' There were two problems he had to deal with—the impact his job was having on the family, and the impact of the turmoil at work on his own work pride, which coupled with the frustration of being unable to do what he set out to do.

'I got to the point of asking "How important is achieving career goals at the expense of a whole lot of other things?"' he recounts. It took both Andrew and Brigid to the edge. Andrew was torn up trying to make it all work; Brigid was at her wit's end and ready to pack.

'I was just trying to hold my tongue,' says Brigid. 'I could see Andrew was moving down that track—but it needed to be his decision.' In the end Andrew decided to end his contract early and the family bolted back to Sydney and, with no job, moved back in with Brigid's parents.

Now, a couple of years later, Andrew says the whole experience made him more reflective about what he wanted and where the balance lay. He's rethought some of his own career goals and has taken a longer-term view of the experience.

'I had to re-evaluate all the things that were important in my life, and work just became a component of that—"this is a career issue, this is a family issue," he says, weighing one hand then the other. 'There doesn't seem to be harmony here, so how do I make them in harmony? I try to juggle the ambitions and what I'd like to do with what pays well and what's affordable and what's doable for us.'

The time trap

There was a time when office, factory and shop required twelve to fourteen hours daily and there was an excuse for heavy fatigue. That era is past. Today, overwork is largely a fiction and the male need for rest scarcely justifies a release from the obligation to be companionable.
—Ira S. Wile, *The Man Takes a Wife*, 1938

The inescapably bad news is that 'work issues' remain one of the main reasons divorcing couples say they split.[1] And the number one culprit? Time—or lack of it. A survey by Relationships Australia found that the biggest difficulty people in relationships face is the inability to spend sufficient time together.[2] There is now a considerable body of research that makes it clear that heavy workplace demands spill over negatively into marriages,[3] a fact that is hardly surprising given that having time together is a vital ingredient for a happy relationship.

The statistics tell the story: by the late 1990s, the average working week in Australia had stretched to 43 hours, and one third of full-time employees worked 49 hours per week or more;[4] between 1986 and 2000 the proportion of employees who had worked some of their hours at night or on the weekend in the previous month increased from 56 per cent to 64 per cent.[5] The proportion of all male employees working 50 or more hours has increased from 15 per cent in 1985 to 25 per cent in 2000. Of male full-time workers, 35 per cent worked 50 or more hours per week in 2002, up from 23 per cent in 1982.[6]

With figures like this it's not surprising that six out of every ten workers say work interferes with the amount of quality time they spend with their families, more than half agreeing they're too tired to go out or work around the house.[7] So in such a time-squeezed world, how do happy couples manage?

For Barry and Emma, awaiting the birth of their first child, the answer is to simply not allow time to become a problem. Their formula is: life first, then career. This agreement was forged early in their relationship when they first moved from Adelaide to Sydney. Emma was juggling work and study while Barry laboured long hours as a concreter. They barely saw each other. To kill time after work, Barry would go to the pub with his workmates, which soon gave him a clear picture of what his future could look like.

'All these guys were alcoholics,' he says. 'You could see yourself going down that path, and I thought "this is just stupid".' Nowadays he has more rewarding work, managing a community centre, but while dedicated to the job, he's strict about the limits. 'I work nine to five, Monday to Friday, and I get paid well for it and the rest of the time is me,' he says. 'I don't think about work when I'm at home.'

'It's not that we're anti-career,' says Emma, adding that both are prepared to work hard to get the things they want. 'But I've always got fulfilment from my relationships with people rather than my job. I just don't believe in working overtime. I think you're paid to do a job, and it should take you roughly 40 hours a week. Occasionally you have to stay back and do something,' she continues, 'but if there was a culture that you had to be there until seven or eight o'clock every night, I just wouldn't do it. We prioritise our life together over work because that's where we get our satisfaction from.' In fact, Emma and Barry's dream is to one day own their own business together. Then they would be together even if they had to put in the overtime.

'Because then you're working for your own goal, that's different,' says Barry. 'It's worth putting in the hard yards for it.'

A similar idea, but different strategy, is expressed by Steve and Shannon, both technical writers. For them time became a commodity as valuable as money after they had their son Gabriele, now six. And to get more time they decided they were willing to trade off the money.

'We went about trying to find jobs that would allow us to earn what we needed and also allow us to have time to spend separately

> **Strong marriages are good for work**
>
> Even though work–family conflict is linked to increased levels of depression, alcohol use, marital tension and poorer health, overall dual-earner couples report more positive than negative effects from the family-to-work spill over—though the research shows family life enhances work life to a greater degree than work life enhances family life.[8] Being in a mutually satisfying marriage is associated with taking less time off work and greater career achievement.[9]

with Gaby and together as a family,' says Shannon. Since then, they've tried plenty of combinations to find a balance that works: at various times each has stayed home while the other worked, or one has worked from home. Right now each works part-time, three days a week. Thursdays are free for both and they tag-team it so each can take a languages course that day—Steve learns Spanish in the morning, Shannon learns Russian in the afternoon—which still leaves plenty of time for Gabriele.

Steve points out that they have the luxury of doing this (and they do consider it a luxury) as they had worked overseas for some years and saved, and were then able to come back and put a substantial deposit on a house, so they're less cash-strapped than other couples. Though, adds Shannon, 'If we wanted a four-wheel drive and I wanted diamonds, we'd both have to work. We just decided, we just don't need certain things, and don't necessarily want them.' In fact, Shannon points out, over the past few years they've reduced their combined salaries. 'But while other people are going up we get more time and a better life.'

They're still a two-career couple, but a pragmatic one. 'I always say I'm sort of anti-career, in a way,' says Shannon. 'No, we're a zero-career couple,' says Stephen as they both laugh. 'We don't have a career between us.'

While this isn't strictly true—Steve and Shannon do have careers—they have decided not to climb the corporate ladder, at least for now. What they've really abandoned is the 'idea of career' and that is something they're still grappling with.

'It's only three days a week but sometimes I think, "If I'm going to spend eight hours a day, three days a week here, then I should try to make it useful, worthwhile and satisfying",' says Shannon. 'I start investing time trying to make the work better and then I start questioning myself: "Should I be bothered trying to make the work situation better, or should I just go to work?"'

When work is home and home is work

One of the good things that comes to a home from which both the husband and the wife go forth to business every day is a new comradeship—a new sort of partnership. A working wife has a better chance of being friends with her husband than a stay-at-home wife.
—Jane Littell, 'Meditations of a wage-earning wife', *Atlantic Monthly*, 1924

A lack of time isn't the only issue in the work versus life struggle. In 2000, the Australian Bureau of Statistics surveyed workers, asking them if they would prefer to: work less hours and earn less; work more hours and earn more; work the same amount as now; or had no preference. The results? Nearly two-thirds answered they would prefer to work the same amount of hours as they actually worked, including six out of ten of those who worked more than 60 hours per week.[10] Another survey has found that the managers who put in the longest hours were in fact the least stressed by their family life—suggesting they didn't feel the work–life collision—that is, so long as the rewards were there at work. And before you go thinking this is mostly absent fathers dodging mundane home responsibilities, fascinatingly, regardless of the number of hours they worked, all the male managers spent the same number of hours on childcare and housework.[11] Clearly something more complex is going on.

In a dimmed conference room a couple of years ago, Rosalind Barnett flashed up the slides of a Powerpoint presentation reporting the results of her research into the effect of working hours on relationships. One said: 'In some studies, long work hours is related to positive outcomes'. The next read: 'In some studies, long work hours is related to negative outcomes'. She followed this with: 'In some studies, long work hours is unrelated to quality-of-life outcomes'. Then a few slides later she delivered her findings on a study of women doctors: 'Contrary to what "commonsense" might predict, the women doctors who worked MORE hours reported BETTER relationships with their husbands than those who worked fewer hours!' Barnett then zeroed in on the real issue: 'The impact of work hours on the marital quality of female doctors in dual-earner couples cannot be determined without knowing how these doctors spend their non-work time.' The key to a good married relationship, Barnett found, isn't just the hours working on the job, but how each partner negotiates the hours they do spend together.[12] So those kitchen sink negotiations are the ones that really matter.

This is something that deeply interests sociologist Arlie Hochschild. She has a theory that one reason work has been able to suck up so much extra time from families is that it is literally a less stressful place to be than home. In her book, *The Time Bind*, she

---

Who blinks first?

Among professional dual-income couples, when faced with a turning point, the husband's career is the one usually given priority. Women are less likely than men to make career choices that will disrupt the lives of their family members and men are more likely than women to move the family for their job.[13]

describes how for both women and men home can become a gladiatorial arena of tension and chaos, with unrelenting and unmeetable demands that offer little space for relaxation, meaningful conversation or appreciation. Work, on the other hand, offers plenty of personal rewards: the opportunity to be recognised for a job well done, and the chance to work as a team and develop challenging adult relationships.

'Nowadays, men and women both may leave unwashed dishes, unresolved quarrels, crying tots, testy teenagers, and unresponsive mates behind to arrive at work early and call out, "Hi, fellas, I'm here!"' she writes.[14] In other words, home is work, and work is more like, well, home.

It's a compelling case. Home for our generation is often ground zero where everything comes to a crunch, particularly when it comes to our careers. After all, when we have to work back, if there's a job offer in another city, or a promotion that comes with longer hours or an opportunity for study that will help us climb the ladder, who do we really negotiate with? We don't ask our employers to pick up the slack or make the sacrifice, we ask our spouses. And the more time one half of a couple spends at work, the more the other is lumbered with home duties.

Is career inevitably a zero-sum game? How do couples cope when crunched between ambition and lack of time and energy?

Joanne and Luke, both university administrators, met at work, 'in divorce alley' they joke. The already separated Joanne provided an emotional bolster for Luke when his marriage broke down. Now happily married, like so many parents they faced an inevitable dilemma with the arrival of son Lachlan, born 18 months ago. The interesting thing is, each responded in a different and unexpected way. For Joanne, herself cared for by her grandmother when her careerist mother went back to work, at first there was no work–life conflict and she happily returned to her job when Lachlan was three months old, Luke's mother stepping in as the carer.

'I'd always been a career person and I was really funny about becoming a mother,' she confesses. Aged 35 by the time she'd had Lachlan, she'd had plenty of time to develop her career identity. 'It was the "mother" tag I had trouble with,' she says. 'I was Joanne, I wasn't "mummy" and consequently I didn't see myself as a mother figure. I saw us as a couple and as a family but I saw myself in terms of my career.' But when Lachlan was around six months old she felt a twinge.

'When they're a blob lying there, that's nice and pretty because they're a baby, but once they're interactive with you . . .' She shrugs a wry grin. She was suffering from guilt—about not feeling loyal to her career.

'I thought "I actually like this child and I could stay home a day or two a week with him and teach him things,"' she recounts. 'But then I thought "No, I define myself as a working person, my career is who I am."' With the career part of her life for so long, accepting another identity wasn't going to be easy.

Things started clicking into place when, undertaking tutoring work at a university, she started reading research that sounded very familiar; she realised it wasn't just parents like her who were feeling a tug between life and work, it was her whole generation. More to the point, no matter how ambitious or hardworking her peers were, they all seemed to be finding that the job payoffs weren't there.

'The X generation coming through, we're following the baby boomers who thought one should stay at work from eight until eight,' she says. 'Our generation feels pressure to do that. But because there are so many baby boomers we're not really rising through the ranks like we should be.' Reading that, she adds, made her rethink her plans. 'I thought "How stupid, you've wasted how many years?"' Now she looks to the future when inevitably the baby boomers will retire, so there'll be opportunities coming. And she's slowed down, started saying no to more work, and has begun looking for a better balance. It was a change that spilled over to how she managed her staff.

'I started treating them so much differently,' she says. 'I became more family friendly and friendly towards their outside life.'

She had experienced what happens when the girls-can-do-anything generation meets you-can't-do-it-all reality. We've seen superwoman collapse on the floor and we're vowing that won't happen to us. It doesn't necessarily dampen the ambition, but it puts the brakes on what we're willing to sacrifice for little reward.

Joanne isn't kidding herself about how hard it is to find a balance, pointing out that she has friends who gave up their careers entirely to stay home when they found the juggle with young children too difficult. And she also knows other women who have chosen not to have children because they're on a career treadmill and can't find the time or opportunity even for a relationship.

While Joanne was discovering that she could take things more slowly with her career, Luke was reassessing the importance he placed on having a job at all. His work hadn't been rewarding for some time.

'I was getting really depressed knowing that life ended at the job wall—you left work and that was it—but not being valued in your job doesn't mean you're valueless,' he says, scooping up the scrambling, squirming Lachlan. Having experienced this value change, Luke decided to turn his attentions closer to home.

'I want to be around the family and Lachlan gets value from me being around him more,' he says. So it's Luke who does the dropping off and picking up of Lachlan from his grandmother during the week, while Joanne commutes all the way into the city working twelve-hour door-to-door days. 'Right now I'm not being career focussed,' says Luke. 'I just don't feel as motivated by work things now.'

What Luke was saying is similar to what Steve said earlier—both still had careers but both had stopped being willing to do absolutely anything for a job when they had something just as rewarding at home.

Indeed, when it comes to assessing career priorities, parenthood seems to have almost as great an impact on men today as on women. Australian surveys show that when they become fathers, men take the emotional role they have with their children more seriously than any breadwinner role. The same research shows that men think they do not spend enough time with their children and believe overwhelmingly that the major barrier to their spending more time is their paid work.[15] The fathers of this generation are changing their priorities, even though the work–life balance is still often referred to as a 'motherhood' debate.

Are two careers bad for one marriage?

You've heard about DINKs (double income, no kids), now we have DINS—double income, no sex.
—Internet joke

You don't have to look far to find the stereotype of what won't work in a marriage—the accepted wisdom on dual-career couples is that when presented with a situation where they have to choose, someone will lose. So the first surprise is that this belief isn't backed up by the research. Instead, studies make it clear that dual-career couples have a high degree of love, sexual satisfaction, good communication and general higher marital quality. That is, with two provisos: this works so long as each partner is committed to both their career and their marriage;[16] and both agree that work is what they want to be doing and should be doing. Which is to say, traditionalists generally aren't happy if wives are forced to work because of financial circumstances.[17]

Overall, women who work full-time experience less anxiety and depression and better physical health than full-time homemakers. Unsurprisingly too, husbands of career women are more involved in caring for their children.[18] So how are these happy couples doing it?

Kate, 29, a plaintiff lawyer, and Julian, 30, a cardiac surgeon, have been juggling careers since they met not long after each had finished their initial studies. After a whirlwind romance—within six weeks of meeting at a dance party Kate moved in with Julian—they've been following each other around ever since.

'There was no real decision to be made,' says Julian. 'It was just "this feels right".' Still, the breeziness with which they tell this belies the sometimes complicated arrangements they have had to make. Five months after they shacked up together, Kate moved overseas to Montreal for a long-planned year of study. In the months she was away they talked on the phone everyday.

'The bills ran to thousands of dollars,' laughs Julian. 'I had to pay it off in instalments.'

When Kate came back, they moved back in together and bought a house three years later. Then, with Julian in training to be a cardiac surgeon, the couple faced another career tug. Just back from a stint in Bendigo in country Victoria, his college decreed that his next move would to be to Tasmania. But Julian knew that for Kate, Tasmania would have been professional suicide, even though she agreed to go.

'Kate has as much right to do what she wants in her career as I do,' he says. 'But the idea sometimes still seems to be that the female has to sacrifice or has more of a burden of responsibility in the home.' Instead, Julian said no. Though he doesn't say so, this was no mean feat in the arcane world of medical colleges, where patronage and favour rule and questioning isn't encouraged. But Julian knew Kate could find work up north so he transferred training colleges to make sure that his next move could be to Sydney, where they stayed for a year before heading back to Melbourne. As both see it, their story is really a simple tale of juggling two careers and neither sees anything particularly remarkable in that.

'I like it that Kate is in a high status job,' says Julian, laughing that her stories keep him grounded. 'I come home and whinge and moan and she says, "You think your day was hard?" She just tells me to get over it. We can bounce things off each other. There's a real difference between my father and myself in terms of the male perspective. My father felt the need to go out and earn a crust for the family. But with us, we support each other's career.'

> **Work v. Home**
> The three main ways work affects your relationships:
> ○ Time pressures (where work and family compete for your time)
> ○ Stress (where stress at home affects work or stress at work affects home)
> ○ Behaviour (where you have to act one way at work and another at home).
>
> These work both ways—work affects home and home affects work.[19]

The key to what makes a happy dual-career couple, according to Ellen Galinsky from the Work and Families Institute in Boston, isn't to do with work at all, but how you handle your priorities. Galinsky, with others, produced a study of 1200 dual-career executive couples. In her study six out of every ten high-achievers described themselves as 'work-centric'. No surprises there. But more intriguing to Galinksy was another group—the happiest group—the three in ten couples who gave equal priority to their lives and job. She coined the term 'dual-centric' to describe them. These couples worked a little less—around five hours fewer per week than the work-centric couples—but significantly, they felt they were more successful in their jobs than the workaholics or the family-focussed group on either side. And fewer of them experienced high stress, an affect particularly notable in women. In fact, the authors found that women at the very highest levels in companies were more likely to have children and feel a sense of balance than women at the next rung down. These top women were also no more likely to have delayed or decided against committed relationships than women in lower status executive jobs.

'Managing work and personal/family life is not a zero-sum game, where if people give to one aspect of their lives, they necessarily take away from the others,' writes Galinsky. She also noted that even calling them 'dual-centric' wasn't strictly true for some, who also maintained other interests in the arts or sport. So how did they do it?

Galinsky found these jugglers were effective at separating the competing demands in their lives, and didn't let one area intrude into another, so they'd tell her things like: they wouldn't come home with work; they didn't work on weekends or in the evenings; and they mentally kept work at work, so at home they were 100 per cent there.

Talking with Kate and Julian I heard similar principles. 'I work really hard at work but I have a rule—I don't work weekends,' says Kate. 'I'm a plaintiff lawyer so every day I deal with tragedy—injured people and awful cases like the death of children—but home is your sanctuary. It's no use unburdening that on your partner. I prefer to come home and walk the dog and get on with domestic bliss. I don't even like discussing work now. It's not about not enjoying the job—but I like to keep it in work hours. Your partner's not for work, they're there to make your life happier and more joyous.'

'The real issue of managing work and personal life boils down to how people assess and decide about priorities, about what's most important for them to do at any given moment and over time,' concludes Galinsky.[20]

Home-work

> Today English-speaking women expect more of life and often demand it. This naturally applies to their husbands. The husband usually leaves the house in the morning not to return until evening. His varied contacts during the day, his experiences, trials, successes and accomplished plans may gladden his hours of work. When he returns home, his running comment may be his wife's greatest diversion, and he, the chief entertainer.
> **—Ira S. Wile,** *The Man Takes a Wife,* **1938**

It's not just the dual-careerists who find there's work and life tension to be negotiated. Thomas, 36, and Nancy, 34, look for all the world like a traditional white-picket fence family. Dating since they were teenagers and married since they were in their early twenties, Tom's now an executive, Nancy the stay-at-home mother of their three children. As we sit chatting around their kitchen table in the midst of a chaos of fresh paint and renovations they're clearly happy, but I find out that for them it's been quite a journey to get here.

Having grown up in the city, in their mid-twenties they moved west to the country, pursuing a career opportunity for Tom, who was working in real estate at the time. The job soured and they came back to the city. With Tom out of work, Nancy became the bread-winner and she took a job working at a supermarket.

'I wasn't too proud,' she says. 'It was more important for me to bring in the money. I could wait to find something I wanted to do.' As they were trying to also save for a house deposit, Nancy took on as many shifts as she could, sometimes working a 90-hour week. Then came the crunch. First Nancy hurt her back and shortly after came down with a bout of glandular fever. She was exhausted. Still, for six months she kept trying to work the long hours.

'It was really chronic fatigue,' she acknowledges now. 'But I never really accepted it. I was having injections as I was determined that that wasn't going to be the case.'

It wasn't working and Tom, by this stage employed in corporate finance, finally said, 'It's either our relationship or your job and I don't think your job's that exciting.' Nancy cut back to working five hours a day and started doing some training that was steering her along a management track. She also enrolled at university. Then they sat down and did the sums. With Tom also studying, and their courses coming in at $1000 each, it didn't add up.

'At that stage it was either "you can get these qualifications or I can get mine",' says Nancy. 'We were still renting, so we decided that his study was more important because eventually we were going to have children and I'd decided I wanted to be home with my children. That was our turning point.'

They set up some five-year plans, focussing on where they wanted to be. Tom's career became a joint project. To save for a house and so Tom could study for his Master of Commerce full-time, they bit the bullet and moved in with Tom's parents. Nancy found work in a bank to support them. Despite the family goodwill, it was, they agree, 'very strenuous on the relationship'.

Now, three kids and a renovated house later, Nancy happily stays home and Tom is on track with where he wants his career. Neither have regrets about the decisions they made.

'I involve myself with my children's lives. I am involved with preschool on the management committee and with playgroup co-ordinating so I'm using my skills, which I'd used in my management career,' says Nancy. 'I suppose I've got a bit of a hunger that I've got to feed for my own self.' Tom, for his part, says that while the hours he works mean that he's not always there for his kids, supporting Nancy at home means he never has to worry about them having the care they need. He also points out that just because he's the one who is paid to work doesn't mean he thinks any less of Nancy's judgement—he uses her constantly as a sounding board even as he knows others can underestimate her.

'I think the thing that most people miss with Nancy is she's the person that read my graduate diploma thesis and my masters thesis, she read all my MBA papers,' he says, adding she's more perceptive than him. 'She'll look at someone and say "don't like him, don't know why" and bugger me, six months later she'll be right.' Nancy, for her part, says they treat each other's work as equally important and whether they're talking about the playgroup or the management board they'll always talk out the day's problems. Most of all, she says, at the end of the day, they agree on what matters most: 'Everything's always centred around the family unit and about what we're wanting for our family.'

Crash and burn

> It must be admitted that the entangled motives of modern life have put a tremendous strain on the marriage relationship . . . instead of mutual respect for individuality the marital state may promote by the raw and primitive exhibition of human nature only mutual disillusionment and despair. There is no greater test of character than daily association with another person.
> **—Mabel Barbee Lee, 'The dilemma of the educated woman',** *Atlantic Monthly,* **1930**

While dual-career dynamism or a two-for-one work effort is fine while you're on the up, what happens when one of you goes into freefall? What do you do if what you're bringing home is nothing but grief?

Georgina and Martin moved to London five years ago in pursuit of work and adventure. At first it went well for both of them, Martin finding work in design and animation, and Georgina a job at the BBC. But in 2001, things suddenly went south for Martin and the jobs he'd found so readily when he first arrived dried up. He fell out of the industry, was unemployed, poor and the best work he could find was in a pub. Georgina, on the other hand, was hitting her stride. She had begun working in documentaries, a field she'd long aspired to.

'It was very depressing at times,' she says. 'We did have a few teary, big fights. Getting rejected is hurtful and Martin's pride was hurting. I wanted to help but instead it sounded like nagging: "Did you call X?"' They had to tighten their belts and Georgina became the main breadwinner. Dreams of travel and owning a house were put on hold. They soon weren't feeling like a dual-career, dual-income couple anymore.

This is the key to the problem. If you have difficulty in one area—work, for example—it can cascade into others, like income. So in one fell swoop you've just collected two tickets in the relationship-stress lottery, rather than one.

For Martin and Georgina's relationship to survive they had to go back to first principles. 'One of the most important things is that we have to share the same goals,' says Georgina. So a bit of adjustment was required. Georgina had to acknowledge she was probably the more ambitious of the two. 'I have to get to the top,' she says. Martin, for his part, let go a little. 'I have this strength that verges on a flaw in that I can make do. I can give very little importance to just about everything.' He clung to the mantra 'this too will pass'.

They decided that if simultaneously good careers couldn't always be a goal, they'd look for what else could be.

'We're both interested in travel,' says Georgina. 'And we both want to have kids.' In fact, rather than pulling them apart, both say coming through this period showed the strength of their relationship. Three years down the track the good news is that Martin is now back working in the design field—teaching design—and is studying for his masters. They're also travelling again and yes, looking for a house.

> **Grumpy old men**
> Husbands are more likely than wives to bring stresses home from work that then affects their partners. Husbands who have conflicts at work are also more likely to have a fight at home. By contrast, wives' workload and work-related stresses have little or no relationship to the wellbeing of their husbands or their interactions at home.[21]

Working it out

In the end it doesn't seem to matter if you're an ambitious dual-career couple, a traditional couple or a couple negotiating a set of different roles. Time after time, everyone I spoke to said pretty much the same thing: 'work is only one part of life'. It was as if having a career was somehow finally put back in the box. It's important, but it's not the only thing. And no matter how ambitious, they stopped being willing to do anything for a job. Instead, work had to function on their terms, which often meant coming to see a job as a means to an end—a financial end, a personal goal or a lifestyle—not a means in itself. But in such a work-oriented world, this stance is radical.

More than one person I spoke to made the point that they treated their marriage as well as they treated their career. And if they were willing to invest long hours and extra training to get ahead in work, they had to be willing to do that for their marriage as well. That included investing in their spouses' careers too, and this applied to dual-careerists who found ways to give each other the mental time-out from high pressure jobs, traditionalists who had two people working on one career, or jugglers taking turns. For all the importance of both respecting and working for each other's career success was hard to miss.

Interestingly, making those choices doesn't cost the other their career. Researchers have found that men who place a high priority on family earn more; and just as significantly, that women who place a high priority on family do not suffer in terms of subsequent earnings as much previous research has assumed.[22]

Extreme solutions

If ever a couple had to think about constantly maintaining what's important it's Leonie, 30, a film director, and Brad, 29, an engineer, who have made the dual-career juggle an extreme sport. Married for eight years, they moved to the United States two years ago when Leonie got a job offer in Los Angeles she couldn't refuse. Brad followed. The catch was, the job transfer he was able to make with his company saw him heading to another city—San Franscisco.

'I got offered the job I'd been aspiring to since before we got married,' says Leonie. Brad says he had always known that he was the one who would probably have to do the moving, acknowledging the nature of Leonie's industry meant that there were only a few companies in a few cities where she could make a good living. Engineering was a lot more portable. And he points out, 'The job opportunity for me over here has been good for my career too.' So the question wasn't whether Leonie should take the job, but rather, how could they make it work? From the start they agreed the one thing that wasn't negotiable was their marriage.

When they began their two-city living they set out a few basic rules to make sure they maintained a real sense of intimacy and connection. 'When I first got here I got instant messaging for my computer,' says Leonie. 'We both did. So we message each other three or four times a day. We speak on the phone at least once a day.' They also spend every weekend together and for two years now, every Friday one or the other has hopped on a train to commute to the other's city. Occasionally, both will catch a train somewhere new that they can explore together.

They make sure the time they spend together is very organised and focussed. 'We're conscious we don't fritter away the time spent together,' says Leonie. 'I tend to invest heaps of time in figuring out what we can do together that's fun. One day one might go the gym while the other does the washing, then we might go to an art gallery. Or if Brad wants to watch a game, that gets scheduled in.'

Not that they're pretending it's easy: to have a full life, each has also had to carve out separate interests in each city. 'It's actually very hard to make friends when you are in the other person's city every second weekend,' points out Brad. 'It took me two years to make a group of quite good friends.'

How long can they keep this up? Two years into a three-year contract, Leonie says confidently, 'We can do another year.' But she adds, 'You've got us on a good week.'

Last September was a different story. Things weren't going well at Leonie's work. 'I was sitting there thinking, "What am I doing? I'm sacrificing my marriage for a job that sucks".' She had a holiday by herself back in Australia for three weeks as Brad didn't have leave available. The last straw came when she returned. Flying back to Los Angeles, Leonie had wanted Brad to pick her up at the airport. But he had been training for three months to run a half marathon at the time she arrived.

'I took it as "You love the marathon more than you love me",' she says. 'I landed back in Los Angeles with no one to greet me.'

'And I did the half marathon with no one to greet me either,' counters Brad.

It was their sorest point. 'By far most of our arguments are when one or the other feels like the other person has higher priorities than you,' says Leonie.

Both had had a gutful. But somehow, the crisis passed. 'As soon as we saw each other again it all worked out,' says Leonie.

They agree the hardest part is maintaining intimacy. 'I think one of the toughest things for me is when it comes to emotional support,' says Brad. 'Your primary emotional support can shift from your partner to your colleagues. It's probably happened to both of us. The first person you turn to if you're having problems is one of your colleagues.'

'There are worse things than cheating,' agrees Leonie. 'I think worse is either or both of us finding our primary emotional support is someone other than the person you're married to.' She goes on to say, however, 'I can't think of a time we thought the marriage is on the skids. If there's a problem we just negotiate.'

'I agree,' says Brad. 'I have never even thought the marriage was on its last legs. I'm a ridiculous optimist. I've never thought there was a crisis that was unsolvable, though that's not to say we haven't been through points when it's been stressful.'

While both say the next move will have to be in the same city— 'I think we need a period of consolidation,' says Leonie—they also say they'd probably do it again if the need arose.

'We both know the relationship is a priority,' says Leonie. 'We make that the centre.'

To sum it up

- Finding time for a career and a marriage is one of the biggest challenges for couples.
- Even the most ambitious couples can find ways to communicate to each other that their careers are but one part of their lives.
- Happy couples find practical ways to support each other's careers as well as their own.
- Finding a way to achieve balance not only makes you happier at home, it makes you more successful at work.

9

THE 'C' WORD:
CHILDREN

Bearing and rearing a child should withdraw a mother from fixed outside occupation for at least a year. Arrangements born out of conflict cannot change this primitive fact. Women should not do shop- or factory-work during the last months before childbirth, and babies should be nursed from seven to nine months. A baby should be nursed for twenty minutes every two or three hours of its waking time, and since it does not always waken regularly, the nursing mother is debarred from continuous work even if it does not interfere with her effectiveness as a milk producer.
—Earl Barnes, 'Women in Industry', *Atlantic Monthly***, 1912**

It's a sultry, overcast Monday morning in Sydney's pretty Petersham Park. Standing next to a big yellow truck, Trisha is eyeing the sky doubtfully.

'We'll set up,' she says. 'Hopefully the weather will hold.' Trisha runs the Magic Yellow Bus, a thirty-year-old local institution that travels around five inner-city parks each week as a mobile playgroup. Today they've pulled over in a park that also sports a pool, playground and track, so there's plenty of curious passing trade to join the regulars who are drawn to Trisha and her two assistants as they busily assemble the soft, squidgy clambering equipment, rocking horses, tables with painting and drawing activities.

By 9.30 a.m., the first groups of parents have arrived and are spreading out blankets, pushing kids on swings and sipping takeaway coffee. Anywhere up to 100 adults and children can turn up on Mondays, the busiest day. Mostly they're mums, rolling up in the twos and threes that are mothers' groups, though half a dozen dads are scattered across the ground, along with a couple of grandparents and nannies.

It might be the groovy inner city but it's fair to say the majority of parents here are married. Most are stay-at-home parents too—the full-time workers can't generally make playgroup. I wander over to the baby section, where a group of mums are playing with their rolling, lolling pre-toddlers on a big vinyl square. There are Lisa and Rebecca, mates from their mothers' group. Lisa is here with her third child, young Zac, while Rebecca, watching one-year-old Jade, now has a second on the way.

'Does having a child change your relationship?' I ask. Both chuckle. Wrong question. I rephrase: 'How does having a child change your relationship?'

'Lots of ways,' says Liz. 'Less time for each other.'

'You're less focused on your relationship,' reels off Rebecca. 'When you're having problems they can escalate simply because you hardly have the time to chat about what the issue is.'

'And good, there's also good,' she hastens to finally add as both laugh again. 'It's a different level obviously, sharing the joy of raising the kids together and talking about what you see is the future for your kids. There's a good, fun part as well.'

Many experts will tell you there are only two kinds of marriages:

those with children and those without. The differences don't always look pretty. Because while you might be walking about love-struck by baby, that little bundle of chaos can soon make your marriage look like a disaster zone—you spend less time alone with your spouse and are doing fewer of the joint things you used to love doing together. Almost inevitably you're fighting more while having less sex.[1]

It's the great irony, really. Not only is having a baby—a rite of passage nine out of every ten couples will choose[2]—the worst thing you can do to your sex life, it's also one of the worst things you can do to your marriage: two-thirds of couples say their 'marital quality' declines following the birth of their baby.[3] So why are babies bad news for marriage?

> **What baby bust?**
> Married women are no less likely to have a child today than they were twenty years ago: 87 per cent of wives have a child by the time they reach the ages of 35–39, compared to 86 per cent in 1986. What has changed is the proportion of women marrying in their twenties and early thirties. It's this and the decline in having larger families that is really contributing to lower fertility rates.[4]

First of all, there's the shock of the new. Researching first-time mothers, Dr Wendy LeBlanc of Macquarie University concluded that the vast majority were stunned by the impact the arrival of their first child had on their lives. LeBlanc describes mothers as feeling isolated and undervalued, with the vast majority believing they're coping badly.[5] Brigid, now 34, remembers the sheer shell shock of coming home with baby Patrick.

'I found it really difficult. It was a very big shock because as a woman, I'd always done what I wanted to do,' she says. 'I got up when I wanted to get up and I went home and did whatever. It just didn't work like that anymore.' She was also having trouble breastfeeding. 'I don't think I got up from the lounge room for four months except to go to bed and come back.'

Nor were she and husband Andrew, 37, on the same page, at least at first. Married for seven years, Brigid's pregnancy was a surprise for her. She was 29 at the time. 'I thought, "I'm far too young to have a baby",' she says. However, she quickly embraced her new direction: 'I became focused and oriented on being healthy and sidelined work.' But at the same time, Andrew was going in quite the opposite direction, having just begun a challenging new job. 'You're not experiencing the body stuff and we didn't have any previous children, so why would it have to change?' he says of his expectations, admitting, 'I was a little work-obsessed in some ways.' It wasn't until after Patrick arrived and Andrew realised the impact parenting had, that his priorities changed.

Andrew and Brigid's experience is typical. Most relationships feel this stress. Indeed, some can't endure it. In LeBlanc's study seventeen per cent of the women said their relationship didn't survive the first three years after baby—a factor they directly attributed to having their child. Another third said they stayed with partners they would otherwise have left because they felt the partner provided greater security.[6]

The baby blues

The baby blues are a fact of life for eighty per cent of women who give birth. These appear somewhere between the third and tenth day after giving birth and bring changeable moods—both high and low—tearfulness and feelings of being overwhelmed. These feelings usually only last a couple of days. But around 10 per cent of women will get the more serious postnatal depression, the symptoms appearing within the first three to six months after giving birth.[7]

Then there's the challenge of suddenly changing roles. In her book, *Misconceptions*, Naomi Wolf describes with surprise how, 'All around me, it seemed that the baby's birth was cleaving couple after couple—once equals in roles and expectations—along the lines of the old traditional gender roles.' It was an experience she saw reflected in her own life when she found herself, 'with a tiny baby, staring out the kitchen window into the backyards of the suburbs, living life much as I had read about it in *The Feminine Mystique*. The baby's arrival acted as a crack, then a fissure, then an earthquake that wrenched open the shiny patina of egalitarianism in the marriage of virtually every couple I knew.'[8]

It's true: research consistently shows that new parents do divide chores along gender lines. And because it's hard to feel on the same side if you stop feeling like equals, unsurprisingly, this division of housework is often a source of dissatisfaction and conflict, particularly if the traditional gender roles become crystallised in daily routines, something, just like Wolf, most new mothers don't see coming.[9] Indeed, it's estimated that when an infant joins the household, the total workload of the household goes up by one quarter, with an additional 400 tasks to be performed. It's an extra load which, statistically, the wife almost entirely picks up on their own.[10] Unsurprisingly then, one of the easiest ways to predict if a woman is happy in her relationship is the extent to which her partner meets her expectations in terms of support and shared parenting responsibilities.[11]

There's also the unexpected baggage you bring to parenting from your own childhood. Darren, who I met in the park with eight-month-old Lily, puts it this way: 'Because you're both brought up differently, you have different ideas on about how to bring up a baby. It's the clash of two ideologies—"my mum brought me up this way". You rear your kids how you were reared. For me this created arguments.' He adds that for fathers these differences can be particularly difficult to negotiate. 'Because mums are home all day with the baby, they look after it a certain way. When you come home they give it to you, but then they want you to look after it their way.' In other words, you may also be ricocheted back to how it was at the start of your relationship, when you were negotiating all the rules of how you were going to live together.

Still, more than anything, it's worth revisiting that old relationship-stress list at the beginning of chapter 7: money, careers and kids. You don't have to think too long to see that a baby hits you with this triple whammy. All of a sudden the household income drops just when you get the additional expenses of a child. Someone has to put their career on hold, at least for a while. In LeBlanc's study, new parents found one of the biggest stresses was the conflict between pressure to return to work and the desire to stay home with their child. It's a lose–lose scenario: those who stayed home felt isolated and undervalued, while the majority of those returning to work said they'd rather be home with their children. Add to this the sleeplessness, the repetitive manual labour and sheer exhaustion of parenthood. Cumulatively, all these differences place enormous pressure on relationships. Something has to give and, unfortunately, that can be the two of you. The only worse patch for marriages—the lowest point in marital satisfaction in the life course of the marriage—is around the time when the first child becomes a teenager.[12]

> **Actually, your kids aren't driving you crazy . . .**
> Australian researcher David De Vaus has found that when it comes to parental sanity (he was looking at mental health statistics) the good news is that children don't increase or decrease a parent's risk of developing a mental illness; so contrary to what you might think, your kids aren't driving you crazy. In fact, they're doing the complete opposite. De Vaus' research showed that the women at least risk of a mental disorder are married, working and had children. The next least-at-risk women are the married full-time mothers. And the people most at risk? Men who aren't married and don't have children or a job.[13]

All this might seem like the bad news. The good news, though, is that not every couple is the same. After having a child some couples show significant *improvements* in their marriage, have more sex, feel closer and solve problems better.[14] And we're only just starting to understand what it is that makes the difference.

Research by Alyson Shapiro (from John Gottman's Relationship Research Institute) turned up something very interesting. While she did indeed confirm the quality of marriage declines for most couples after the arrival of a baby (a downward slide that might not show up until a year or even two after the birth) the surprise was, kids don't deliver a marriage hit for everyone. Around a third of couples found their marriages either improved or stayed stable. Where it got really interesting was when Shapiro teased out the key to these happier couples—and found it was the husband.

'If the husband is aware of his wife and attentive, it helps them make it through this stressful time,' she writes, pointing particularly to the importance of the husband expressing his fondness for his wife. 'Similarly, when the wife is aware of her husband and his contribution, she is more likely to give him the benefit of the doubt when she may be preoccupied with the baby.' So, once husbands actively come on board and support their wives—as well as their babies—the relationship gets a whole lot better.

The three big keys for husbands that Shapiro lists are:
- building a fondness and affection for your partner;
- being aware of what is going on in your spouse's life and being responsive to it;
- approaching problems as something you and your partner have control of and something you can solve together as a couple.[15]

Being in this together—being allies—is something that matters in big ways and small. It can be about husbands being willing to take on additional household tasks (something that Michael Bittman's research shows they're starting to do) but it's also about finding ways to create a sense of family together—particularly when, in addition to all your concerns about jobs, finances and extra workloads, just like at the wedding, all of a sudden your families are back. If you're lucky they're there with help, but at other times it's more 'helpful advice'.

Consider Catherine, whose mother and mother-in-law had both worked professionally with children for years. One day, after too many tips from them, she finally turned to husband Greg and said, 'I feel like I'm on work experience. Everything I say and do with my children is being analysed.' It's not like Catherine was being a slouch: she was doing parenting classes. And the mothers were being helpful, but Catherine's sense of being able to cope by herself was being steadily undermined. More than anything, though, she needed an ally. So obeying the golden rule—you deal with things within your own family—Greg had to find a way to talk to his mother about toning it down.

'She was going to write down some helpful points,' recalls Greg. 'So what I said was, "Catherine really appreciates that neither her mother or you tells us how to raise our children".' Score one point for a better marriage.

Stay-at-homers

> I believe that a woman who wants both career and children should delay the children until she has achieved such permanence in her art that she can lay it aside temporarily without injury, or until she has had such success that she can ensure her future by the employment of capable household assistants. To care for a young career and a young child at the same time is to run the risk of making a weakling of each.
> **—Worth Tuttle, 'A feminist marries',** *Atlantic Monthly,* **January 1934**

One of the most vexed questions is, of course, does how you structure a household make a difference here? Are stay-at-homers better off than dual-careerists when it comes to marriages with children?

In the park, Louise, 35, is spreading down a tartan picnic rug alongside Ann and Libby, two members of her mothers' group. They have been meeting together for four years—ever since the Sydney Olympics, when their first children were born. Now each has a second child as well and all three are full-time mums. This is a choice around one third of women with children will choose according to the work of British sociologist Catherine Hakim.[16] Talking to each of these women, it was interesting to hear the very different reasons they'd made the stay-at-home choice.

For Louise, formerly a solicitor and married to a partner in a law firm, this decision was borne of traumatic circumstances. Her first pregnancy was terminated at 19 weeks when the baby was found to have very serious, and unsolvable, health problems. 'You're planning a new life together and then all of a sudden you're planning a funeral, all in the space of a couple of days,' she says, her voice still cracking with the memory. 'We both changed a lot with that experience. I think if it hadn't been for Eve—that's her name—there would have been a lot more pressure from Patrick for me to go back to work,' says Louise. 'I think that's probably what I would have done. It just made us pause and take stock about what's important.' So rather than letting the grief wedge them apart it drew them closer together. But it also changed Louise's perspective on what really mattered to her. So while her husband is still logging the long hours, Louise is taking a step back for a few years with only vague long-term plans to return to work— perhaps part-time.

For Ann, 34, the decision to stay home was as much about commonsense as anything. A preschool teacher, it just didn't seem smart to put her two kids, Harry and Samantha, into day care, and then go teach children the same age somewhere else. Even so, she says, she found the transition from worker to stay-at-homer hard.

'You go from working with adults and being out and about all the time, to being at home on your own with a baby,' she says, 'just not feeling as independent and earning your own money.' It was a theme I heard often. Ann and her husband had always pooled their earnings and hadn't done the 'my money/your money' system for years but even so 'that was really hard in the beginning,' she confesses.

Rebecca, who's with a different group here, found her hand was forced when it came to being a stay-at-home parent. She was expecting to go back to part-time work with her firm after she finished her maternity leave, but when she was ready to return the part-time work option was refused. Having also had an earlier offer of promotion retracted when she announced her pregnancy, she took her company to court. Her case was upheld on the promotion, but not the right to part-time work. This decision thrust Rebecca and her husband into a very traditional arrangement where he worked extra hours to make up for the income shortfall. That, too, took its toll.

'We'd be niggling at each other at little things,' she says. 'And the feelings I had about not contributing to the household income brought in a whole mixture of emotions. Dropping a whole income meant losing a whole complete freedom in choosing what I bought and when I bought.' They resolved some of those feelings by moving control of all the household finances over to her. Still, Rebecca recently confronted the identity of motherhood versus career again.

'I signed myself up recently to do some market research on the side,' she says. 'They always ask you your profession and I looked at the form and thought, I can't answer that, because I'm not one anymore.'

'What did you put?' asks Lisa.

'I put unemployed,' says Rebecca. 'These surveys don't have the option of "home duties" or "full-time mum" so I found myself ticking the "unemployed" box because there was nothing else.' Negotiating new identities can be an ongoing process for some.

Libby, 39, here with Ann and Louise, has no regrets about giving up work. 'I certainly don't miss it. I don't have this yearning for full-time work, and certainly not a career,' says the former recruitment manager. 'Now the biggest thing is trying to think of things to do every day.' And while she says she might go back to work in a couple of years, 'I just want something simple, no big responsibilities.'

Still, while they've revelled in the time at home, they are all enjoying the fact that their kids are getting older so they can start thinking like being part of a couple again. Ann's now celebrating the fact that with the kids old enough to go and stay with their grandparents in the country (three-year-old Henry has already been for his first solo visit) she and her husband can begin to find time just for the two of them again. But for Ann, just like Louise, what's made the biggest difference through this period is having a supportive partner.

'He works for himself, so if I really needed a break or time out he'd come home early or go in late.' He's also hands-on with bathing and nappy changing. 'I'll go out for girls' nights and he stays home with the kids,' Ann says, adding, 'I don't think I would have married somebody who wasn't that way inclined.' And they make plans to help stay connected as a couple. 'It's making time to have a chat about ourselves and where we see ourselves. Talking about five-year plans and two-year plans so there is a focus of life beyond kids, for us as adults.'

'How about your friends who have gone back full-time,' I ask the group. 'Do you think there's a difference?'

'Definitely,' says Louise. 'They're all so stressed I don't see them that often, trying to balance family and work.'

'I actually don't know anyone who has,' says Libby.

'Not that works full-time, no,' agrees Ann.

'Wow, if I was to return to full-time work . . .' begins Louise, shaking her head with wonder. 'You'd have to buy in a lot of help, which would defeat the purpose of going back to work—pay for childcare, cleaning, people to help you out . . .'

'Takeaway,' adds Libby.

All three sit in silence shaking their heads. It doesn't make sense to any of them.

Still, while these women are in a fairly traditional arrangement right now, they don't seem to have traditional attitudes. They expect their husbands to be hands-on, and the fact the guys have been has clearly made a difference. For this group, at least, this is a temporary state of affairs and a few of them assume they'll be back in the workforce soon, at least part-time. What about a couple who are more conservative, I wonder. How do they square their roles with each other and is their experience any different?

> **The opt-out revolution**
> In a comparison of dual-career couples across eleven countries, researchers found the most educated and economically privileged women—who in theory could wield the greatest career power—were in fact less likely to be employed and more likely to chose the 'traditional sexual division of labour'. The bewildered researchers concluded that that this 'casts doubt on whether women wish to achieve economic autonomy of equality', and instead suggested that the interplay between personal and families strategies was complex. Dual-income earners were also likely to have less children, but this effect was smallest in Belgium, Sweden and Italy, 'countries with more generous social provisions in support of maternal employment'. Australia, with few provisions in this area, ranked lower.[17]

Andrew and Sarah describe themselves as traditional and for them the decision for Sarah, 31, to stay home was made easier—and more complicated—by the fact that Andrew, 47, had two teenage daughters by his previous marriage, who were spending increasing amounts of time living with the couple. Today, with three daughters of their own, Andrew and Sarah's house is filled with kids from nappies to high school.

'We're at the stage where Sarah's been introduced to lying awake at one o'clock in the morning waiting for someone to come home,' admits Andrew grimly. 'It does put stress on the two of us. Most marriages have stress. This really doubles it I think. We don't get a lot of time with each other because of the young children and because of older children.'

In fact, it was his previous experience that coloured Andrew's views on what worked and what didn't in a marriage with children. Previously married to a driven career woman—'everything had to be equal and split down the middle'—the relationship ended acrimoniously. He wasn't keen to go down that path again.

'When Annabelle was born one of the first things Sarah said was, "Now I've got to work out when I'm going back to work",' he relates. 'I said, "Why do you want to do that?"' Her reasons, he says, sounded more like social expectation than something she actually wanted. But having had a rising career in the advertising industry and a significant salary, work wasn't something Sarah was initially willing to drop. When the baby was nine months old, Sarah took up a one-month contract to test the waters. It was this experience that sealed it.

'It was just a disaster,' she says. 'It was too hard and trying to get childcare and dropping off and picking up—I didn't have the energy or time to do anything else. Just go to work and come home, try and cook a meal. For me it wasn't satisfying at all and I'm not the kind of person that can put my children in day care for ten hours a day.' So staying home it would be. Still, the decision took some psychological getting used to.

'I think society sees staying home as a poor option,' she says. 'You're a nobody, you've got no brains and you're not an interesting person. It took me a while to realise it is a valuable job.' Nowadays Sarah and Andrew are happy to describe themselves in traditional terms. 'I think another reason why it's worked really well is because we're defined in what we do,' says Andrew. 'I do change nappies but Sarah takes on ninety per cent of the mothering. She's a great mother.'

For Sarah, the kind of emotional support she gets from Andrew is also something she looks for in her friends. 'When you opt out of the workforce and you become a mother, you don't get a lot of praise,' she says. 'You don't get your boss coming to you and saying you're doing such a good job here's a pay rise, and you don't get a review every year. Now I socialise with other stay-at-home mothers. We praise each other because not many other people give you praise for it. We all build each other's morale and cheer each other on.'

> **Don't mention the 'm' word**
> A recent study by Curtin University Business School found that some young women feel it's embarrassing—and a risky career move—to even mention they would like to be mothers. The study also found that women feel they face stark choices and substantial costs when it comes to children: they fear the economic penalties for being absent from the paid workforce, the loss of financial independence and the lack of recognition and status of those who stay home.[18]

The careerists

> The wage-earning wife is quite likely to love her husband the more because of his limitations. If his limitations extend to his earning capacity she is not helpless before it, for she appreciates her own capacity to earn.
> **–Jane Littell, 'Meditations of a wage-earning wife',** *Atlantic Monthly,* **1924**

While the stay-at-homers are the biggest group at the Magic Yellow Bus, they're not the only ones here. At the top of the park pushing blond, curly-haired Oliver on a swing is Louise, 34. Unlike most women here she is a full-time worker, but because she works shifts as a flight attendant, she can still meet with her mothers' group on Mondays. Unlike what some stay-at-home parents imagine, Louise says she hasn't found having a child and working full-time a problem for her relationship.

'I love being married,' she says. 'And the commitment between my husband and I is deeper, just seeing what we've created. With a child you just basically look into their cot and fall in love everyday.' It's a feeling she contrasts with how you can come to see your partner.

'With a husband, you have the initial falling in love but then you just love each other—it's not a constant feeling of awe,' she says, adding that having a child enhanced their feeling for each other. 'I think it deepened our relationship. It made it stronger when we worked together. Of course now we might get more snappy with each other,' she admits of the increased workload, 'but we don't actually spit insults at each other. We normally start talking and working it through.' Again, it's that sense of teamwork, of each putting in the effort that Shapiro identified, that seems to be what's making the difference. It's something that becomes very important when two careers are part of the parenting–relationship mix.

If there ever was a couple who had the dual-career, dual-parenting marriage thought out and lived out, you'd be hard pressed to find bigger champions than Juliet, 39, and Ian, 46, who have been married ten years. I'm meeting them from precisely 7 p.m. until 8 p.m. on a Tuesday night in a cafe. The time is exact because with two careers and two children, everything is precisely scheduled, and this is when the regular babysitter is booked. Both originally lawyers, Juliet and Ian met at work and were friends before they became lovers. They had also both been in previous long-term relationships—Ian had been married thirteen years, Juliet part of a long-term de facto couple—which they say colours how they treat this relationship.

'We give it priority,' says Ian.

Children were also part of their picture from the start, with Juliet falling pregnant on their honeymoon.

'It was all legit,' she laughs, 'though some of our friends were counting.' Equity, too, was part of the plan and when Jesse, now nine years old, was born Juliet looked after him for the first three months, then Ian took the next three. After that they hired a nanny. But when Eliza, now four years old, came along the pattern had to change. Ian, by now a barrister, couldn't take the same time out, so the primary care fell to Juliet, who had by then also moved on to running her own business. But both say the original experiment made a difference.

'I think it was very important to do that with Jesse,' says Juliet to Ian. 'It gave you a sense that you could do the job and me a sense that I could let you do it—I didn't have to be in control all the time.' That's important, she says, because she travels more than Ian to conferences and while she's away, 'Ian has full-time custody and I have no concerns about that.'

With both working long hours they've also been careful to find ways of putting the family first. For example, Ian always gets home between 6 and 6.30 p.m. each night to have time with the kids, and it's only once they're in bed that he'll often turn around and go back to work—a benefit, he says, of choosing to live close to the city. 'I can drive into town and I'm there in five minutes. There are too many lawyers who spend enormous hours—you hear stories of barristers who don't know their children's names and it's just not worth it.'

Juliet and Ian are continuing to find creative ways to adapt. With Jesse now in school and Eliza there next year, the nanny has recently gone. So, today Ian took the morning off while Juliet went to a meeting. Apart from that, most days Juliet juggles her time around preschool, some very helpful grandparents and a babysitter. They still, however, also concentrate on keeping the relationship front and centre; since Jesse was born they've set aside Tuesday night for each other, a strategy Juliet picked up years before when she was a nanny and the couple she worked for did the same.

'It's really important to the kids that mummy and daddy are having time alone together,' she says. 'They see us prioritising our relationship and they feel quite content that we have a good relationship.' It's a strategy they highly recommend to everyone—dedicated, structured time together every week.

'If you don't schedule it, it won't happen,' says Juliet. 'There's always something that comes up. It's only two hours, but it's quite workable.' And Friday nights are set aside for family.

It makes sense why this works for them. One study found that women are more likely to rate their work patterns as fair—and be satisfied in their marriages—when they get companionship and emotional support for themselves and interest in the children from their husband. Another study found that when partners spend social time together and achieve a sense of intimacy, both men and women rate the division of labour as more fair, and are appreciative of what each other does for a day's work.[19]

'Underlying it all is a respect for the other person's work,' says Juliet. 'We know the other person's priority is the family. If they're working back, it's because they have to do it.' So passionate is Juliet about this area of work and family balance that she's set up a company called Life+Work Balance that helps businesses implement anti-discriminatory work practices. She leads by example. Having established the company shortly after the birth of her second child, she quickly laid down the rules to clients. 'I don't start work until ten in the morning, and I'm breastfeeding, so you'll need to provide me with breastfeeding facilities,' she tells them. It was a risk, she admits, but if she wanted to help companies become more family friendly, there was no better place to start. She's also turned her attention to how businesses—including her own—measure professionalism, success and delivery of service.

'Some of my clients pay me in hours but others pay me in the outcome of the project,' she says. 'They don't care how many hours I do or where I do the hours or when I do the hours, so long as I achieve it. Prioritising work and family doesn't have to be mutually exclusive.'

The jugglers

> It has been repeatedly shown that only around half of the women graduates of our colleges and universities marry; and those that do marry give birth to strikingly small numbers of children, their average being less than two per couple.
> —**Louis I. Dublin, 'Homemaking and Careers',** *Atlantic Monthly***, 1926**

As is fitting for Generation Choice, the largest group of parents are at the halfway mark between the stay-at-homers and the full-time workers. These are the jugglers—couples who try different work arrangements that they adjust as their circumstances change. It's a description that fits almost six in ten parents with dependent children: they're dual-income earners, but most frequently the woman is working part-time.[20]

They're couples like Andrew and Brigid who we met earlier. After the initial shock of adjusting to family life they have gone on to try nearly every combination imaginable when it comes to caring for their two sons Patrick and Joseph. With Patrick, Brigid had a year off on maternity leave and then Andrew took the next year off.

'You don't get many opportunities like that,' he says. 'I was really happy to do that and make the most of it.' After that, both worked part-time. Not all couples could make this work financially, but for Andrew and Brigid this juggling was made viable by an unusual family set-up. When Patrick was born they sold their own kit-built rural log home to move in with Brigid's family. Subsequently they built their own home on the same large block. Now seven years later, the families still cook together most nights, and Brigid's mother often helps with the kids during the day. It's a very normal arrangement for Brigid, who grew up in her grandmother's house with her extended family all around.

'I'm very close to my mum, so when things aren't going well here I can easily just go there,' she says with a glint. 'I don't have to pack my bags, I can just walk across. To be able to live with all that,' she adds, 'makes Andrew a remarkable person'.

They admit, though, the closeness can have its downsides. 'At some of the more difficult times when I just wanted to say "Why am I married to this person?", pack my bags and get out, you think "Right, and we've tied up all our investments in her family too",' admits Andrew. But the upside of on-tap family support—and reduced financial pressure—has made it worthwhile.

'We definitely wanted to share the upbringing,' says Brigid. 'We wanted the boys to know both of us really well—that they didn't know just one, and the other one was off to work.'

When it came to looking after their second child, however, they weren't able to split the time 50/50. Andrew had just landed a challenging full-time job in Tasmania (chapter 8 tells you how well that went) and the family moved there, Brigid staying home with Joseph.

'It was the second child that was the huge lifestyle change,' says Andrew, who adds that the job change was in large part motivated by trying to get greater security over the long term. It didn't turn out to be a happy experience and, compared to the first time around, Andrew lost the close bonding time with his young son. Brigid, meanwhile, despite feeling isolated in Tasmania, came to revel in full-time parenting.

'I much prefer parenting to work. Much more fun,' she says. Two years on she's only recently returned to part-time work now that Joseph's reached preschool age. Now Andrew is looking forward to the kids getting older, when he and Brigid can share the income-earning burden more.

'I can see myself doing more and more community voluntary work,' he says, then looks at Brigid with a grin. 'And you're looking forward to the days when I take them camping for weeks on end.' Each having done parenting and earning, they understand each other, as well as their kids.

This 'walking-a-mile-in-another's shoes' is well understood by another of the dads by the bus, Hugh, 36. Bravely wearing a white shirt, he is holding a piece of paper at arm's length against an easel while his middle child, Aiden, 2, smears on a painting. Aiden's sister Madeline, 4, is in preschool and there's a third child on the way.

'That should be it,' says Hugh, 'then I'll have the operation.' Hugh and his wife Heather both work part-time—she's a casual drama teacher, he's in ministry and the media—which he says, 'allows us a 50/50 share of taking care of the children.'

'It's really healthy that I get to experience that so I can appreciate the importance of not staying at the office—getting some extra calls done—between five and six,' he says knowingly. 'I've felt how great it is when Heather comes home at that time when I'm getting the dinner ready and I've had a full-on day and it's so great that she comes home and has got energy for the kids because she's really missed them.' That attitude, he says, means their priority is keeping the relationship front and centre, which for him is also a Christian world view.

'God created Adam and Eve and there were no children at that time and he said it was very good. If you take that first model you find husband and wife are a family. If the child makes the family, they become the centre of the family and they're surpassing the importance of your partner. We don't want to be like couples can turn out to be when, after eighteen years, children leave home they're like, "What have we got? Nothing", because they've been orientated around their children's lives.'

Hugh says the great challenge is to maintain intimacy. 'With a child's demands it's very hard to do that,' he says thoughtfully. 'We work really hard getting babysitters and making sure we have time to ourselves to develop our relationship. A child can come between you and your partner or he or she can become an extension of your love together.'

Robyn Parker and Dr Michelle Simons from the Institute of Family Studies in Melbourne say there's an irony in how focused on the child marriages have become. 'Families become so child-centric—everything's for the child,' says Parker. 'We're having fewer children and they become little projects.' But, she points out, the research is clear. 'One of the best things you can do for the child is to maintain a connection with the person who is their biological mum or dad.'

'It's almost counter-intuitive,' agrees Simons. 'Do you have a choice of spending an extra fifteen minutes playing with your child on the floor, or do you put them somewhere safe and go and spend fifteen minutes talking with your partner?' It's something, she adds, that kicks against the grain, 'particularly when everyone else around you is focusing on the baby.' The big trap, she says, is kids defining the hours rather than making couple time, 'That's when you want to cuddle up in bed, and you want to have sex, but you're just so tired. It's about prioritising the couple.'

Simons and Parker can't help reflecting on their own lives. 'One of the things we did is that we trained our two children very early on to understand what Saturday mornings were,' says Simons. 'Saturday mornings were the time when Mum and Dad got a chance to spend time together. Originally we didn't have a lock on our bedroom door, but we ended up putting one on because the kids would sometimes forget.' She laughs, 'I remember when our daughter was about seven or eight, she'd come and stand outside and knock on the door—"Are you finished yet?" She'd have no idea what we were doing—"Are you finished yet? I want my Weetbix now".'

The mummy wars and the fatherhood revolution

> Without doubt, the lives of our women in Victorian days were far too monotonous. They were brought up to think of nothing but marriage and when married their thoughts hardly ever strayed beyond the four walls of their cages . . . men had the best of it. For they all had some interest outside the four brick walls—either in their professions or business, or in the outdoor work connected with their estates.
> **—Eileen Terry, *Etiquette for All*, 1925**

While most of the parents I talked with seemed happy enough with their choices, even as they all complained about not enough time to themselves or to spend on their relationships, it was interesting at times to hear their attitudes to each other.

'Why bother?' muttered more than one stay-at-home mother of the working mothers. 'I get quite angry with feminism,' said one juggler who reluctantly worked part-time, 'putting my child in day care isn't a choice.' Meanwhile a happy working mum looked at me bewildered at even the suggestion that she stay home. 'I'd go crazy if I was home all the time,' she said.

These different attitudes have been fashioned by commentators in the 'mummy wars' and they've spawned a whole literary genre that runs the gamut from the eternal struggle of parenthood—*The Price of Motherhood* (subtitled: *Why the most important job in the world is still the least valued*) and *What Our Mothers Didn't Tell Us* (subtitled: *Why happiness eludes the modern woman*)—which decry the domestic gulag. In the middle is, *She Works, He Works: How two-income families are happier, healthier, and better off*, which gives away it's own ending. While on other side of the fence is homemaker porn, such as the recent fictional sensation *I Don't Know How She Does It*, which sees the careerist-mother heroine eventually ride off into a muffin-baking sunset. But while they seem to take different sides, all these books have one thing in common: they mostly concentrate on what women are doing and sacrificing.

I think they're all looking in the wrong place and if we're after ways to improve the relationships parents have with each other they're giving us a false battle. Michael Bittman, the time-use researcher, pointed out that the sole area every survey could agree on was that today's fathers are spending more time with their children. That's the big change and it's happening now, in the space of one generation. The fathers I met pretty much felt they were facing the same choices as the mothers. Evan at the poker night, a former actuary now stay-at-home father, echoed the experience of stay-at-home mothers, by telling of people walking away from him at parties thinking he has nothing to say. Andrew, an IT professional, who planned for parenthood by rethinking his career; around the time he and wife Mandy started talking about babies he was offered the job he's always wanted—'lots of travel and car and lots of money, lots of hours,' he says. He knocked it back in favour of going out on his own and setting up his own small business from home. Why?

'It was definitely a conscious decision, knowing we were going to have kids, in a year's time,' he says. 'I didn't want to leave at six in the morning and get home after they got to bed. I wanted to be there as much as possible.' Four years on he's working from nine to five in a studio at the back of their house and sees his two kids at lunch as well as dinner.

There's also another Andrew. After the birth of his second child, Phoebe, he swapped being a journalist—which he'd always seen himself as, but which didn't pay well and didn't have family-friendly deadlines—for better-paid work in public relations. Now on firmer financial ground it would be wrong to say he's thrilled with his new profession.

'But in the context of marriage I did the right thing. If I was still a journalist the financial difficulties would have put such a strain on the family that we could have broken.'

These are all pragmatic choices, each with similar financial, personal or career penalties that women have long known come with parenthood. Evidence is increasingly showing that younger men mostly don't aspire to a model of traditional breadwinner–homemaker in a relationship, one United Kingdom study showing that the majority of younger men no longer endorse such a model as the one they aspire to.[21] And if you ask Australian men what model they prefer for a family, only just over one quarter are in the breadwinner camp, the majority preferring a more collaborative approach.[22] Men are changing, and new ways of parenting are being forged.

However, some are straining under the burden of it all. There's even a term for it—the Atlas Syndrome, named after the mythological figure forced to carry the sky on his shoulders. Sufferers are the have-it-all fathers trying to be breadwinners, cooks, cleaners and nappy changers, who are left 'exhausted, anxious, unfulfilled and depressed', according to Dr Tim Cantopher, who coined the term. In his practice he lists 34 doctors suffering from the syndrome as well as police officers and teachers.

> **Squeezing time**
>
> Men are spending more time with their children—considerably more than previous generations. The catch is that for eighty per cent of the time men are doing things with their kids, the mothers are present as well. This means they're not really freeing up much of their wives' time. Using paid childcare doesn't significantly lesson the amount of time women spend with their children either: they don't reduce their time on doing things like reading to their kids or playing with them. Women are squeezing this extra time by literally sleeping less, taking less time showering and dressing.[23]

'It's the curse of the strong,' he's quoted as saying. 'A modern condition, caused by the social and political changes affecting the role of men in society.'[24] To me this also sounds suspiciously like the problem dogging supermums. So really we have two terms for the same phenomenon: parents going under while trying to do it all and be it all, trying to play by this generation's values—be better parents, better friends, better lovers—while working to a previous generation's set of rules. For couples this means going out there without a guidebook—if you're making your own rules you have freedom, but you don't have guarantees. To make it work often requires very big changes.

The creatives

> Idealists and ravelers among primitive people love to tell us how easily women meet their special functions: carrying burdens equal to those carried by men, when on the march, and dropping out from the caravan for only a few hours to give birth to a child; but the fact remains that women in all primitive societies age quickly, and that those who are spoiled are thrown aside and forgotten. Women's handicap as a working animal in competition with man is too obvious and too deep-seated to be idealized away.
> —Earl Barnes, 'Women in Industry', *Atlantic Monthly*, 1912

For Kip, 40, who's in the park at the squidgy-soft clamber gym with daughter Leah, 21 months, deciding to have a family meant radical career changes, and career sacrifices, on both his and his wife's part. Having first met as research scientists specialising in environmental science, five years ago they started talking about children and realised a life in academic research wasn't going to work for them.

'It's quite clear cut—it's a very competitive environment to get research grants,' he relates in matter-of-fact British cheeriness. 'There are a lot of women I worked with who had probably given up the idea of family to do research.' He relates a surreal conversation with his head of department—a woman, childless—who urged him not to go down the family path as it would damage his career. Taking heed, he and his wife instead decided to change tack and moved into policy work in the public sector. This meant they were also able to share the parenting. In the year Leah was born, his wife took off the first six months, while he took the second, then after that, both went part-time, and on Wednesday Leah goes to family day care. In this work environment Kip's not a part-time oddity, with three women in his department doing the same, but he does say that 'the colleagues I have that are quite a lot older—in their fifties—find what I'm doing quite foreign. Certainly the people I was with in research don't understand my giving up my career. A lot don't see why I'd even advocate taking time out to be a dad.'

Changing careers wasn't the only radical step Kip and his partner took, though. An hour later as I'm sitting under a tree writing up my notes, Kip circles back around pushing Leah's pram energetically out in front. 'There's one other thing that we've noticed with all of our friends with children like ourselves,' he says. 'The main thing that constrains them from having the balance we've got is the money it costs to live in Sydney.' What Kip and his partner have done—which their friends haven't—is delay getting the mortgage, so they currently still rent. With Leah heading towards two years of age they're looking to buy a home on the outskirts of the city rather than in the fashionable inner west where we are right now.

'We'll still commute by public transport,' he says. 'But it means we'll get a mortgage based on our two part-time salaries, rather than our two full-time salaries. All through the inner west people need two salaries to buy a house and it's a lot more difficult in their marriages, the stress comes because they're working five days a week each and they're trying to do all the family things on the weekend.'

A surprising number of couples I met were experimenting with new ways to keep their relationship healthy, their career on track and still be hands-on parents. Like Anthony and Eleanor, who would be the first to tell you they were in a fortunate position. Shortly before their first child was due, Anthony, a financier who had worked around the world, found his company was in the middle of a takeover. His job was changed, but rather than go with redeployment, he asked for a redundancy. This meant he was at home when daughter Brigid was born.

> **Does it pay to have children?**
> In the past there were two obvious reasons to have children: firstly, there was poor birth control, so you didn't have much choice; secondly, children were there to work and support their parents in their old age, so raising them was an investment which offset the costs of raising them. But today, in economic terms at least, parental investment is being diminished. The earning power of children has dropped and children's support of parents in old age has disappeared from family accounts. At the same time, child-rearing costs have escalated and the length of time children are dependent on their parents has increased. In short, parents have effectively been disinherited from the payoff of family, while the costs have risen enormously. So from a simple economic standpoint, parents are being asked to do more and more with less and less.[25]

'At first it was a blissful dream,' he says of the two-parent solution. 'It wasn't the dramatic shift people characterise, more an emerging change. It was a gradual shift into parenthood. Brigid was a completely easy kid. I guess the biggest thing for me was being home and better understanding.'

'I didn't experience what a lot of women go through—the isolation—I always had intellectual stimulation,' agrees Eleanor. 'Other mothers with similar aged children would say, "Oh, you seem really happy," and I was. I could see what they were going through and it was just a different scenario. Their husbands just didn't understand.'

It was a revelation for Anthony too. 'It was completely counter-culture in my family to not have a job,' he says. 'As a kid I'd always been trained to have this terrible skepticism of housewives. It was quite an eye opener in terms of what happens in a day.'

Originally intending to take six months off, industry circumstances meant Anthony stayed out almost two years before he went back to work, though he also worked from home. But this changed with the arrival of their second child. So Eleanor then found herself catapulted very quickly from being part of a team of two-parents-one-child, to being one-parent-two-children. But as with other fathers who had taken time out, Anthony hasn't quite returned to his old hours, however, and he has an early-morning start to ensure he's home by early evening. 'He is devastated if he can't be home by six-thirty to spend time with the children,' says Eleanor.

'It made me realise how much emphasis society places on where you work and what you do,' says Anthony. 'And it's interesting how many fathers—old ones—came up to me at the time and said "I wish I'd done that".' Now one of his best friends has decided to take a year off to be with his child as well. Anthony also points out he has a real insight into what parenthood can do to your self-esteem.

'I can understand why you get a bit depressed doing it,' he says. 'Your self-esteem drops, your rewards system goes, you are a second tier in a marriage.'

Both he and Eleanor roar with laughter as they recount the exchange that brought this problem home. Anthony was sharing with Eleanor's priest his concerns that she was too shut in and was struggling to find the time to maintain her previous interests in charity work. He was worried about her frustrations looking after the kids and thought she needed to get out more, be it for work or her other interests.

'There he [Anthony] was thinking, "I'm a really caring husband"' laughs Eleanor, turning to Anthony with a grin. 'And what did he [the priest] say?'

'You're not doing your job. You're not stimulating her enough,' laughs Anthony.

'He really did,' says Eleanor. 'Basically he said, "You're part of the problem".'

Psychotherapist Marie Burrows would agree with that. She often finds couples in her office struggling to stay together after having a child. 'I see it over and over again in therapy,' she says. 'They're wonderful parents to their babies and children. They're not wonderful mates or lovers to each other anymore because the baby has become the central focus and they put their needs—their individual needs and the needs of the relationship—on hold. You've got to consciously make the time as a couple, right from the beginning.'

Research shows that what tears a relationship apart is when husbands or wives feel a major time squeeze and the thing that goes

Caging the kids

William Doherty, therapist and author of *A Strong Marriage*, believes one of the greatest traps for marriage is to let children dominate a marriage. 'Parenting has become like operating a 24-hour, seven-day-a-week store, with service on demand,' he says. In his books he outlines a raft of tips for parents to get their marriage back, including:

- understanding that, more than almost anything, good marriages lead to good parenting
- having a fixed bedtime for children, after which you are off-duty and are alone as a couple
- making sure you plan time to hang out together, as well as time as a family
- remembering your children are probably better at fighting for their needs than you and your spouse are at fighting for your marriage
- carving out private time for yourself as a couple every day, such as a 15-minute coffee break together
- making sure your children know your bedroom is private when your door is closed
- getting babysitters and going on regular dates.

is the couple time.[26] Burrows points out that even a year after the baby is born parents can often be in a negative cycle with each other where either they don't talk, or they only talk about the baby and forget to make time for the intimate pillow talk. Fortunately, she says, the solution doesn't have to be complex.

'It doesn't mean they have to go out for dinner. It means someone might take the baby for a few hours and they might sit in a garden or go out for a walk. It means when the baby is sleeping they've got to find the time to share their feelings. It's finding that intimate time.'

This is similar to the idea of 'intentional marriage', a term coined by William Doherty, a US-based marriage therapist and researcher, to describe the attitude people need for a marriage to succeed. He believes the single greatest threat to a good marriage is everyday living. That is, we can be very good at scheduling and managing the family, but we often put off the things that make us feel connected as a couple.

To sum it up

- There are two kinds of marriages—those with kids and those without.
- Having kids is the greatest test you can place on your marriage.
- Most mothers are shocked by the impact of children on them.
- Yes, your families are back.
- It can be a one-two-three hit: less money, career compromised, baby-shock.
- Some marriages get better with kids—this is mainly down to the father.
- Real partnership in parenting is important, even if only one of you is staying home.
- Loss of an independent income can hit a woman hard.
- Teamwork and planning is important when you both work.
- The relationship still has to be the number one priority.

- If the personal intimacy is there, both of you will feel like you're sharing parenting more equally.
- The most common family has two incomes, but with one parent working part-time.
- The mummy wars are one big distraction—there is no such thing as an ideal model. It's the fatherhood revolution that's the real news.
- Men today want to be different fathers than their fathers.
- Couples are making big changes and compromises to maintain a lifestyle.
- Children don't make a marriage—happy couples keep their marriage at the centre.

10

The Sticking Point

> The longer we dwell on our misfortunes, the greater is their power to harm us.
> **—Voltaire**

When you stand in front of each other making your vows, you'll probably say a word or two about sticking by your spouse through thick and thin, sickness or health, better or worse. It's a lovely sentiment, and one you probably don't think too much about. After all, you wouldn't marry someone you didn't think you could make it last with, no matter what, would you? I know Rob and I—if we thought about it at all—figured that after a sometimes rocky courtship the worst was well and truly behind us. We'd lived together for several years, we'd done most of the tough negotiating about housework and careers, what could possibly go wrong?

Well, I found out what can go wrong sitting on the toilet, six and a half months pregnant, bleeding. Despite what you might expect, at first an eerie calm of crisis washes over you. You call your doctor who says, 'go straight to the hospital'; you call your partner and say, 'meet me there'; you call your work to say, 'I won't be back'. Then when you get to the hospital you get hooked up to monitors that record your heartbeat and the baby's and you listen to the baby's galloping patter drifting in and out of range as you both wonder if all the hard work, misery, pain, expense, sorrow and finally elation of the last three years are all about to come down to this—a baby arriving far too early, who may, or may not, survive. But wait, I'm getting ahead of myself.

Having babies is meant to be the most natural thing in the world. And quite frankly, those first few months of trying were a whole lot of good ol' fun, just like it's meant to be: lots of laughs; lots of sex; lots of wondering, 'Did we just make a person?' But nothing happened. So I went to the doctor.

'Don't worry,' she said. 'We'll get you a referral but it hasn't been a year yet.'

The gyno said the same. 'A few basic tests,' but, 'don't worry'. We tried not to. The tests showed up nothing. 'Come back in twelve months if nothing's happened,' he said breezily, in a tone that suggested, 'I don't expect to see you.'

At the twelve-month mark we went back. Apparently a lot had changed. Like one in ten couples, we now officially 'had trouble conceiving' and were suddenly flung from reassuring 'it'll happen' to 'big problem' territory. There were more, and more invasive, tests—some involving hospital admissions—and for the first time we had some inkling of where the trouble may lie. It turned out there was a problem with Rob's sperm.

Eavesdropping on a phone conversation between my GP and the gyno one day I heard him say, 'that's IVF'. We were summoned to another consultation. By then I was prepared. We were going to try the alternatives before we went down that pathway. The gyno looked doubtful when we told him, but wished us well.

At the naturopath's clinic we filled out questionnaires detailing the cleaning products we used, what we ate, where we worked, what electrical appliances were in the bedroom. Our diet became organic, our house non-chemical. Rob gave up the nicotine gum. I realised I wouldn't be going back to my beloved, but stressful, television work anytime soon. And because we were now charting my monthly cycle, sex was programmed, and on demand.

'You'd better be ready tonight,' I'd say waving the thermometer. It wasn't as much fun anymore. And Rob was now feeling like a failure. We'd joke about his sperm problem (poor morphology, or not enough 'good sperm') as 'too many sherpas, not enough Hilarys to plant the flag', but neither of us really found it funny.

Months passed and still nothing. All around us people were carelessly, easily, falling pregnant. We'd summon up the energy to be happy for them and come home after seeing the new babies and quietly wilt. Our reserves were worn down. Infertility may be a couple problem, but it's still hard to not start looking for someone nearby to blame. So we'd be snappy, but not talk about why. We weren't pulling together, just pushing on. Rob admits now he was so despairing of it all that had we conceived then, he wouldn't have even been sure it was his. Not that anyone knew any of this. In public we still put up the same happy-go-lucky front we always did.

In the end we admitted defeat and went to the fertility clinic. Now I wasn't happy. My feminist hackles were up.

'Why is it when the problem's with you I'm the one injecting the drugs, having the operation?' I fumed. Then I'd panic about my disappearing career. The finances were pinching too—we calculated we'd already spent over $10 000 before we even went to IVF, and that was going to cost thousands more. I retreated into myself. We agreed to three rounds of IVF before putting it aside and saving for an overseas holiday. I started planning the holiday. Some days I wasn't entirely sure it was going to be with Rob.

How do you deal with the 'for worse' when it hits you? Infertility, illness, death, or any number of other things beyond your control, place huge stresses on your relationship. And the truth is, for all the opinions freely available about what people could and should do to save their marriages, when they're in a major crisis we still don't know what it is that makes some couples pull through and others bail out.

In chapter 5, Jenny and Craig's marriage survived his affairs because they'd decided that regardless of the pain that had been caused, what they had together was better than what they'd have apart. But what if you can't see that light at the end of that tunnel, or if you're plummeting in freefall?

Fortunately for us, IVF was the answer and we got pregnant first go. So, despite how horrid the process was, it had a payoff and I'm now holding our baby girl, but it wasn't smooth sailing.

After IVF treatment, our relationship just fell back into place again, though when we look back we still wonder at how we survived. It took us a few months after to get back to each other and get in sync again. Then I bled and I didn't get out of hospital that day. In fact, three months later I was still there, but the good news was I was still pregnant. Sitting in the delivery room that first day, thinking we were about to have a very premmie baby we found ourselves naming her, because she at least needed a name. And we held hands and told each other, no matter what, it would be okay. Which it would be. Because we were okay. In the end, that was what mattered most of all.

Circumstantial evidence

> There is a limit beyond which free and independent thought and action cannot be carried by the average man except at too great a cost ... The vague discontent, the nervous pursuit of pleasure, the high rate of divorce, are suggestive of general moral discomfort and the increase of mental disorder and crime which has accompanied our liberation from the bonds of custom may well be the price of our new privilege.
> —**Margaret Carey Madiera, 'Our burden of choice',** *Atlantic Monthly,* **1934**

Not everyone gets the time to build a strong base on their marriage first, before a hurdle looms. Some couples deal with difficult circumstances right from the start. I first met John, 39, and Ronelle, 31, a stand-up comedian and school teacher respectively, at a friend's wedding. Sparky, creative, chatty and married for four years, they seemed like the perfect couple. But sitting down to interview them I found they were still coping with a very bad start to their marriage. Twelve months before their wedding, as John finished a comedy gig, they were held up in an armed robbery. Forced to the floor, John had a gun placed in his mouth. Understandably, it caused them both great trauma, and it didn't end on their wedding day.

'The robbery stole our first year of marriage,' says John. 'We were getting over pain instead of enjoying each other's company.' They had therapy, but Ronelle found the experience especially hard to come to terms with. She was highly strung and emotional, couldn't sleep, felt scared and didn't want to be in the house alone. And it killed her libido. They settled into a not-very-productive routine.

'When someone's been emotionally scarred, the other partner doesn't want to exacerbate it so they tiptoe around and put their own needs on hold,' confides John. 'You end up being comforting rather than sexual and playful.' After a while that took its toll. 'We found we were starting to not relate as lovers but as flatmates,' he adds.

The old demand–withdraw cycle appeared—the more John wanted sex the less Ronelle wanted anything to do with it. He felt rejected, she felt put upon. The hit on their sex life put a hit on their emotional relationship.

'If someone wants sex and then masturbates alone,' says John, 'if he's honest, he'll resent it just a little.' It is, he says, a way of not really being with your partner. 'You aren't thinking sexy, loving thoughts about your wife if she's rejected you.'

Still, they weren't giving up without a fight. John began buying books with tips on how to be romantic and Ronelle went into therapy. They both went to couples counselling.

'It's a big commitment,' observes Ronelle with a dry laugh. 'One of my sisters pointed out that at $600, it is cheaper to get divorced.' They had to try a couple of therapists before they found one they both liked.

'One, I thought, was just rubbish,' said John. 'Her approach to solving our physical intimacy problems was to divide Ronelle's body into segments that I could touch or not touch, depending on whether I'd been given permission the week before.' Finally though, third time lucky, they found someone who seemed to be getting to the heart, and groin of the matter. Then two weeks before John was due to go on a six-week work trip overseas Ronelle pulled the plug.

'For two years we've been unhappy,' she said. 'John's a normal guy with normal needs and I'm not fulfilling them. John doesn't understand and I barely understand myself,' she continued. 'What we both want is a happy marriage and it's not. This really sad stuff has hung around so long it's making happiness impossible.' She moved out to do some soul searching. Two weeks later John called me.

'What more could I have done?' he pleaded. What more indeed? They seemed to have tried it all. It wasn't looking like a storybook ending.

Where can you really go when things aren't good between you? The answer isn't always as obvious as it looks. The shameful secret of the relationships therapy industry is that while some couples (between a third and half) find marriage therapy helps them in the short-term, research indicates only a small percentage actually see any lasting change in their relationships.[1]

'It's a crap shoot,' says William Doherty, who now trains therapists on how to do it right. The problem is, while anyone can hang up a shingle claiming to be a relationship therapist, not all are properly trained in the specialised skills that this requires. Doherty says the two biggest problems are therapists who are 'trained to work with individuals and then can't handle the hot conflict that occurs in the room'. Or, just as bad, therapists who 'give up on you because they can't handle what's going on'.

For couples looking for some extra help, it's worth looking to registered organisations, such as Relationships Australia, for a referral to someone who is actually qualified to counsel couples. It also pays to know what to look for when you visit one for the first time.

In *A Strong Marriage*, Doherty lists the classic signs. A bad therapist is someone who:
- lets spouses interrupt each other, speak for each other, make attacks and counterattacks
- does not recommend any changes in the couple's day-to-day relationship
- gives up on the relationship because they feel overwhelmed by the couple's problems
- chooses a side
- believes a good marriage or good divorce are equally acceptable outcomes
- believes women should behave a certain way and men a different way
- spends a lot of time exploring your pasts and but doesn't help you develop strategies to deal with the present.

A good marital therapist:
- doesn't take sides
- is compassionate towards both of you
- structures your sessions
- offers some perspective on your problems
- challenges each of you
- offers you specific strategies
- checks for individual matters like depression, alcoholism and illnesses that could affect both of you
- is alert to whether there are problems of physical abuse.[2]

I thought I'd seen the last of John and Ronelle after they split up, but a couple of months later I heard on the grapevine they were back together so I called them for a follow-up interview. Meeting them again was like seeing an entirely different couple. Plonking themselves down in the cafe they brimmed with the easiness that happy couples have in each other's company. What on earth had changed?

'I moved back in,' laughs Ronelle. 'It was a good break for me, even if it wasn't a good break for John.'

'Well,' drawls John in his best cowboy accent, 'the results were good. I came back married instead of not married.'

So what had made the difference? Ronelle had finally been diagnosed with depression, was on anti-depressants and was seeing a psychologist. She was also seeing a naturopath to clear up some allergies that had been troubling her for years.

'I've just started feeling better within myself,' she says, 'instead of carrying around everything and not really acknowledging that I had a problem. I thought the problem was the marriage,' she says. 'But I realised it was the depression. I haven't got the sort of depression where I couldn't get out of bed—people can get that bad—but mine manifested itself in terms of motivation and I think the motivation for the marriage suffered.'

She'd also been burning the candle at both ends, not allowing herself the emotional space she needed. So she negotiated a better school timetable. A dedicated school teacher, Ronelle had also been forcing herself to be happy in the classroom and then pushing herself through choir practice in the evenings.

'It was all getting ready to blow up in my face,' Ronelle says. Once John left on his overseas trip, 'I really missed him, and I didn't realise I'd miss him so much. I feel like I'm halfway through a tunnel between how it was and how it's going to be,' says Ronelle. 'I know we have a good relationship—we're so well suited to each other—and the thought of not being with him is devastating. John's been very supportive. He realises there's a reason behind the problem and he's changed how he's been dealing with things. Instead of being selfish about the way things are in the relationship he's been more caring and it's become a team thing.'

'I'd agree with that,' says John. 'One of our major, major things was in the bedroom. It was just getting unbearable. We'd negotiate every aspect of our lovemaking with the therapist. It'd be so black and white—why we're doing it, how, reporting back to them how it went. It was just cringe-worthy. But it was what we had to do. That side of things we're slowly working on and it's much nicer now. We've still got miles to go but it's a good start.'

'He's a sex maniac,' laughs Ronelle.

'In two words,' agrees John proudly.

What ever happened to your equal relationship?

Black cat on my doorstep, black cat on my window-sill
Black cat on my doorstep, black cat on my window-sill
If one black cat don't cross me, another black cat will

It's bad luck if I'm jolly, bad luck if I cry
It's bad luck if I'm jolly, bad luck if I cry
It's bad luck if I stay here, it's still more bad luck if I die
—*Black Cat Hoot Owl Blues*, **Thomas Dorsey, 1928**

In our choice-ruled world our actions are meant to inoculate us against risk. We pay for insurance against fire, theft and accidents, we get an education to avoid unemployment. But what insurance can you take out for a marriage?

For a start there are the basics words of wisdom that John Gottman discovered:
○ spend 15 minutes a day staying connected
○ find ways to stay more positive than negative with each other
○ fight fair.

Talking with couples who've made it through unemployment, career crises and the demands of children it's clear how important these basics are for maintaining a sense of connection. But in big crisis there is another element: It's often not a shared burden. Illness, particularly, can tip the balance—like it or not, one of you is suddenly dependent, the other a carer. This challenges modern marriages in the most fundamental way: 50/50 goes out the window, and often for the first time you aren't and can't be equals. Depending how debilitating the illness is, one partner can often end up bearing the entire financial burden as well as supporting their partner emotionally.

When Lara was 21, she didn't even plan on getting married. Then she met Charles, 22, who was studying at Duntroon. They went out for two years. When Charles graduated Lara decided that she needed a bit more than hope if they were going to stay together through the intransigencies of army life. So she proposed. Fortunately the idea wasn't a rude shock to Charles.

'I'd already told all my mates I was going to marry her,' he deadpans. 'I'd just neglected to tell Lara.'

Two years later in Townsville, Lara was pregnant with their first child. It should have been a happy time. Expecting a baby fills most mothers with happy hormones, but not all. Late in her pregnancy Lara started feeling down—really down.

'I was really anxious and obsessive,' she says, recounting how she repeatedly asked herself, 'What if I'm going to be a bad mother?' She was crying all the time, didn't want to see anyone and had vivid dreams about stabbing her family. In a small country town no one believed that you could be depressed when you were pregnant so she tried to put it aside.

They moved back to Melbourne just before their son was born, but then Lara progressed to panic attacks—the first occurring ten minutes after Joshua's delivery. Unhelpfully, the midwife had told her to pull herself together, while her mother instructed, 'You should suckle him'. Charles threw them both out and held Lara until the shaking stopped. After a week, a psychiatrist told Lara she'd needed to take medication. Still no one mentioned postnatal depression.

A fortnight later, Lara saw a brochure on the condition. 'Maybe this really exists,' she thought to herself and rang the number. She found a doctor and was put on new medication.

'Once we were diagnosed—had the name for it—it was easier,' says Charles. Still, Lara struggled to get out of bed in the morning, and hated leaving the house. As the year progressed the family became more and more isolated. Finally out of options, Lara was admitted to a hospital psychiatric unit with Joshua to get some counselling and was put on Prozac. Charles came in every day and stayed until midnight, then was back at 5 a.m. for breakfast.

Then three weeks in, it was Charles's turn to have a meltdown. It seemed he now defined their relationship by Lara's condition.

'All of a sudden I had this fear—"What if she comes out of here and doesn't need me anymore?"' he says. Fortunately he joined a group for men to learn about postnatal depression.

'Charles said that once he accepted he couldn't make it better— that all he could do was listen—that helped,' recalls Lara. She and Charles also did courses at the hospital together. They had to learn to be husband and wife again, says Charles, 'we weren't anymore. We were carer and caree.'

The next year was a bumpy ride. Trying for another baby, four subsequent miscarriages saw Lara relapse. She got more therapy and did a cognitive behaviour course. And three and a half years ago she finally gave birth to Isabella. This time, under the watchful eye of her doctor, she went on low doses of antidepressants during her pregnancy.

Lara is also working on not letting the condition define her. Formerly a spokesperson with the beyondblue postnatal depression information group, she's now left so that she can move on. Lara and Charles have also fostered a close friendship with another couple who also have two children—'every weekend they're here or we're there,' says Lara. 'So it's like one big family.'

That Charles and Lara have remained together is a huge testament to their strengths as research shows depression *is* a major problem for relationships. 'It breaks up an enormous number of marriages,' says Professor Ian Hickie, clinical advisor to beyondblue, adding that a big factor is that the normal emotional cues couples give to each other are disrupted. 'The other person can often feel ignored and neglected, "I cried and he took no notice". It sounds like they didn't care, but really they didn't see the cue. People who are depressed really need the people they live with, but they don't respond to them.'

Depression sees couples fighting more and having greater distress than non-depressed couples. There's also often a lot less affection. Add to that sexual dissatisfaction, boredom, stubbornness, financial disagreements, difficulties communicating, conflicts about children and lack of respect and you have a marriage-killer combo with the works.[3]

Knowing the failure rate of marriages and depression, Charles admits he finds it hard to say what the differences are between him and the guys who leave.

'I really get upset about the loss of our twenties,' he admits. 'We had a really good love life and it all disappeared up in smoke. The years we should have had fun and carefree are gone. Depression is not a straight-line recovery—you've always got to keep your guard up,' he admits. 'You learn pretty quickly not to believe what they're telling you. You wait six months to see if it's consistently looking good.' He deals with that 'a day at a time'.

'Maybe because I grew up in a farming community, where people don't quit on marriage, we work well together,' he says. 'Sexually we're compatible. Mentally Lara drags me kicking and screaming through the world—she'll go and do stuff. We have similar values, likes and dislikes. I view Lara as having depression—not being depressed,' he says. 'It's a thing, a critter. The same Lara I've known and loved is there. She'll still give me a pinch and a punch for the first day of the month—silly stuff like that.' And he focuses on what they have together. 'We've grown at the same speed. We both like just being at home, just like having kids.'

> **Women's illness more likely to break a marriage than men's**
> According to research by Dr Michael Glantz, a US oncologist, married female patients with brain tumours and other life-threatening illnesses experience a much higher rate of divorce compared to their male counterparts. Women with brain tumours were eight times more likely to undergo separation or divorce than men. Women with other diseases also experienced high rates of marital breakdown—those in the MS group were seven times more likely to suffer this outcome and those in the general oncology group were nearly twelve times more likely to divorce or separate.[4]

Separating the illness problem and the marriage problem

> It seems preposterous to urge the necessity of health; but when we consider the many ways in which it is heedlessly injured, we reason as if it were considered of little importance. Want of exercise at one time, and too violent exertion at another; exposure to cold and dampness; imprudence in dress and diet; all these conspire to impair the constitution, and produce premature old age.
> —Mrs Louisa C. Tuthill, *The Young Lady's Home*, 1847

Ingrid and Izars, from Melbourne's Latvian community, met when Ingrid was just 18 years old and Izars 23. Within six weeks Izars had popped the question and six months later, with the doubts of both families, they married. Recently, the businesswoman and general manager respectively celebrated their twentieth anniversary. Few predicted they would make it.

Ingrid had the cards stacked against her early; her parents divorced when she was young and her bipolar mother introduced a new stepfather into the household who was an alcoholic. By the time she met Izars, Ingrid was also beginning to show the signs of the manic depression that had dogged her mother.

'It didn't put me off,' says Izars of Ingrid's strange behaviour—including her 'suicide hints'—'In a strange way it was all the more intriguing.' Still, it wasn't a good start.

Then not long after they married, Ingrid's mother had a mental breakdown. And Ingrid and Izars were also fighting a lot, feeling the pressures of having married so young. They were dealing with coming from very different families. Ingrid's depression deepened. 'Barely surviving' is how Ingrid recalls that period. She became convinced Izars was on the verge of leaving her.

Izars was lost. 'I didn't know what it was back then,' he says. 'I didn't know it was depression though I knew there was trouble in the family.'

Unlike in some couples, Izars realised early on that he wasn't the problem—and that he didn't have the solution. One night he simply told Ingrid, 'I can't help you. I can give you love, but I can't give you self-love. If you keep saying you're going to leave, you'll make it happen.' Then he got Ingrid into therapy.

'I didn't think much of it,' he says. 'I thought something had to be done. I knew there was only so much I could do and I knew she needed an outside perspective.'

Therapy was a big step for Ingrid. 'I was so ambivalent,' she says of her attitude. 'It's not me that's the problem—it's everyone else.' Family and friends didn't help either, simply thinking she was being indulgent—'Why don't you just sort yourself out.' Fortunately she found a good therapist who, unusually, insisted Ingrid meet her at her house twice weekly, which helped Ingrid unpack the baggage of her own dysfunctional family experience. 'She wanted me to see what it was like to be part of a normal family unit.'

It was a slow process—Ingrid says it took her five years to accept Izars wasn't going to leave, and a long time to learn how to fight without thinking it was the end of the world. Now twenty years later she says, 'I'm still here because of her [the therapist] and my husband.' There have been crises since—both their mothers died within six months of each other which sent Ingrid spiralling dangerously back down again. But while she still battles depression, Ingrid's now managing it. She takes daily medication and is more alert around times like Christmas when she feels vulnerable.

The couple say their marriage remains strong because they have always managed to keep the outside pressures—the family politics, the difficulties with Ingrid's mother—outside. Both agree their families' opposition to their match was a strength they drew on.

'We didn't allow them to come between us. There was never a question of allowing the family to take sides,' says Izars. 'We always recognised we were the family and that letting others in is a recipe for disaster.' Six years ago they also had a daughter.

'Life just changed completely. We had more focus,' says Ingrid.

How have they stayed together when depression and crises like those have broken other couples? 'I don't think we've ever really been in trouble,' says Izars thoughtfully. 'I know personally I'm old-fashioned. Once you decide to get married it's a real commitment. It's exactly what marriage is about—you make a promise. There was no question of not following through. Sometimes everything fits together. We're strong individuals. We've always enjoyed the adventures we've had. We're certainly not alike—in music, sport we're poles apart—but in the things that matter, we're close and supportive. It's a positive marriage. I can't imagine not being with her. There's so much we want to be and do—you're always looking forward to something.'

'Every day we say, "I love you",' says Ingrid. 'There hasn't been a day I haven't run up to say "I love you" or "have a nice day" and not meant it. He will kiss me every morning. My marriage is the only normal thing in my life. We have had it tough, we have had it hard. He's taken me warts and all. The reality is in this illness, you do become irrational. But Izars is not the one I have a void with, neither is my daughter. They're my anchors. Me and my husband, we're friends, we're mates, we're soulmates. I love talking to him—he's interesting, he's supportive, stable, reliable, trustworthy and he's given me freedom.'

Choosing what matters

> Fortitude, like Integrity, may be termed one of the severer virtues; but it is not the less necessary for the weaker sex, since with less physical strength, and fewer opportunities of improving it, either mentally or corporeally, woman is yet called upon to exert great powers of endurance, both actively and passively. The pains of sickness, the misfortunes of life, the inflictions of calumny, call upon her for patience under suffering; and firmness, resolution, and perseverance in conduct; without these qualities, a woman, however engaging or attractive as a companion, must be found deficient in all the nearer relationships of life, and incapable of fulfilling its more important duties, all of which, in her own person, or that of some near connexion, demand the assistance this virtue, in one of its many forms, can alone supply.
> —*The Young Lady's Book: A manual of elegant recreations, exercises, and pursuits*, **1830**

The more I talked with couples who'd made it through the dark times the more sense William Doherty made when he talked about the problem with what he terms consumer marriages—the constant cost–benefit analysis many couples indulge in that consists of a running tally of who's doing what.

'The market-based consumer culture feeds on the idea that our primary role in life is to pursue our individual desires,' he says. 'We tend to define ourselves by what we buy and what we own—the one with the most toys wins . . .' The problem is, according to Doherty, that consumers are inherently disloyal: if a better product comes along we will buy it. So a marriage that is constantly evaluated in terms of, 'am I getting enough out of this relationship' or 'will this relationship meet my needs?' is asking to be made redundant.

'While there's nothing wrong with asking the questions,' says Doherty, 'if they dominate our reflections on our marriages, commitment is up for grabs. These are the opposite values necessary to withstand the challenges of long-term marriage. A cost–benefit attitude towards marriage actually erodes marriage satisfaction.'

Faced with a crisis, not only is this consumerism unhelpful (of course someone's putting in more and someone's putting in less), it's going to aggravate your sense of unfairness about the whole situation. Then it won't seem like the two of you facing it together at all. Come a calamity, that kind of thinking won't get you through.

It's fair to say six-foot and red-haired Richard, 32, is a knockabout kinda guy. A state-level rugby player in Tasmania, in his early twenties he signed up with the Air Force to play for the Australian Combined Services. Newly married to Jacqui, now 31, the couple happily packed up together for six years of air force life—'we just had itchy feet doing stuff,' she says. In the military, Richard was able to pursue his rugby career until a serious injury to his neck eventually put him off the field. Jacqui, meanwhile, built a career with a bank, working her way up to managing a call centre for 200. When his service was up both decided it was time to head back to their home state and after a three-month trip around Australia they moved back to Tasmania.

The first twelve months were a bit rough as, while Jacqui had secured a job in Launceston, Richard couldn't find work. Still, that pales in comparison with what was to come as in 2000, the fitness fanatic started to get sick.

'He picked me up from work and said, "I've been to the doctor—I have this lump",' Jacqui recalls of the day they got his diagnosis. Richard had testicular cancer. 'I freaked out a bit,' she admits. A major and immediate concern—and the main reason they'd moved back was their desire to have children.

'Are we ever going to be able to have kids?' she asked. They decided quickly to start trying. Miraculously, with a window of opportunity of around a week before Richard's treatment was to begin, they hit the jackpot.

'She was suffering morning sickness and I had the chemo drugs so I was suffering nausea too,' he recalls with dry humour. 'We'd be patting each other on the back as we drove the porcelain bus.' The next year when son Isaac was born their two mothers made up a roster and came to help with chores while Richard recovered.

The worst seemed behind them and later that year, despite still undergoing radiation therapy, Richard was able to land his dream job as a fireman, one of only ten applicants to make it through from a field of 3000. Then the following year, with strange bruises appearing on his body, he started feeling unwell again. He again went to the doctor. That evening he was admitted to hospital with leukaemia.

'I went from having a barbecue at home to intensive care and the following day started massive chemotherapy,' he recalls, adding with understatement, 'It knocked us for a six.'

This time the condition was even more serious. The treatment compromised Richard's immune system so he spent much of the time in hospital in isolation. He couldn't kiss Jacqui and he couldn't pick up Isaac. He nearly died twice from infection.

'It's very uncomfortable, very isolating,' he remembers. 'I was in with another fellow who died while I was in and that freaked me out a bit.' Jacqui, meanwhile, was holding down a full-time job and holding the family together.

So how did they cope? 'You just do,' she says. 'You take each day as it comes. There's no question of not seeing it through together. It's certainly stressful. I know I got emotional, but I never really let Richard see my emotion. You realise if you're not going to be the strong one, who is? You put it in perspective. It's Richard lying there in bed feeling like he's been run over by a truck—so get a grip. He's doing the suffering. You need to be positive and upbeat when you walk in the room even when you don't feel like giving it.'

Incredibly, in the midst of this, Richard and Jacqui decided to try for another baby, refusing to countenance that something like cancer would get in the way of their plans. Neither finds this a strange decision.

'We just wanted to go ahead as a family,' says Richard. 'It didn't cross my mind that I wouldn't pull through.' And, he adds, with an extensive family network in Tasmania, 'Even if I wasn't here, there are grandparents, aunts, uncles...' So having finished one treatment cycle he went off the drugs for 72 days—the amount of time it takes sperm to mature. Again, miraculously, they quickly conceived their second son Angus, now one. And in 2004 Richard was given a clean bill of health.

Looking back, what effect has all this had on their relationship? 'For a start,' says Richard, 'it puts things in perspective. You really don't sweat the small stuff. If the kids do something we don't tend to get stressed about it too much. We look at the lighter side of things.'

'We're a lot more forgiving of each other,' agrees Jacqui. 'We let things go. It's not worth arguing. You get over it really quickly.'

'And,' adds Richard, 'it's strengthened the relationship. If we disagree, we disagree. We don't try and force opinions on each other—we compromise and try to find common ground.' Jacqui says they were fortunate in having a strong base from the start.

'When he joined the military it wasn't just his decision, it was ours,' she says. 'Throughout the relationship if either of us is unhappy we've encouraged the other to change. One of the things we're really happy about with our life is we really don't have regrets. We've done the stuff we wanted to do and done it together and I want to continue that.' Richard adds that all their experiences have let them see a change in the meaning of their relationship over time.

'It's become more understanding, more like friends, less based on the sexual. As time's gone on we've grown closer, we talk about stuff that in the past we couldn't talk about.'

Endurance

> . . . the arduous, imperative duties that in life's progress devolve upon woman call for physical, as well as mental, vigour. To hover around the couch of sickness, and smooth the pillow of the dying; to bear patiently with the querulous impatience of the aged, and the petulance of childhood; to lead into the right path the boisterous waywardness of youth; and to soothe, by unwearied kindness, tempers rendered harsh and irritable by intercourse with a cold, unfeeling world;—are not these a part of her humble ministry?
> —**Mrs Louisa C. Tuthill**, *The Young Lady's Home*, **1847**

Daniel, an investor and athlete, has been paralysed since the age of seventeen when he was hit by a drunk driver. So you might suppose that his and Julianne's story begins with him being in a wheelchair. You'd be wrong.

'I didn't even see the chair,' says Julianne, a nurse, who's worked with quadriplegics and also has a brother-in-law in a wheelchair, confessing, 'I'd book restaurants that were up a flight of steps.'

It was a swift romance and they moved in together after eighteen months. Then, aged just 21, Julianne fell pregnant. Things didn't go smoothly.

'It was hard,' she confesses. She'd been raised in a strict Catholic household. 'My mum didn't approve of our relationship and she didn't approve of my being pregnant. She and Daniel had issues. I was 21 and terrified.'

Still, they went ahead with the pregnancy and had baby Michelle. But from the start, Michelle had problems. So Julianne took her to Tresillian, a centre for women and babies, who agreed something was wrong. A month of tests followed, each coming back clear. It was the final test that cruelled everything. At four months of age, Michelle was diagnosed with I-cell disease—in effect, a death sentence. Julianne and Daniel were told she would only live until she was three or four. They went into shock.

'I went from being this carefree twenty-year-old to a mother with a child with a terminal illness,' recalls Julianne. 'I went onto anti-depressants and didn't get my life together at all.'

Within three months she and Daniel separated. Still, they continued to share the care of Michelle. Julianne went back to work part-time. Then they got back together, separated, and made up again. Throughout all this time family opposition continued to exert pressure on their relationship. Finally, when Michelle was three, Julianne took a stand and confronted her mother. 'Accept this is what I want,' she said to her of her relationship with David.

Things between her and David got better, though they still had to deal with Michelle's illness. They were told that it was pneumonia that would eventually end her life. 'So every cold, every sniffle . . .' says Julianne of watching for the worst. 'Her whole life was an emotional roller-coaster. It was like a time bomb waiting to happen.'

They fought to get Michelle into a normal preschool and when she was three she got into her first wheelchair, 'and then she was off'. Fortunately, although her condition was serious, with Julianne being a nurse, Michelle could mostly be managed at home and didn't have to be admitted to hospital too frequently. None of it was easy, though.

'I'm not proud of how I acted or reacted sometimes,' admits Julianne. 'You always hurt the ones you love. I took my stress out on David.' But by now, despite the initial rocky times, they made the decision that they were in this all together and when Michelle was four and half they got married.

It was a morning wedding. 'A perfect day,' says Julianne. 'Nothing went wrong.' Michelle was the flower girl 'and stole the show'. For their honeymoon they went to nearby beachside Manly for three nights, then another three nights in Terrigal, on the New South Wales central coast, the first time they'd been alone together since Michelle was born. Then nine months later Michelle got sick. A low-grade temperature and runny nose turned into pneumonia. She went into intensive care and died on Christmas day.

What got them through those next few months, says Julianne, was their friends. Partly as the result of her work as a nurse, they weren't alone in their experience. 'We had lots of friends who'd lost children,' says Julianne. Their friends gave them permission to both talk about Michelle or not. 'There could be silences, and they weren't awkward.' And they were given good advice. 'Everyone said don't do anything—and don't separate—before twelve months.' Another friend who'd lost two children to the same syndrome said, 'Accept you'll grieve differently.' So, adds Julianne, 'Knowing that, we did.'

Coming up to the one-year anniversary of Michelle's death, Julianne started having some counselling. 'That first year is all about survival,' she says on reflection. 'Daniel had to say, "Michelle wouldn't want to see you like this".'

Now fifteen months later, having looked after herself, they're pulling back together. 'We have so many happy memories—they far outweigh the sad,' says Julianne. And they're finding out new things about each other. 'From the day we had Michelle, she was the number one priority for both of us,' she continues. 'Every hour from 7 a.m. to 8.30 p.m. had meaning, our whole focus was her—feeding, doctors' appointments—we did it all together. Now we're discovering our relationship again.'

It's not been all plain sailing. They've been trying for another child and are having problems conceiving. 'I'd still be disappointed if we couldn't have more children,' says Julianne. 'But I'm at peace with how I feel. We've been through too much to let it affect us too badly. And,' she adds, 'most importantly, I'm enjoying our relationship. I don't want to give all that away again so I hope I have the insight, even if we do have more children, to make time for that.'

The bad comes good again

> A successful marriage represents the triumph of will over the immediate needs of the moment.
> —**W.H. Auden**

William Doherty and his colleagues found something really interesting after interviewing people who said their marriages were rotten—to the point where they almost walked away—but had then salvaged them. Bad marriages, and bad times in marriages, don't necessarily stick.

'It's very important to know that even when marriages go bad they can go good again,' concludes Doherty. 'It's not like fruit, once it gets rotten it's not getting ripe again.'

Teasing out the details they found what made the difference in these tested relationships was a whole raft of commonsense strategies that hadn't appeared before in the research.

'For example, "put one foot ahead of the other, day after day", "we talked it out and things get better",' he says, adding that much of it came down to simply outlasting the problem. 'The stress that they were under went away—their husband got a job, the mother-in-law died, the kid left home.'

Compiling the results, Doherty and his colleagues found that spouses' stories of how their marriage survived and then thrived again fell under three main categories:

1 A marriage endurance ethic
This was the most common strategy. Rather than resolving problems, partners simply outlasted them. Financial problems, career setbacks, depression, problems with children or even infidelity, all eased or disappeared as marriage pressures over time.

2 A marriage work ethic
Here partners actively worked to solve problems, change behaviour or improve communication. One group are the 'husbands behaving badly'. Issued with a 'shape up or ship out' ultimatum by wives at the end of their tether, these husbands do improve their bad behaviour, not wanting to lose their marriage.

3 A personal happiness ethic

Here, where the actual problem didn't seem to go away, couples found ways around it by finding ways to improve their own happiness and build a good life despite a mediocre marriage.[5]

Stickiness

> In my pocket not one penny
> And my friends I haven't any
> But If I ever get on my feet again
> Then I'll meet my long lost friend
> It's mighty strange, without a doubt
> Nobody knows you when you down and out
> I mean when you down and out
> —*Nobody knows you when you down and out*, **Ida Cox and B. Feldman, 1929**

If ever there was a couple with a marriage endurance ethic, it's Steve and Vicki. When they married fifteen years ago, Steve, now 52, and Vicki, 48, had a right to think the worst was behind them. Not long before they wed, Steve had had a bicycle accident that left him broke and without a livelihood. Vicki already carried the scars of an abusive childhood and had also survived a violent first marriage.

Initially things were better than they had been in a while. Both were keen competitive cyclists who rode up to 500 kilometres a week and Steve, a musician, trainer in personal development and meditation and something of a jack-of-all trades, began building an eco-friendly house he had designed himself. Nestled down by a river it has a passive solar design with vaulted ceilings, a big open plan and a meadow garden by the side. Vicki, a chef, was working hard in a local restaurant.

Two years into their marriage, Steve started to get muscle twitches. In constant pain, he was sent from his Goulburn home to Sydney for a month of tests. Vicki, working back home, could only see him on the weekends. But despite getting every type of test in the hospital's large neurology ward, nothing yielded any information. At the end of his tether he eventually grabbed an intern and demanded some information. The young doctor flipped open the chart open and read out 'Amyotrophic Lateral Sclerosis—Motor Neurone Disease' (ALS/MND)—a progressive, usually fatal neuromuscular disease.

'I did a B-movie double take,' says Steve of his shock, while the intern stood there with his eyebrows raised. With Steve too stunned for words, the doctor simply left.

Get MND and your muscles will atrophy and cease to function. Your nerves and nerve connections may be damaged. In its final stages you lose the ability to do even simple things like cough, or scratch an itch. You are an active mind trapped in a body that can't work at all. The most famous of all sufferers is Stephen Hawking, who has a particular slow-developing version of the condition.

Given the diagnosis Steve rapidly progressed through the classic five-step response—denial, anger, bargaining, depression and acceptance. Still, when Vicki next came to Sydney, Steve couldn't bring himself to tell her. Hungry for any information—and hope—he eventually found out from the head of neurology that the 'diagnosis' of MND is basically what's left to doctors when every other medical explanation is exhausted. That didn't change his prognosis, though, which was basically that he had two to five years left to live. He finally told Vicki.

Like Richard and Jacqui earlier, Steve and Vicki simply got on with business.

'It wasn't like it was the end the world,' says Vicki of her practical response. 'It was just something I had to do—look after him.'

'I have never admitted I *have* MND,' says Steve. 'I've just been *diagnosed* with it.' Still, coping with a traumatic illness doesn't inoculate you against other pressures. While Steve and Vicki were finding a way of getting on with business together, Steve found himself becoming isolated by a world that doesn't cope with his kind of disability.

'If they think you're dying or in a wheelchair people start speaking loudly,' he observes. The support groups weren't helpful either. 'Horrific,' he says. 'You see people in the last stages of the illness—they just reaffirm that you're dying.'

To cope, Steve tried seeing a psychologist and even though 'he was nonplussed by me and didn't know what to say' Steve found talking to a neutral party cathartic. Finally though, he says he realised it was up to him. 'It was either heal yourself or die.' He devoted his next year to studying the illness and began experimenting with every treatment he could glean from a mountain of research. High on the list was taking lots of antioxidants, which he started doing. He began to show results and his mobility improved.

'I'm the first person in Australia to send a wheelchair back to the MND Association,' he says with pride. He started a website on his illness that lists all the research and posts an online diary of his experiments on himself. After initial hostility from the medical profession for providing false hope, Steve—now stable for ten years—finds his site is recommended at neurology conferences, though, he adds wryly, not funded by any. He's also been able do a bit of guitar teaching, and still performs his beloved blues when he can. Things should have been settling down for them both, but then Vicki started to collapse.

During Steve's illness Vicki had become the breadwinner and she was working very long days, up to eighteen hours, earning money to support them both. She initially put her fatigue down to the fact that the restaurant she worked at had changed hands, and with inexperienced new owners she'd ended up pretty much running the show. Without the staff she needed she was getting skinny with the stress of it all. Things came to a head one Easter—the busiest time of the year—when Vicki saw she alone was rostered to work. She told her boss if they didn't get extra help she would resign. They didn't. She resigned then she went home to bed. She didn't get out for six months.

'I would get up and sit on the couch and wait four hours to get enough energy for a shower,' she recounts. She subsisted on a diet of yoghurt and crushed lemonade and put on thirty kilograms in two months. But the doctors didn't seem to be able to find the problem.

'I kept getting diagnosed with severe depression,' she says. 'I'd go to the doctor, burst into tears and say "I'm so tired I can't move, I can't eat, I can't wash my hair".' For the next two years Steve, still struggling with his MND, had to look after her, including washing her hair and making the meals. It was only when Vicki started to get night sweats she was finally diagnosed with Hashimoto's Thyroiditis, a disease of the thyroid that's related to chronic fatigue. After this diagnosis and seeing another doctor's report Vicki finally also owned up to depression and went on a diet. Now she's pulled out of the worst of it and is back to being the main carer for Steve.

They've both faced major health crises. Each has endured the loneliness of being the sole carer. Vicki is still loath to leave Steve for any length of time—he is on a lot of painkillers, some of which he reacts to badly. 'Basically I need to be with him 24 hours of the day,' she says. She says it's her friends that get her though, and they now have home care coming in once a fortnight for two hours, which at least sees the kitchen and the bathroom cleaned. But that kind of narrowing world leaves you vulnerable. This wasn't the last test Steve and Vicki had to get through.

A neighbour and long-time friend of Steve's had become a de facto helper to both of them. 'I thought she was just helping,' says Vicki. 'I couldn't drive, couldn't go out. Then it got a bit tangled up.' It began to become clear the helper had an agenda. 'She started being really horrible to me,' says Vicki. She'd cook for Steve, but make nothing Vicki could eat. 'But to Steve she was like an angel and because she was so good to him he couldn't see what she was doing to me.' That, says Vicki, after everything she'd been through— her childhood, Steve's illness, her illness—was the hardest. 'It really tested my strength of character.'

While Steve didn't have an affair, the wedge driven between them was getting worse. Finally Steve saw what was going on. 'Once he agreed with me, we worked as a team,' says Vicki. 'I said "I don't want her in my life".'

So Steve confronted her. 'Vicki will always win,' he said. 'Even if she dies you and I won't be together.' He had to do this more than once.

'It could have ruined our marriage,' says Vicki. 'But we had the strength to stick together.'

They're still not doing it easy. With two disabilities pensions they live on less than $400 a week. Nine weeks out of the last sixteen they haven't been able to buy groceries. They miss their social life—with the bike-riding days gone, they found there was little to talk about with some friends. But someone recently bought Steve a really nice guitar, and his story has been published in six books. They try and look out and connect as much as they can.

'Stephen and I do things for the community—we write hundreds of letters to politicians,' says Vicki. 'We fight for other people not able to fight for themselves.'

'Even now I'm determined we have a future,' says Steve.

So what's the glue?

'Oh my God,' he says thoughtfully, 'what would I do without her? We're together 24 hours a day in an open-plan house. Where would I go? Fundamentally, it's a friendship,' he says. 'I would trust her with my life. I'd stop at nothing to protect her. It's just tremendous respect.' Even at their lowest, when Vicki wants to talk it out, Steve wants to solve things first—'Essentially we have the same goal in mind; we love each other and have never ceased to.'

Towards the end of our conversation Steve comments: 'Most marriages I observe are 50/50 affairs—"I'll mow the lawn if you do the washing".' But, he says. 'With us it's 100 per cent/100 per cent. If I have to do all the washing, I'll do it. It's a 100 per cent marriage.

You just do as much as you can for the other.'

That's just what William Doherty says too. Instead of 'consumer marriages' he advocates 'intentional marriages', where couples find ways to concentrate on constantly putting in rather that taking out.

Later, I read Steve's website. On it he's posted his philosophical musings. One really catches my eye: 'Each day I wake up and decide that today can be a good day or a bad day—it's my choice. I can feel sorry for myself or I can take charge and do what I can with what I've got—my choice.'

It's tempting in all these examples to look at the obvious—the depression, the illness or injury, dealing with death. And it's true: all of these can and do place enormous stresses on marriage— stresses that each carry unique elements and, thankfully, stresses not all marriages will face. When you look closely at these stories the one commonality is the choice each couple had to make. Whether they got hit with sickness, poverty, betrayal or loss—all things out of their control—they all did the one thing that was in their control. They chose every day, day by day sometimes, that the marriage was going to make it through. It's really all about the oldest 'c' word of them all. Commitment. And you can't get more intentional than that.

To sum up
- Admit it when you can't solve the problem by yourself and get professional help.
- Look for a well-qualified couples therapist who wants to work with both of you to preserve the relationship.
- Don't be afraid to invest in individual therapy as well, especially if you think you may suffer depression.
- When the relationship becomes unequal, find ways to connect as husband and wife, not just carer and caree.
- Admit you can't solve all your partner's problems for them.

- Keep pressures, like family relationships, outside your marriage.
- Abandon the 'what-am-I-getting-out-of-this?' tallying up of a 'consumer marriage'.
- Take responsibility for your emotions.
- Don't sweat the small stuff.
- Give yourselves time to recover from trauma.
- Accept you may cope with crises and grief differently.
- Bad marriages can come good again.
- Choose to stay married.

Conclusion: Having it all

The most superficial observer must have noticed that there is being gradually built up in the community a growing dread of the conjugal bond, especially among men, and a condition of discontent and unrest among married people, particularly women.
—**Maud Churton Braby,** *Modern Marriage and How to Bear It,* **1908**

When I started writing this book the question 'How do you stay happily married?' was really a theoretical one. I was married, and happily so. Sure, we'd had our moments, and a somewhat turbulent relationship in the nine years we'd been together before we got hitched. We'd survived a seven-month separation as I backpacked around the world, a career change on my part, a career crisis on Rob's, but by the time we married we thought the worst was behind us. If you've just read the last chapter you'll know it wasn't. I think we're still too close to it all to know entirely what kept us going together through all the drama of my pregnancy, but I do think we knew that while we felt awful at the time, that feeling wouldn't last forever.

That experience did make reading the original outline for this book rather interesting. At the outset, I had a fairly simple idea. I was going to write about how marriage had changed, how our marriages are different to our parents' and grandparents' marriages and how we're forging new models and ways of making it work. I still think that's mostly true. Today we do have ridiculously complicated lives. We don't have fixed roles. The art of marriage has become the art of continuous negotiation. We're creating something new almost daily. But now, I'm also not sure that marriage hasn't always demanded this. And the clues have been there all along.

For a start, to make my point I asked Flora and Gordon Aris (that would be Mum and Dad) what they thought it took to keep a marriage happily together. The original idea was I'd compare what they said to what the experts said and young couples were telling me today, then I'd track the changes.

Gordon and Flora have been married forty years. They've lived that entire time in the same quarter-acre blocked house they came home to when they wed. They share a profession (teaching) and the same religion. Their two children (one girl, one boy) turned out to be a writer and an engineer. They agree marriage is harder today.

'It is more difficult with two needing to work to afford a home,' says Dad. 'And if a marriage fails one is not necessarily considered "a loser" now.' They think choosing the right person from the start (compatible, shared values) is important.

Here's my problem: when it came to actual marriage advice, first they insisted on being contemporary by quoting television shrink Dr Phil: 'Make the right *decision*—then make the decision *right*'. But then, true to form, they jotted down a list:

1 Practice the Golden Rule; *mutual* loyalty, respect, support, patience, understanding, sincerity, generosity, flexibility.

2 Cultivate a happy and positive outlook on life in general. When you have a 'downer' learn to deal patiently and kindly with yourself and get help if you need it; you'll eventually bounce back.
3 Learn to prioritise what really matters.
4 Have a great sense of humour and a sense of the ridiculous. Cultivate one's inner child—be playful!
5 Good communication is essential!
6 Make sure there are lots and lots of cuddles and affection and expressions of appreciation.

This last one was amended by email from Mum: 'Did I make it clear? That includes sex though I prefer to call it "making love".'

Unfortunately for my theory those ideas didn't sound so different from what I had been hearing from younger couples.

'I come from a background where you don't quit on marriage,' said Charles when dealing with his wife's depression.

'I'm old-fashioned,' said Izars, facing a similar situation. 'I feel a real commitment once you decide to get married.'

'It's about friendship and respecting the other person and valuing them,' said Juliet. 'I made a good choice when I married Ian. I was very fortunate, and he's a good partner.'

'It's a matter of constantly reminding yourself of the importance of acknowledging the other person,' added Ian.

'We're a team,' says Andrew. 'The bottom line is we love each other in a broad rather than narrow context of the words. That means you accept that other person has needs and you're prepared to sacrifice your own needs for that. You're prepared to look at whatever you can do to make that person's life as good as it can be.'

'The thing about our marriage is we promised to do certain things—and we realised you can live into your word,' says Sarah.

'You make a promise because you choose to make a promise,' said her husband Matt. 'Choice is a very powerful thing. If you choose something, you can make it work. If you make a commitment, you draw a picture for yourself to live up to.'

In other words, couples are choosing to stay married over and over again. It doesn't quite have the ring of grim drudgery that the word 'commitment' has taken on, but is it so different? Indeed, in many ways commitment is back.

Like an increasing number of couples, Juliet and Ian recommit regularly—every fifth wedding anniversary. The first time was with the same minister in the same church. The second, last year, was in front of a celebrant, on top of the lighthouse in Byron Bay. 'It's indicative of the commitment we gave the relationship and the kind of ongoing commitment,' says Juliet. 'We both are very private about that type of stuff, so to make a very public commitment each time is a declaration.'

Tracy and David thought the same thing when they renewed their vows on their tenth wedding anniversary with a big party, including a jazz band, 60 adults and 22 kids. David's kids and their son Max—'the mortar between two gorgeous bricks', according to a friend who spoke—were made part of the ceremony.

'You tell your partner all the time that you love them,' says David. 'But to go through that process in front of witnesses was intimidating. I'm generally easygoing, so saying the vows like that was a really nice thing to do.'

Making it that far was such a big deal, says Tracy, noting both of them have failed relationships behind them. 'It was just a great day, a happy day, such a peak experience,' recalls Tracy. 'The ritual of marriage is an ancient ritual. There is such an energy shift verbalising a commitment in front of your friends.'

Since the beginning of the twentieth century moralists have worried that marriage is on its last legs, that the new modern woman and the jazz age would kill off the institution. Since then we've had the pill, the sexual revolution, feminism, legalised abortion, women's entry into the workforce, women's economic independence, rock 'n' roll, punk, no-fault divorce laws, increased hours at work, the end of job-security and increased expectations of marriage. Yet still we marry. It's not going away anytime soon.

Even the high divorce rates are deceiving. Yes, divorce is at an all-time high, but then the past wasn't entirely golden there either: in the 1920s, the US state of Wyoming had a one-in-three divorce rate[1] and, Michael Bittman points out, if you include desertion rates in Western Australia's gold rush over a century ago, one in four men lived away from their wives. We don't know if they ever came back. It's a mistake to think marriage was somehow a lot easier in a supposedly rosy earlier age.

Certainly there are things that have changed. Marriage was once a grand institution based on solid commitment, duty, raising children, economics and stability. There were roles that, if not entirely agreeable, were set. It made sense when women were dependent on men for a livelihood, when marriage was as much business as romance. But to paraphrase that early feminist, Mae West, today we don't want to live in an institution. We have set a higher bar. We don't just want an economic transaction of convenience with the bargain of a breadwinner husband for a look-after-you wife. We don't need to marry for social acceptance, even if there is still a level of family and social approval that follows. We won't simply, grimly settle for 'until death you do part'. Today we want a partnership based on love and friendship that is still passionate. Above all we want to marry the soul mate who will make us happy. We want more and demand more. We have chosen, in fact, what the marriage emancipists wished for the future a hundred years ago.

> The husband and wife of the future will no more think of demanding subordination; on the one side or the other, than a couple of friends who had elected to live together would mutually demand it. That, after all, is the truest test. In love, there ought to be *at least* as much respect for individuality and freedom as in friendship.
> **—Mona Child, *The Morality of Marriage*, 1897**

So what are the keys? The handful of researchers who have turned their attention to long-lasting marriages have turned up an intriguing fact. Far from change being the enemy of marriage, the old-timers are telling them that their marriages lasted precisely *because* they changed. What makes a long-term marriage succeed is:

1 Ability to change and adapt to change
Long-lasting couples see changes to their social foundations—like women entering the workforce—as developmental rather than destructive, and subsequently adjust.

2 Ability to live with the unchangeable
Couples accept from the start that marriage isn't perfect and that not every difference needs be resolved or solved. They could let some things be. They find ways to work around the things they can't change or to avoid needlessly expending energy trying to settle things 'once and for all'.

3 Assumption of permanence
Couples have an attitude that the marriage must last because, even if it isn't perfect, it is important to them. They are committed to 'the marriage' as well as each other and are prepared to compromise to protect and nurture the relationship. They see marriage, despite its individual constraints, as a haven rather than a prison.

4 Trust
Trust is a constant among the ups and downs of marriage and underpins the sense that marriage is a sanctuary along with a commitment to, and expectation of, fidelity.

5 Balance of power
Even very traditional couples who said they were mutually dependent also said that their relationship did not compromise their sense

of individuality. While spouses need and depend on each other, they are also capable of surviving as individuals.

6 Enjoyment of each other
The spouses in the happiest long-term marriages share values—if not interests—but do not agree on everything. They enjoy spending time together but do not see spending time apart as a minus from the relationship. Each maintains individual pursuits so when they do spend time together they are fully engaged with each other.

7 Cherished shared history
Each couple values the story of them. They see their past with affection and as having significance. Their history helps them hold the relationship together when it is tested by current difficult events.

8 Luck
All couples agreed that in marriage, as in life, a little luck made a big difference. Luck in finding a partner who grows with you, luck in being able to break free from an unfortunate background, luck in avoiding some of life's devastating events. But even if they said they had been lucky, the couples in happy long-lasting marriages, while acknowledging the hard times, gave greater weight to the positive aspects of their marriage.[2]

(Based on a list from *The Australian Institute of Family Studies*.)

Jim, 64, and Helen, 61, have at various times been farmers, bookshop owners and gold miners, and have been together since Jim crashed Helen's sixteenth birthday party. Last year they celebrated their fortieth wedding anniversary. In that time they've survived raising their babies on a bush property without electricity while Jim still worked the nickel mines at night. After that they put in eighteen-hour days raising chooks and after that it was the gold mine. Then, as if they hadn't had enough of each other, when they retired they opened a bookstore just so they could spend time together.

What's their secret? 'Back then you just did things,' says Helen. 'You didn't think what the future was. If something had to be done, you just did it.'

'If you start at the bottom there's only one way to go,' says Jim.

'We always made sure we made time for each other—we still do,' says Helen. 'When we were newly married we used to talk all night and then we'd see the sun come up. Then it's like, "Hell, there's chooks to be fed".'

'You don't want to spend too long thinking about what you want to get out of the relationship,' adds Jim. 'You want to think about what you can contribute. A lot of it is making time for each other. No matter what—kids or business can always get in the way—you have to make a habit to switch off for a while and enjoy each other's company. With us, we've always been able to shut the rest of the world out.' And, he adds with a twinkle, 'Never stop courting. Whatever you were doing before you were married, don't stop after. Forty years on we're still doing it.'

When a study asking fifty-year-plus married couples what factors accounted for their marriage lasting, the following responses were given:
- trust (82 per cent)
- loving relationship (81 per cent)
- willingness to compromise (80 per cent)
- mutual respect (72 per cent)
- need for each other (70 per cent)
- compatibility (66 per cent)
- children (57 per cent)
- good communication (53 per cent).

The researchers also noted that 'sense of humour' was commonly added to the list.[3] All of which sound like pretty timeless reasons to me.

When couples go through the bad times, what keeps many of them going is the faith that on this journey things will get better.

'Marriage is like a huge trek through Europe,' says John, who went from married to separated and back again. 'There's the honeymoon period when you get to France and you start going around Paris. Then something goes wrong and you're in Spain and you get all your luggage stolen and you realise, "Oh they freak out, this person, over a little stress". Then you work through that and by the time you hit Eastern Europe you're back to friends again and you know too much about each other,' he continues. 'But then you come out the other end so at peace with that person, you know the bad, you know the good and even how to ease them to the halfway point of what you can put up with and what you don't mind or what you like. I think most people aren't forced to do it until they move in with someone or get married.' It's seeing through the crap to what matters most.

'At the end of the day, when something interesting has happened, the first person I want to tell is Andrew,' says Tiffany. 'It's interesting watching someone else's life from a close perspective. I've watched Andrew go from job to job and he's changed a lot, and that's fascinating. When we first got together I remember Andrew saying, "I'm looking forward to growing old with you. I just think its going to be really interesting, as our hair goes grey and we shrink a bit," and there's a truth in that. Like the email he sent this morning going "we're going to have so much fun in our forties". We think about it, stuff we're going to do a lot further down track.'

But keeping a marriage together isn't just up to two people. One of the smartest things anyone said to me was by Jennifer, who was talking about how she kept her marriage going after her husband's affair. 'If I was getting married today, knowing what I know today, it would be to say to my friends "we need all of you to help us be a family" and to celebrate us starting off that family unit with two and we're going to need all of you as friends in your different capacities to offer us something during our journey.'

This made me start thinking. Much as couples cherish each other, set aside regular time to keep their marriage healthy and look forward to the future, it isn't just the internal world of the couple that holds a marriage together. There's also a village of friends beyond that. Barbara Defoe Whitehead once wrote, 'Every divorce is the death of a small civilisation.' The community needs marriages and marriages need a community.

William Doherty tells of when he first realised he didn't have that community. Driving to a meeting he asked himself, 'Who are the people who have helped me be a parent, people who have helped me raise my children?' The car, he recounts, was suddenly filled with faces of people—relatives, teachers, friends—who had helped him and his wife raise their two children. People that had supported them when they were reeling under the effects of small babies, people who told them they were doing a great job. Then he thought, 'Who has helped me grow my marriage, people who have known my marriage well?' The car suddenly emptied of faces.

Some people are lucky and have that community to surround them. Tiffany has a friend, Phil, who rings her and asks, 'So how are things between you and Andrew?' She admits it was a shock at first. But she also points out, support doesn't just have to be talking either: people can babysit your children or take your children off your hands for short periods of time to help—especially if they can do it for free.

There's a step beyond that too. We know the stress points for marriage: financial troubles, career worries, the crunch that comes with young children. Weigh a marriage down with too much of any of these and it will buckle under the stress. A couple can't always make it through that alone. Nor can friends or family bear it all as well. If we as a society are really serious about the benefits of marriage, then we have to support it practically. This means if governments genuinely have the family values they say they do, they must take the stresses on young parents seriously: reduce the financial crisis that hits with a baby and pay parents something real; facilitate ways for men and women to get some time out; find practical incentives that help address the work versus life balance that don't just run families off into the shunted-to-the sidings parent career path.

Business too, which benefits from marriage (married couples are better workers) has to make sure that benefits also flow back the other way; more companies need to wise up that it's cheaper to keep parents employed. Measures here include ensuring real work flexibility, gauging work by output rather than time spent desk sitting and seeing the value in job-sharing and part-time work. All of which are better than watching parents run out the door, taking their valuable training, corporate knowledge and memories with them because they are just too squeezed.

If we can agree that the whole community benefits from intact marriages and families, we all have an obligation to ensure families aren't left alone to bear the financial, career and childhood risks that threaten marriage. It doesn't seem like too much to ask.

Will this happen? Maybe there is one unlikely source of optimism, from the current debate over gay marriage. No matter which side you sit on, the fact that people are choosing sides shows that they still think marriage matters. Marriage is the bridge between two political philosophies and it matters too much to be left to either. It's too important to be left in the hands of the conservatives, the churches and the crusaders who can make marriage sound as good for you as wholegrain muesli and as fun as a low-carb diet, who are big on telling individuals how to run their lives but reluctant to regulate the social institutions, such as banks, business and government, whose practices impact on people's ability to stay married. Marriage is also too important to be dismissed by the cynical left or the literati, who either equate marriage as a servitude second only to the salt mines or as a repression of individual freedom, who are all too willing to demand social change by institutions but decry any attempt to promote or support changes to how individuals behave toward each other.

Marriage sits directly in between these two spheres and is so much more than either would contend.

There is a sea-change of attitude going on. It's something people only really say out loud once, when they say their wedding vows, but still this new attitude is rippling out, and it is this: marriage matters. It does make a difference, and it is worth it. Standing side by side with someone going into the future is a hell of an adventure and far more interesting than bailing out every time the new best thing comes along. That's the easy way. Marriage is a guarantee of more. More fun, more friendship, more understanding, more heartache, more pain and most of all more joy.

Notes

Introduction
1. Arndt, B., 'Young men in fear of a life stifled by marriage', *Sydney Morning Herald*, 5 June 2003; Maley, B. 'Marriage is the weakest contract of all', *Sydney Morning Herald*, 16 December 2003; 'Women reject the chore of marriage', *Illawarra Mercury*, 7 August 2003; Hudson, P., 'Call for inquiry into the decline of marriage', *The Age*, 4 August 2003.
2. Australian Bureau of Statistics, figures for censuses 1911, 1986 and 2001, compiled in Birrell, B., Rapson, V. and Hourigan, C. 2004, *Men and Women Apart: Partnering in Australia*, The Australian Family Association and Centre for Population and Urban Research, Monash University, Melbourne.
3. McDonald, P. 1995, *Families in Australia: A socio-demographic perspective*, Australian Institute of Family Studies, Melbourne.
4. Halford, W.K., Wilson, K.L., Lizzio, A. and Moore, E., 2002, 'Does Working at a Relationship Work? Relationship Self Regulation and Relationship Outcomes' in Noller, P. and Feeney, J.A. (eds), *Understanding Marriage*, Cambridge University Press, Cambridge, pp. 493–517.
5. ibid.; L. Clark and A. Berrington, 1999, Socio Demographic Predictors of Divorce, Lord Chancellor's Department Research Secretariat Research Series, vol. 1, no. 2/99, p. v.

6 Story, L., Rothman, A. and Bradbury, T., 2002, 'Risk Factors, Risk Processes, and the Longitudinal Course of Newlywed Marriage', in op. cit. Noller D. and Feeney J. A. (eds) *Understanding Marriage*, pp. 468–92.
7 Wolcott, I. and Hughes, J. 1999, 'Towards understanding the reasons for divorce', Australian Institute of Family Studies, Melbourne, working paper no. 20, June, p. 3.
8 ibid., p. 22.
9 Klagsbrun, F. 1985, *Married People: Staying together in the age of divorce*, Bantam Books, Toronto; Lauer, J.C. and Lauer, R.H., 1986, *Til Death Do Us Part*, Haworth Press, New York, both cited in Parker, R., 2002, 'Why marriages last: A discussion of the literature', Australian Institute of Family Studies, research paper no. 28, July 2002.

1 Why Marry?
1 Sassler, S., 2004, 'The Process of Entering into Cohabiting unions', *Journal of Marriage and Family*, May, vol. 66, no. 2, pp. 491–505.
2 Bateman, G. and Conroy, R., 1999, 'The 1998 Relationships Indicators: Views on relationships now and in the future', papers to celebrate 50 years of Relationships Australia, Relationships Australia Inc., Deakin, ACT.
3 ibid.
4 National marriage project, Rutgers University <www.marriage.rutgers.edu>.
5 Australian Institute of Health and Welfare, 1997, Australia's Welfare, AIHW, Canberra, cited in Disney, H. and McPerson, A. 1999, 'Changing Family Structures and the Impact of Economic and Social Factors on Family Well Being', papers to celebrate 50 years of Relationships Australia, Relationships Australia Inc., Deakin, ACT.
6 Cherlin, A., 1992, *Marriage, Divorce, Remarriage* (revised), Harvard University Press, Cambridge, MA.
7 Haskey, J., 1995, 'Trends in marriage and cohabitation: the decline in marriage and the changing pattern of living in partnerships', Population Trends; Marriages and Divorces, Australia 1998 (cat. no. 3310.0), Australian Bureau of Statistics.
8 Dr David de Vaus, 2003, 'Living together before marriage', *La Trobe University Bulletin*, April.
9 Brown, Susan L., unpublished, 'Moving from Cohabitation to Marriage: Effects on relationship quality', Social Science Research.
10 DeMaris, A. and MacDonald, W., 1993, 'Premarital cohabitation and marital

instability: A test of the unconventionality hypothesis', *Journal of Marriage and the Family*, vol. 55, 2 May.
11. op. cit. Bateman and Conroy, 1999.
12. Smock, P. and Manning, W., 2002, 'First Comes Cohabitation and Then Comes Marriage?', *Journal of Family Issues*, November.
13. Marriages and Divorces Australia 2002, Australian Bureau of Statistics, cat. no. 3310.0.
14. Nock, S., 1998, *Marriage in Men's Lives*, Oxford University Press, New York.
15. Piquero, A., 2002, 'Marriage can reduce a life of crime', press release, University of Florida, 12 September.
16. Research by David de Vaus from La Trobe University, Melbourne, cited by Hatfield, P., 2002 'Women's Lib got it wrong in the 1970 . . . marriage makes both sexes happy', *New Scientist*, vol. 176, no. 2363, 5 October.
17. Halford, W.K., 2000, 'Australian Couples in Millennium Three', Department of Family and Community Services, Canberra, ACT.
18. ibid.
19. Williams, J., 2003, 'Talk before tying the knot', *Psychology Today*, New York.
20. Parker, R., 1999, 'A framework for future research in premarriage education', Australian family briefing no 8. Australian Institute of Family Studies, November.
21. Parker, R., 1999, 'Research in Premarriage Education', *Family Matters*, Australian Institute of Family Studies, no. 54, Spring/Summer.
22. Cost of Love Survey, 2000, *Bride to Be* <www.i-do.com.au>.

2 Nice Day for a White Wedding
1. Cost of Love Survey, 2000, *Bride to Be* magazine <www.i-do.com.au>.
2. ibid.
3. ibid.
4. Australian Bureau of Statistics, 'Marriage and Divorce in Australia', March 2002, catalogue no. 3101.0.

3 The Honeymoon is Over
1. Quoted in Quilter, H. (ed), 1888, *Is Marriage a Failure?*, Swan Sonnenschein London. Reprinted in 1984, Garland Publishing Inc., New York.
2. Michael, B., 2003, 'Scratch the seven-year itch—its down to two', *Sydney Morning Herald*, 18 March.
3. 'All downhill after "I Will"', *Sun Herald*, 21 September 2003, p. 49.
4. Dalton, A., 2000, 'The Ties that Unbind', *Psychology Today*, Jan/Feb.

5 Halford, W.K., 2000, 'Australian Couples in Millennium Three', Department of Family and Community Services, Canberra, ACT.
6 Kiecolt-Glaser, J., Bane, C., Glaser and R., William B., 2003, 'Love, Marriage, and Divorce: Newlyweds' stress hormones foreshadow relationship changes', *Journal of Consulting and Clinical Psychology*, vol. 71, no. 1, February, pp. 176–88.
7 Doherty, W., 2003, *A Strong Marriage*, Finch Publishing, Sydney, pp. 80–1.
8 Bryant, C.M., Conger, R.D. and Meehan, J.M., 2001, 'The influence of in-laws on change in marital success', *Journal of Marriage and Family*, August, vol. 63, no. 3, pp. 614–26.
9 Kurdek, L.A., 1991, 'Marital stability and changes in marital quality in newly-wed couples: a test of the contextual model', *Journal of Social and Personal Relationships*, vol. 8, pp. 27–48.
10 Esmond, J., Dickinson, J.I. and Moffat, A., 1998, 'What makes for Successful and Unsuccessful Relationships?', paper presented to Changing Families, Challenging Futures, 6th Australian Institute of Family Studies Conference, Melbourne, 25–27 November.
11 Karney, B., study conducted at University of Florida, quoted in, 1998, 'Study reveals that partners' self-delusion contributes to their successful marriages', *Jet*, Chicago, 26 January, vol. 93, no. 9.
12 Gottman, J., Murray, J., Swanson, C., Tyson, R. and Swanson, K., 2002, *The Mathematics of Marriage*, A Bradford Book, MIT Press, Cambridge Massachusetts, p. 294.
13 op. cit. Esmond, J., Dickinson, J.I. and Moffat, A., 1998, 'What makes for successful and unsuccessful relationships?'.
14 Aron, A., Norman, C.C., Aron, E.A. and Lewandowski, G., 2002, 'Shared Participation in Self-Expanding Activities: Positive effects on experienced marital quality', in op. cit. Noller P. and Feeney J.A. (eds), *Understanding Marriage*, pp. 177–94.
15 Halford, W.K., Kelly, A. and Markman, H.J., 1997, 'The Concept of a Healthy Marriage' in Halford W.K. and Markham H.J. (eds), *Clinical Handbook of Marriage and Couples Interventions*, John Wiley & Sons Ltd, Chichester, UK.
16 ibid.
17 Gottman, J. and Silver, N., 1999, *The Seven Principles for Making Marriage Work*, Random House, New York.

4 The Art of Marital Warfare

1. Gottman, J. with Silver, N., 1994, *Why Marriages Succeed or Fail and how you can make yours last*, Bloomsbury, London.
2. ibid, ch 2.
3. ibid.
4. Gottman, J. and Silver, N., 1999, *Seven Principles for Making Marriage Work*, Orion Books Ltd, London.
5. Young, K., 1998, Programs for Perpetrators of Domestic Violence National Campaign Against Violence and Crime research cited in 'Meta Evaluation of the Partnerships Against Domestic Violence Current Perspectives on Domestic Violence: A review of national and international literature', 1999, Strategic Partners Pty Ltd in collaboration with the Research Centre for Gender Studies, University of South Australia, May.
6. Halford, W.K., Wilson, K.L., Lizzio, A. and Moore, E., 2002, 'Does Working at a Relationship Work? Relationship self regulation and relationship outcomes' in Noller, P. and Feeney, J.A. (eds), *Understanding Marriage*, Cambridge University Press, Cambridge, pp. 493–517.
7. Gottman, J., Murray, J., Swanson, C., Tyson, R. and Swanson, K., 2002, *The Mathematics of Marriage*, A Bradford Book, MIT Press, Cambridge Massachusetts, p. 293; op. cit. Gottman, J. and Silver, N., 1999, *The Seven Principles for Making Marriage Work*; pp. 10–11.
8. Waite, L.J., Browning, D., Doherty, W.J., Gallagher, M., Luo, Y. and Stanley, S.M. 2002, 'Does Divorce Make People Happy? Findings from a study of unhappy marriages', Institute of American Values.

5 Men v. Women: Can we be on the same side?

1. Bernard, J., 1972, *The Future of Marriage*, New Haven, Yale University Press.
2. Baron-Cohen, S., 2003, 'They just can't help it' <www.guardian.co.uk>, cited on 17 April.
3. Konner, M., 2004, 'Bridging Our Differences' <www.msnbc.msn.com>.
4. Buss, D.M., 1989, 'Sex differences in human mate preferences: evolutionary hypotheses tested in 37 cultures', *Behavioural and Brain Sciences*, no. 12, pp. 1–49.
5. Wolcott, I. and Hughes, J., 1999, 'Towards understanding the reasons for divorce', Australian Institute of Family Studies, working paper no. 20, June.
6. Yogev, S., and Brett, J., 1985, 'Perceptions of the division of housework and child care and marital satisfaction', *Journal of Marriage and the Family*, vol. 47, pp. 609–18.

7 Blair, S.L., 1993, 'Employment, family and perceptions of marital quality among husbands and wives', *Journal of Family Issues*, vol. 14, pp. 189–212.
8 Guzman, L., 2000, 'Effects of Wives' Employment on Marital Quality', Center for Demography and Ecology, working paper no. 8, University of Wisconsin-Madison, October.
9 Australian Social Trends, 2001, Work-Unpaid Time: Time Spent on Unpaid Household Work, Australian Bureau of Statistics, May.
10 Bittman, B., Meagher, G. and Matheson, G., 1998, 'The Changing Boundary Between Home and Market: Australian trends in outsourcing domestic labour', Social Policy Research Centre discussion paper, July, no. 86, Sydney.
11 Baxter, J., 2001, 'Marital Status and the Division of Household Labour: cohabitation versus marriage', *Family Matters*, no. 58, Autumn.
12 Bittman, M. and Pixley, J., 1997, *The Double Life of the Family*, Allen & Unwin, Sydney.
13 Bittman, M. and Lovejoy, F., 1993, 'Domestic Power: Negotiating an Unequal Division Of Labour In A Framework Of Equality', *Australian and New Zealand Journal of Sociology*, vol. 29, no. 3, pp. 302–21.
14 Gershuny, J., Bittman, M. and Brice, J., 1997, 'Exit Voice and Suffering. Do couples adapt to changing employment habits?', working papers of the ESRC Research Centre on Micro-Social Change, University of Essex, Colchester.
15 Bittman, M. and Wajcman, J., 1999, 'The Rush Hour, the quality of leisure time and gender equity, Social Policy Research Centre discussion paper', February, no. 97, Sydney.
16 Baxter, J. and Westen, M., 1996, 'Satisfaction with Housework: Explaining the paradox', Paper presented to the Australian Family Research Conference, Brisbane, 27–9 November.
17 Paul, A.M., 1997, 'Depressions Dirty Laundry', *Psychology Today*, Nov/Dec.
18 Hochschild, A., 1989, *The Second Shift: Working parents and the revolution at home*, Viking, New York.
19 op. cit. Gershuny, J., Bittman, M. and Brice, J., 1997–8, 'Exit, Voice and Suffering: Do couples adapt to changing employment patterns?'.
20 Gottman, J. and Silver, N., 1999, *The Seven Principles for Making Marriage Work*, Crown Publishers, New York.
21 2003, 'Men, Polish Up Your Act', *Sydney Morning Herald*, 27 August 2003, reprint from *The Telegraph*, London.
22 Gottman, J., Coan, J., Carrere, S. and Swanson C., 1998, 'Predicting marital

happiness and stability from newlywed interactions', *Journal of Marriage and the Family*, February.
23 Miller, N.B. and Kannae, L.A., 1999, 'Predicting marital quality in Ghana', *Journal of Comparative Family Studies*, University of Calgary, Autumn.
24 Interview, Michael Bittman.
25 Waite, L., 2000, *The Case for Marriage*, Doubleday, New York, pp. 25–30.
26 'The more things change, the more marriages stay the same', press release, Penn State University, 4 June 2003.
27 Bateman, G. and Conroy, R., 1999, 'The 1998 Relationships Indicators: Views on relationships now and in the future', papers to celebrate 50 years of Relationships Australia, Relationships Australia Inc., Deakin, ACT.

6 SEX: Are we having fun yet?
1 Laumann, E.O., Gagnon, J.H., Michael, R.T. and Michaels, S., 1994, *The Social Organization of Sexuality*, University of Chicago Press, Chicago.
2 Blumstein, P. and Schwartz, P. in Call, V., Sprecher, S. and Schwartz, P., 1995, 'The incidence and frequency of marital sex in a national sample', *Journal of Marriage and the Family*, Minneapolis, August, vol. 57, no. 3.
3 'Women Turned On By Love And Marriage', *South Wales Evening Post*, 15 November 2002.
4 Spence, S.H., 1997, 'Sex and relationships', in Halford, W.K. and Howard, J.M. (eds), *Clinical Handbook of Marriage and Couples Interventions*, John Wiley & Sons Ltd.
5 op. cit. Blumstein, P. and Schwartz, P. in 'The incidence and frequency of marital sex in a national sample'.
6 ibid.
7 op. cit. Laumann et al., *The Social Organization of Sexuality*.
8 Weiner Davis, M., 2003, *The Sex-Starved Marriage*, Simon & Schuster, New York.
9 Donnelly, D.A., 1993, 'Sexually inactive marriages', *Journal of Sex Research*, vol. 30, pp. 171–79.
10 Smith, A., Rissel, C., Richters, J., Gruilich, A. and de Visser, R., 2003, *Sex in Australia, a summary of finding of the Australian Study of Health and Relationships*, Australian Research Centre in Sex, Health and Society, La Trobe University, Melbourne.
11 Orenstein, P., 2000, *Flux: women on sex, work, kids, love and life in a half-changed world*, Doubleday, New York.

12 Gemmell, N., 2003, interview *Enough Rope* with Andrew Denton, cited at <www.abc.net.au/enoughrope>.
13 C. and Sadd S., 1975, *The Redbook Report on Female Sexuality*, Delacorte, New York, cited in Love, P. and Robinson, J., 1994, *Hot Monogamy*, Piatkus, London.
14 Hurbert, J., 1991, *Journal of Sex and Marital Therapy*, vol. 17, no. 3, Fall, p. 183, cited in op. cit. Love, P. and Robinson, J., 1994, *Hot Monogamy*.
15 op. cit. Donnelly, D.A., 1993, 'Sexually inactive marriages'.
16 op. cit. Weiner Davis, M., 2003, *The Sex-Starved Marriage*.
17 Spence, S.H., 1997, 'Sex and relationships', in *Clinical Handbook of Marriage and Couples Interventions*, Halford, W.K., Markman, H.J. (eds), John Wiley & Sons Ltd, New York, p. 75.
18 Research by Donnelly, D. of Georgia State University, cited in Shellenbarger, S., 2003, 'Not Tonight, Honey: The plight of the dual-income, no-sex couple', *Wall Street Journal*, New York, 3 April.
19 Halford, W.K., 2000, 'Australian Couples in Millennium Three', Department of Family and Community Services, Canberra, ACT p. 21; Acitelli, L., University of Michigan in Tanzito, C., 1995, 'Closeness Calls', *Psychology Today* cited at <www.psychologytoday.com>, July/August.
20 op. cit. Weiner Davis, M., 2003, *The Sex-Starved Marriage*, pp. 56–7.
21 Bradley, M., 2003, 'Magic sex pill a can of worms, says doctor', *Sydney Morning Herald*, 23 September, p. 6.
22 'Women Fake Sex Numbers', 15 July 2003, cited at <www.news.com.au>.
23 op. cit. Weiner Davis, *The Sex-Starved Marriage*, pp. 95–9.
24 Mackay, J., *The Penguin Atlas of Human Sexual Behaviour*, Penguin Group, New York.
25 Scott, J., 1999, 'Family change: revolution or backlash in attitudes?' in *Changing Britain, Families and Households in the 1990s*, McRae, S. (ed), Oxford University Press, Oxford, pp. 68–99.
26 Smith, A., Rissel, C., Richters, J., Gruilich, A. and de Visser, R., 2003, 'Sex in Australia', a summary of findings of the Australian Study of Health and Relationships, Australian Research Centre in Sex, Health and Society, La Trobe University, Melbourne.
27 Weiner Davis, M., *The Divorce Remedy*; Vaughan, P., *The Monogamy Myth*; Shirley Glass quoted in Morano, H., 2003, 'The New Sex Scorecard', *Psychology Today*, Jul/Aug; Lauman, E., *The Social Organization of Sexuality*, Peterson, KS 2002, 'How can you mend a broken vow?' *USA Today*, McLean, Va. Sep 3, 2002.

28 Quoted in Morano, H., 2003, 'The New Sex Scorecard', *Psychology Today*, July/August.
29 'Unfaithfully Yours', *New Zealand Herald*, 1 March 2003.
30 Peterson, K.S., 2002, 'How can you mend a broken vow? Getting past a partner's affair requires new level of honesty and lots of talk', *USA Today*, 3 September.
31 Mitchell, S.A., 2002, *Can Love Last?*, WW Norton & Company, New York.

7 Show Me the Money

1 Batemen, G. and Conroy, R. 1999, 'The 1998 Relationships Indicators: Views on relationships now and in the future', papers to celebrate 50 years of Relationships Australia, Relationships Australia Inc., Deakin, ACT, p. 26.
2 Esmond, J., Dickinson J.I. and Moffat, A. 1998, 'What Makes for Successful and Unsuccessful Relationships?', Changing families, challenging futures, 6th Australian Institute of Family Studies Conference, Melbourne, 25–27 November.
3 op. cit. Batemen, G. and Conroy, R. 1999, 'The 1998 Relationships Indicators: Views on relationships now and in the future', p. 26; Vinokur, A.D., Caplan, R.H. and Price, R.D., 1996, 'Hard Times and Hurtful Partners: How financial strain affects depression and relationship satisfaction of unemployed persons and their spouses', *Journal of Personality and Social Psychology*, vol. 71, no. 1, July, pp. 166–79.
4 McAllister, F., 1999, 'Effects of Changing Material Circumstances on the Incidence of Marital Breakdown' in *High Divorce Rates: The state of the evidence on reasons and remedies*, One plus One Marriage and Partnership Research, vol. 1, Simons, J. (ed), Lord Chancellor's Department Research Secretariat.
5 Research by Smock, P., University of Michigan and Manning, W., Bowling Green State University, cited in Schulman, D., 2003, 'Women Marry For Money' <www.psychologytoday.com>, March/April.
6 Birrell, R. and Rapson, V., 1998, 'A Not So Perfect Match', Monash University, cited in Edgar, D., 1999, 'Thick and Thin: Relationships in the new millennium', papers to celebrate 50 years of Relationships Australia, Relationships Australia Inc., Deakin, ACT, p. 45.
7 Arndt, B., 2003, 'Why going for the money is the natural thing', *Sydney Morning Herald*, 2 April.

8 Ginther, D., 1997, 'Is the Male Marriage Premium Due to Selection? The effect of shotgun weddings on the return to marriage', Federal Reserve Bank of Atlanta working paper 97–5a (revised October 1998).
9 Baxter, J. and Gray, E., 2003, 'For Richer or Poorer: Women, men and marriage', paper prepared for the Australian Institute of Family Studies Conference, Melbourne; Grossbard-Shechtman, S. and Neuman, S., 2003, 'Marriage and Work for Pay' in *Marriage and the Economy*, Grossbard-Shechtman, S. (ed), Cambridge University Press, Cambridge, pp. 234–35.
10 Drago, R., 2003, 'The Role of Economics in Work–Family Research', paper for the BPW/Brandies Conference From 9-to-5 to 24/7, Roland, 3 January.
11 Wilmoth, J., 1998, 'Purdue Study Suggests Marrying For Love and Money', Purdue University press release, 9 January.
12 Lupton, J.P. and Smith, J.P., 2003, 'Marriage, Assets and Savings', in op. cit., *Marriage and the Economy*, Grossbard-Shechtman, S. (ed).
13 Singh, S., 1997, *Marriage Money*, Allen & Unwin, Sydney, p. 53.
14 Woolley, F., 2003, 'Control over Money in Marriage' in op. cit., *Marriage and the Economy*, Grossbard-Shechtman, S. (ed).
15 ABS figures quoted in, 2004, 'Average families can't afford own home: new research', cited at <www.actu.asm.au>, 9 February; Gordon, J., 2003, 'Bleak future for debt-ridden children of the 60s', cited at <www.theage.com.au>, 18 November.
16 ACTU figures, 2004, cited in 'Young Families out of housing market', <www.news.com.au>, 9 February; Allen, B. and Silmalis, L., 2004, 'Average home now costs $500 000', *Sunday Telegraph*, 22 February.
17 op. cit., Singh S., *Marriage Money*.
18 Wolf, N., 1993, *Fire With Fire: The new female power and how it will change the 21st century*, Random House, New York, pp. 249, 304.
19 Average weekly earnings, 2003, Australian Bureau of Statistics, catalogue no. 6302, 14 August.
20 Orenstein, P., 2000, *Flux: women on sex, work, kids, love and life in a half-changed world*, Doubleday, New York, p. 18.
21 Woolley, F., 2003, 'Control over Money in Marriage' in op. cit. *Marriage and the Economy* Grossbard-Shechtman, S. (ed).
22 Commuri, S., 2001, 'Bringing Home The Bacon: Female breadwinners hide financial savvy', University of Missouri, Columbia press release, 26 October.
23 Bittman, M., England, P., Folbre, N. and Matheson, G., 2001, 'When Gender Trumps Money: Bargaining and time in household work', paper presented at Population Association of America, March.

24 Hamilton, C. and Mail, E. 2003, 'Downshifting in Australia. A sea-change in the pursuit of happiness', The Australia Institute, discussion paper number 50, January; Galinsky, E., Salmond, K., Harrington, B., Bond, J.T., Brumit Kropf, M. and Moore, M., 2003, 'A study of executive women and men (executive summary)', Leaders in a Global Economy sponsored by Families and Work Institute, Catalyst, Boston College Center for Work & Family, 14 May.
25 op. cit., Hamilton, C. and Mail, E., 'Downshifting in Australia'.
26 'Women take home-loan lead' cited at <www.news.com.au>, 18 September 2002.

8 All Work, No Play?
1 Esmond, J., Dickinson, J. and Moffat, A., 1998, 'What makes for Successful and Unsuccessful Relationship?', Changing families, Challenging futures, 6th Australian Institute of Family Studies Conference, Melbourne, 25–27 November.
2 Ross, E., 2003, 'Give me one minute more', *Business Review Weekly*, 12 June, p. 78.
3 Weston, R., Qu, L. and Soriano, F., 2002, 'Implications of men's extended work hours for their personal and marital happiness', *Family Matters*, Australian Institute of Family Studies, Melbourne, no. 61, Autumn.
4 Research by Charles Birch and David Paul, cited in West, A., 2003, 'Hi ho, hi ho, it's off to #@*&#!@ work we go...', *Sun Herald*, 17 August, p. 20.
5 Australian Social Trends 2002, 'Work–Paid Work: Employment arrangements', Australian Bureau of Statistics.
6 op. cit., Weston, R., Qu, L. and Soriano, G., 2002, 'Implications of men's extended work hours for their personal and marital happiness'.
7 Robinson, P., 2003, 'No sex please, work's a headache', *Sydney Morning Herald*, 28 July, p. 3.
8 Roehling, P.V. and Moen, P., 2003, 'Dual-Earner Couples, A Sloan Work and Family Encyclopedia Entry', <www.bc.edu/bc_org/avp/wfnetwork/rft/wfpedia/wfpDECent.html>, 5 March.
9 Forthofer, M.S., Marhman, H.G., Cox, M., Stanley, S. and Sessler, R.C., 1996, 'Associations between marital distress and work loss in a national sample', *Journal of Marriage and the Family*, vol. 58, no. 3, pp. 597–605.
10 op. cit. Australian Social Trends 2002, 'Work–Paid Work: Employment arrangements'.